Design in Composite Materials

Conference Planning Panel

J C Riddell, MA, CEng, MIMechE, MBIM (Chairman)
Clayton Son Holdings plc
Leeds

A N Bramley, BEng, PhD, CEng, FIMechE
School of Mechanical Engineering
University of Bath

M W Commander, BSc, PhD, CEng, MPRI
Fiberite Europe (UK)
University of Warwick Science Park

M H Datoo, BSc, PhD
College of Aeronautics
Cranfield Institute of Technology
Bedford

F L Matthews, BSc(Eng), ACGI, CEng, MRAeS, FPRI
Centre for Composite Materials
Imperial College of Science and Technology
London

G Money, BSc, MPhil, AMIM
The Design Council
London

C E N Sturgess, BSc, PhD, CEng, FIMechE, FRSA
Department of Mechanical Engineering
University of Birmingham

J Whiteside
British Aerospace plc
Preston
Lancashire

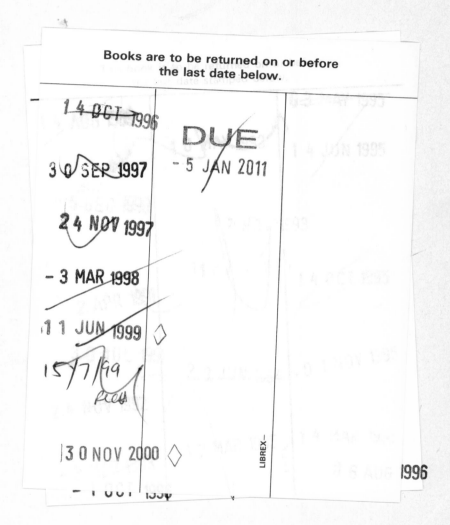

Books are to be returned on or before
the last date below.

14 OCT 1996

30 SEP 1997   DUE
                  -5 JAN 2011
24 NOV 1997

-3 MAR 1998

11 JUN 1999

15/7/99

30 NOV 2000

LIBREX—

Proceedings of the Institution of Mechanical Engineers

Conference

Design in Composite Materials

7–8 March 1989
The Institution of Mechanical Engineers
Birdcage Walk
London

Sponsored by
Aerospace Industries Division of the Institution of Mechanical Engineers

Co-sponsored by
British Composites Society

IMechE Conference 1989–2

MEP Published for the Institution of Mechanical Engineers by
Mechanical Engineering Publications Limited

The publishers are not responsible for any statement made in this publication. Data, discussion and conclusions developed by authors are for information only and are not intended for use without independent substantiating investigation on the part of potential users.

Printed by Waveney Print Services Ltd, Beccles, Suffolk

Contents

The Institution of Mechanical Engineers

The primary purpose of the 76,000-member Institution of Mechanical Engineers, formed in 1847, has always been and remains the promotion of standards of excellence in British mechanical engineering and a high level of professional development, competence and conduct among aspiring and practising members. Membership of IMechE is highly regarded by employers, both within the UK and overseas, who recognise that its carefully monitored academic training and responsibility standards are second to none. Indeed they offer incontrovertible evidence of a sound formation and continuing development in career progression.

In pursuit of its aim of attracting suitably qualified youngsters into the profession — in adequate numbers to meet the country's future needs — and of assisting established Chartered Mechanical Engineers to update their knowledge of technological developments — in areas such as CADCAM, robotics and FMS, for example — the IMechE offers a comprehensive range of services and activities. Among these, to name but a few, are symposia, courses, conferences, lectures, competitions, surveys, publications, awards and prizes. A Library containing 150,000 books and periodicals and an Information Service which uses a computer terminal linked to databases in Europe and the USA are among the facilities provided by the Institution.

If you wish to know more about the membership requirements or about the Institution's activities listed above — or have a friend or relative who might be interested — telephone or write to IMechE in the first instance and ask for a copy of our colour 'at a glance' leaflet. This provides fuller details and the contact points — both at the London HQ and IMechE's Bury St Edmunds office — for various aspects of the organisation's operation. Specifically it contains a tear-off slip through which more information on any of the membership grades (Student, Graduate, Associate Member, Member and Fellow) may be obtained.

Corporate members of the Institution are able to use the coveted letters 'CEng, MIMechE' or 'CEng, FIMechE' after their name, designations instantly recognised by, and highly acceptable to, employers in the field of engineering. There is no way other than by membership through which they can be obtained!

Introduction to composite materials

C S FRAME, BTech
British Aerospace plc, Warton, Lancashire

SYNOPSIS   The paper is a basic introduction to composite materials and the reason for their selection
as an engineering material.   The manufacture of the raw fibre, pre-pregging and basic composite
properties are given.   Matrix algebra for the generation of multi-angular properties together with
general lay-up guidelines are also presented.   Fundamental differences between composites and
metallic materials are discussed together with factors affecting the properties of composites
including environmental effects, stress concentrations and the effects of stacking sequence.   Finally,
basic non-destructive inspection of composites is presented.

1   WHY CARBON FIBRE COMPOSITE?

Aerospace structural engineers are constantly
seeking the means to improve structural
efficiency and thereby reduce structural mass
without compromising structural strength and
stiffness.

Carbon Fibre Composite (CFC) meets these
requirements in that it has low density coupled
with high strength and stiffness along the fibre
direction.   The comparison between CFC and some
basic metallic materials in terms of density,
specific tensile strength and specific stiffness
are shown in Figure 1.

2   PRODUCTION OF CFC

Carbon fibre starts off as a special acrylic
fibre, similar to rayon, known as polyacrylonitrile - PAN for short.   The PAN fibre then
undergoes a series of heat treatments (under
tension and inert gas) which transforms it into
long fibres of carbon with high strength and
stiffness.

These fibres can then be used to produce
continuous fibre products such as:- uni-
directional preimpregnates, woven fabric, filament winding and braiding tows etc. or a number
of short staple materials such as:- aligned
short staple pre-impregnates; sheet, dough and
injection moulding compounds etc.   This paper
will consider only the continuous fibre uni-
directional preimpregnated material.

To fully utilise the properties of the
fibres they need some means of transferring load
from one fibre to another and, in the case of
compression, fibre stabilisation.   This is
achieved by using a matrix resin which, for
example, is assumed to be an epoxy.

The production of the fibres and the
impregnation process is illustrated in Figure 2.

The uni-directional preimpregnate (prepreg) will generally be in the order of 0,125 mm
thick and contain approximately 60% of fibres
by volume.   Although stiff and strong in the
fibre direction it will be weak transverse to
the fibres since this will only be the strength
of the matrix resin.   Typical single layer
properties are shown in Figure 3.

3   LAY-UP AND CURE

The designed component will have fibres in a
variety of directions to take account of all the
various loads.   This means that plies will be
laid, one on top of each other, to produce a
symmetric stack.   This will then be consolidated
and cured by the application of pressure and
heat, usually in an autoclave, as shown in
Figure 4.

A higher degree of molecular cross-linking,
and hence quality, is generally achieved by
post-curing the laminate in an air circulating
oven for several hours.

4   GENERAL LAY-UP GUIDELINES

Although there will always be exceptions to
every rule, the following are given as guidelines and should be considered as good design
practice:-

(a)   Since the material is stiff and strong in
the fibre direction, align fibres to the
loads ($\pm 45°$ for shear).
(b)   Keep lay-ups balanced and symmetric about
their mid-plane to avoid thermal distortion.
(c)   If 'co-curing' skins of a honeycomb sandwich, avoid large cell sizes to prevent
the plies nearest to the core from
'quilting'.
(d)   Keeping external plies mutually perpendicular gives a more damage tolerant laminate.
(e)   Avoid having more than four plies of the
same direction together.   This can lead
long, fibre direction, cracks which will
cause a reduction in strength.

(f) When changing thickness (ie adding plies), interleave the additional plies within the existing ones - do not just add a 'lump' of extra plies onto one surface. Also, keep to a shallow gradient (20:1) particularly in prime loading directions.

(g) If using mechanical fasteners maintain an edge distance of at least twice the nominal bolt diameter.

(h) CFC behaves as a noble material and can cause galvanic corrosion of aluminium and cadmium when in direct contact.

5 ADVANTAGES AND DISADVANTAGES OF CFC

The relative advantages/disadvantages can be summarised as follows:

5.1 Advantages

(a) Weight saving
Due to the high strength and stiffness combined with low density, overall weight savings of 15 to 20% are normally achieved.
(b) Strength/Stiffness tailoring
By changing the ply lay-up and fibre orientation, an almost limitless combination of strengths and stiffnesses can be created. Thus a structure can be tailored to a required strength and/or stiffness.
(c) Good formability
The plies can be laid-up and cured on a curved tool so that the finished component comes off the tooling to the desired shape.
(d) Possible overall cost reduction
The subject of costs is a complex one, since it depends on the type and function of the component, number required, raw material cost, amount of labour and method of production etc. However, composite materials can give overall cost reductions due to:-
-the low scrap rate since material is added where needed as opposed to material removal in N.C. machining.
-low parts counts are achieved by co-curing or bonding of stiffeners so that the final component has integral stiffening.
-automatic tape layers can give a deposition rate ten times that of hand lay-up.

5.2 Disadvantages

(a) High raw material cost
Aircraft specification carbon composites cost about 15 times more (pounds sterling per kilogram) than conventional aluminium alloys.
(b) Environmental degradation
Design strengths and stiffness have to take account of reduction in values due to elevated temperature and moisture absorbtion, although much work is being done to reduce this.
(c) Notch sensitivity
Since most composite lay-ups are fully elastic to failure, holes and possible impact damage must be considered at all loads up to ultimate.

(d) Delamination and out-of-plane loading
Since a composite structure consists of several layers (i.e. a laminate), the design should minimise the possibilites of delamination and out-of-plane loadings.

6 MATRIX ALGEBRA

As has already been stated, a single layer of CFC is stiff and strong in the fibre direction but poor in the transverse direction. It therefore follows that a laminate, consisting of a number of plies laid in different directions, will have different mechanical properties in different direction i.e. it will be anisotropic.

In order to be able to determine laminate mechanical properties in different planes, matrix algebra is used.

Some of the more common expressions are given in Figure 5.

7 FATIGUE

One major advantage of CFC is its good fatigue characteristics. Unlike most metallic materials which have non-linear S-N curves, CFC has a longer endurance at higher loads and the S-N curve is essentially linear. Again, unlike metallic materials, CFC is responsive to compression fatigue but it still maintains a long fatigue life at relatively high cyclic loading.

A typical fatigue comparison between notched CFC and aluminium alloy is given in Figure 6.

8 ENVIRONMENTAL DEGRADATION

CFC can be degraded by the environment i.e. temperature and moisture which can cause a reduction of the matrix dominated properties although the fibres themselves are not affected. Since most laminates have fibres aligned to the loads the problem is only really seen in compression and interlaminar shear and the effect of environmental degradation is taken into account in the design values. Additionally, advances are being made in the matrix resins to improve their temperature/moisture tolerance.

9 STRESS - STRAIN CHARACTERISTICS

Another fundamental difference between CFC and metal is seen in the stress-strain characteristics. Most metallic material exhibit non-linearity and have a yield (or limit of proportionality) followed by a plastic region. CFC on the other hand has no yield point and is essentially fully elastic to failure. A comparison between CFC and aluminium alloy is given in Figure 7.

10 NOTCH SENSITIVITY

The fully elastic behaviour of CFC means that the effect of holes and other stress raisers have to be taken into account at all load levels. Furthermore, the stress concentration factor will vary depending on the lay-up (proportion of 0°/+45°/90° plies) and type of loading (tension or compression).

2

If a notched CFC laminate is progressively loaded in tension there will be a concentration of stress adjacent to the edge of the hole. The stress concentration will remain, until the local stress reaches the ultimate tensile strength for the laminate, when failure occurs. Aluminium alloy, on the other hand, will only show the stress concentration up to the point where the local stress reaches the yield point. More and more of the material will yield, with large plastic deformation, until net area failure occurs at ultimate stress.

This difference in behaviour is shown in Figure 8.

11 EFFECT OF STACKING SEQUENCE

The effect of stacking sequence on CFC lay-ups is best illustrated by considering shear buckling of a panel. For a metallic panel the initial shear bucking stress is a function of Young's Modulus (E), panel length and width (a and b), edge support condition and panel thickness such that:-
$$f_{sb} = K.E.(t/b)^2$$
A CFC panel will depend not only on the above factors but on the ply lay-up and how it is stacked. As was given in the general lay-up guidelines (4.0 a. above) the best lay-up to react in-plane shear in 100% +45.
Using a shorthand notation where + = +45°
- = -45° (135°)
then it is possible to obtain four different symmetric stacking sequences which are still 100% +45°:-
i.e. (+ - - +), (+ - + -), (- + + -) and (- + - +)

Figure 9 shows that, if shear loading is increased with laminate thickness, the initial shear buckling reserve factor (allowable stress divided by applied stress) varies dependant on which of the above stacking sequences are used. The reason for such a variation is that the fibres will only carry load along their length and so the flexural stiffness, or resistance to buckling, will change depending on distance from the neutral axis of the load carrying fibres, as shown in Figure 9.

Not surprisingly, computers are used extensively in the stressing and design of CFC structures.

12 NON DESTRUCTIVE INSPECTION (NDI)

A number of different NDI techniques are used in the inspection of CFC parts but the most extensively used method is that of ultrasonics.

This relies on the fact the ultra sound will be transmitted through a reasonably dense material (including water) but that it will not easily pass through air.

An ultrasonic beam which passes through a known good laminate can be calibrated for the amount of attunuation which that thickness gives. If any defects are present, in the form of voids, delaminations etc., the signal will be more attenuated.

If the ultrasonic probe is then moved over the surface, usually in a recti-linear pattern, the increased attenuation produced by a defect can then be displayed by one or more of the following methods:-

"A" scan - the beam will be reflected from the front and back faces of the laminate which show as peaks on an oscilloscope. If a defect is present, the beam will be reflected by it, causing a shift in the 'backwall' echo. This method will locate a defect depth to an accuracy of about 0,5 mm.

"C" scan - used in conjunction with an x, y plotter. The system is set so that the normal attenuation of a good laminate will give a pen trace but abnormal attenuations caused by defects will give no trace. In this way defects are shown as white patches on the paper. The defect depth can be determined by "A" scan.

"B" scan - a combination of "A" and "B" scans. This system, developed from the medical antenatal one, uses a multi-probe scanning head which displays a pictorial 'slice' onto a television screen. In this way both defect depth and planform dimension are shown.

A sketch of the principles of "A" and "C" scans are shown in Figure 10.

13 CONCLUSION

This paper has been, as it's title says, an introduction to composite materials and has not attempted to discuss any single aspect in detail.

It is recognised that it is extremely unlikely that an aeroplane, ship, motorcar or building will be built solely of one material. Nevertheless, composite materials do have a place in structural designs and can provide high strength/stiffness and low mass structures.

The useage of composites is increasing world-wide and, as developments produce fibre/resin systems with less environmental degradation and notch sensitivity, the increase is sure to continue.

METALLIC vs CFC COMPARISON

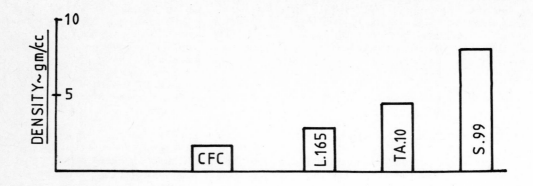

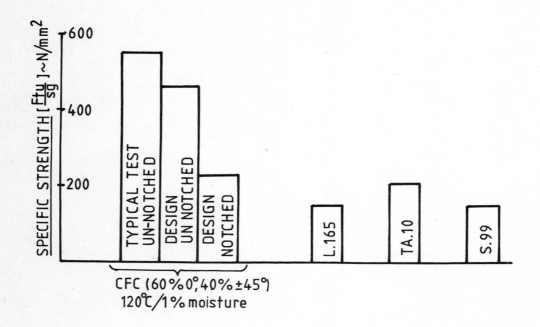

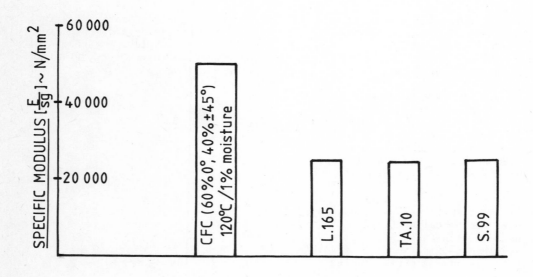

Fig 1   Metallic versus CFC comparison

PRODUCTION OF CFC

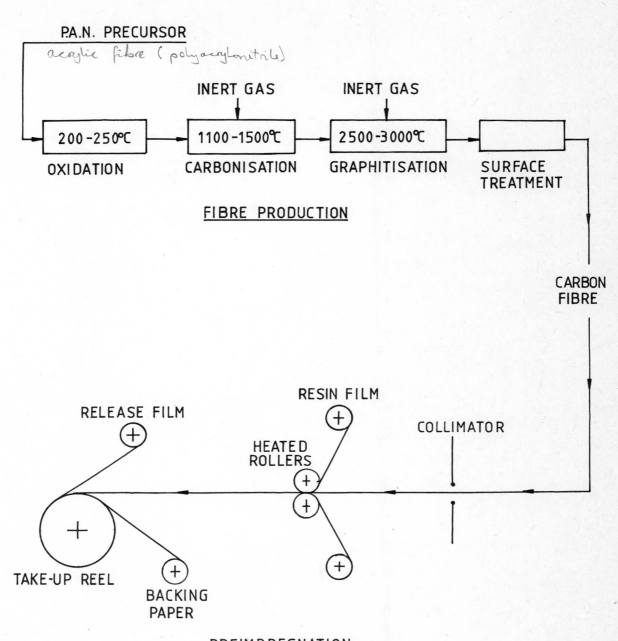

P.A.N. PRECURSOR

acrylic fibre (polyacrylonitrile)

INERT GAS INERT GAS

200-250°C	1100-1500°C	2500-3000°C	
OXIDATION	CARBONISATION	GRAPHITISATION	SURFACE TREATMENT

FIBRE PRODUCTION

CARBON FIBRE

RESIN FILM

RELEASE FILM

COLLIMATOR

HEATED ROLLERS

TAKE-UP REEL

BACKING PAPER

PREIMPREGNATION

Fig 2   Production of CFC

DIRECTIONAL PROPERTIES

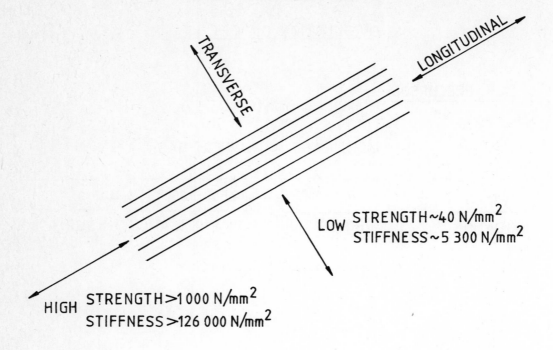

LOW STRENGTH ~40 N/mm^2
STIFFNESS ~5 300 N/mm^2

HIGH STRENGTH >1 000 N/mm^2
STIFFNESS >126 000 N/mm^2

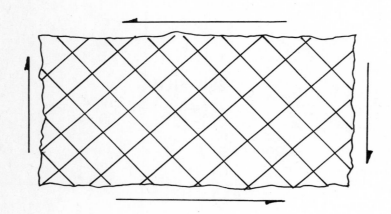

HIGH SHEAR STRENGTH >320 N/mm^2
HIGH SHEAR STIFFNESS >32 000 N/mm^2

(LOAD CARRIED BY FIBRES IN TENSION & COMPRESSION)

Fig 3   Directional properties

EXAMPLE OF LAMINATE LAY-UP & CURE

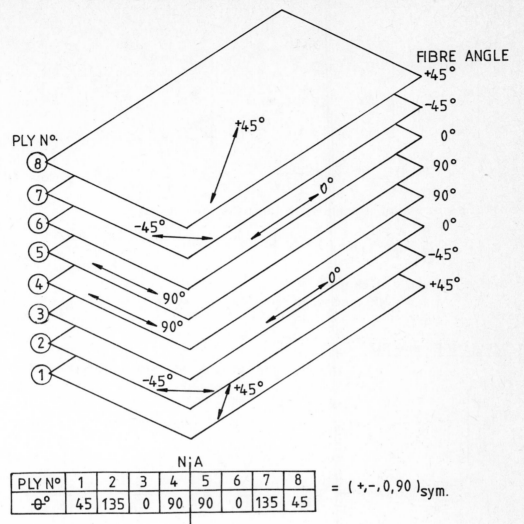

PLY N°	1	2	3	4	5	6	7	8
θ°	45	135	0	90	90	0	135	45

N|A

$= (+,-,0,90)_{sym.}$

N.B. $-45° \equiv 135°$

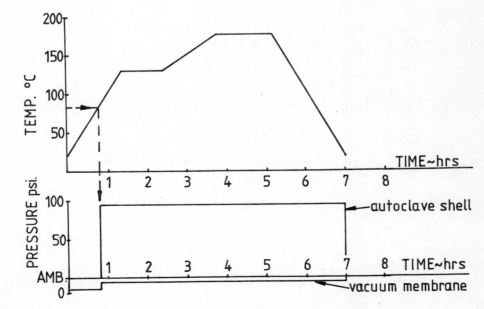

Fig 4   Example of laminate lay-up and cure

MATRIX ALGEBRA

RIGIDITY MATRIX

In bending

$$\begin{bmatrix} M_x \\ M_y \\ M_{xy} \end{bmatrix} = \begin{bmatrix} D_{11} & D_{12} & D_{13} \\ D_{21} & D_{22} & D_{23} \\ D_{31} & D_{32} & D_{33} \end{bmatrix} \begin{bmatrix} K_x \\ K_y \\ K_{xy} \end{bmatrix}$$

where $\quad K_x = \dfrac{\partial^2 w}{\partial x^2} \qquad K_y = \dfrac{\partial^2 w}{\partial y^2} \qquad K_{xy} = \dfrac{2\,\partial^2 w}{\partial x\,\partial y}$ i.e. the plate curvature

For plies of equal thickness it can be shown that

$$D_{ij} = 2\,t^3 \sum_{k=1}^{N} Q_{ij}^{\theta} \left[k(k-1) + \frac{1}{3} \right]$$

where $\quad t$ = ply thickness

$\qquad\qquad k$ = ply N^a measured from axis of symmetry.

COMPLIANCE MATRIX

is the inverse of the stiffness matrix such that :-

$$\begin{bmatrix} \varepsilon_1 \\ \varepsilon_2 \\ \gamma_{12} \end{bmatrix} = \begin{bmatrix} S_{11} & S_{12} & S_{13} \\ S_{21} & S_{22} & S_{23} \\ S_{31} & S_{32} & S_{33} \end{bmatrix} \begin{bmatrix} \sigma_1 \\ \sigma_2 \\ \tau_{12} \end{bmatrix}$$

$$S_{11} = \frac{1}{E_{11}} \qquad S_{22} = \frac{1}{E_{22}} \qquad S_{33} = \frac{1}{G_{12}} \qquad S_{12} = \frac{-\nu_{12}}{E_{11}} = \frac{-\nu_{21}}{E_{22}} = S_{21}$$

STIFFNESS MATRIX

$$\begin{bmatrix} \sigma_1 \\ \sigma_2 \\ \tau_{12} \end{bmatrix} = \begin{bmatrix} Q_{11} & Q_{12} & Q_{13} \\ Q_{21} & Q_{22} & Q_{23} \\ Q_{31} & Q_{32} & Q_{33} \end{bmatrix} \times \begin{bmatrix} \varepsilon_1 \\ \varepsilon_2 \\ \gamma_{12} \end{bmatrix}$$

$$Q_{11} = \frac{E_{11}}{1 - \nu_{12}\,\nu_{21}} \qquad Q_{22} = \frac{E_{22}}{1 - \nu_{12}\,\nu_{21}} \qquad Q_{12} = \frac{\nu_{21}\,E_{11}}{1 - \nu_{12}\,\nu_{21}} = \frac{\nu_{12}\,E_{22}}{1 - \nu_{12}\,\nu_{21}} = Q_{21}$$

$$Q_{66} = G = Q_{33}$$

$$Q_{13} = Q_{31} = Q_{32} = 0 \qquad \text{for specially orthotropic laminates.}$$

For generally orthotropic laminates $\quad Q_{13}$ & $Q_{31} \neq 0$

Fig 5   Matrix algebra

8

FATIGUE COMPARISON

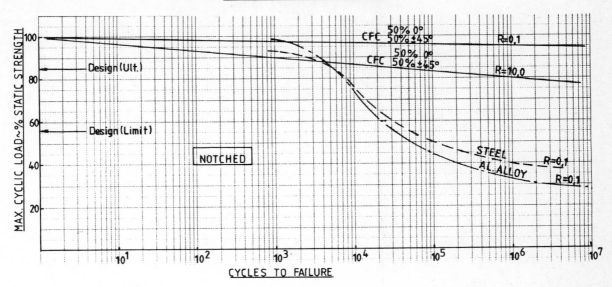

Fig 6　　Fatigue comparison

STRESS-STRAIN COMPARISON

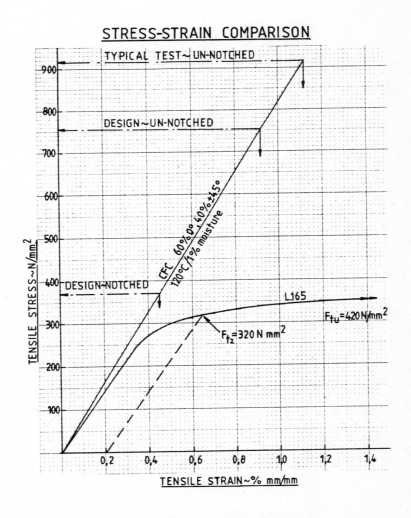

Fig 7　　Stress-strain comparison

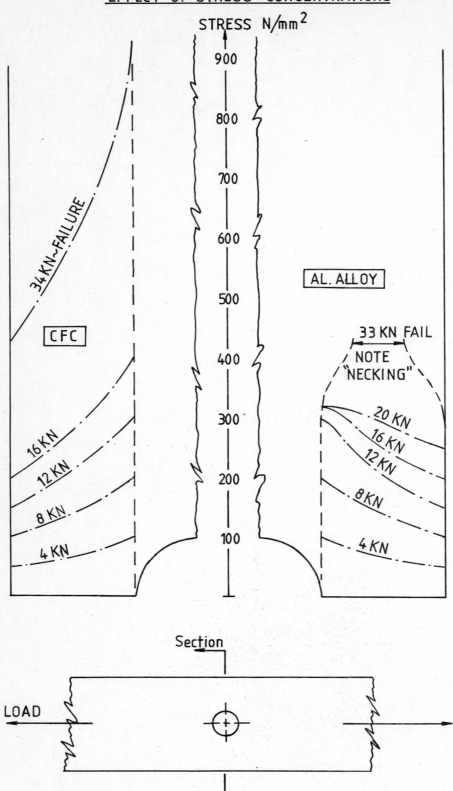

Fig 8   Effect of stress concentrations

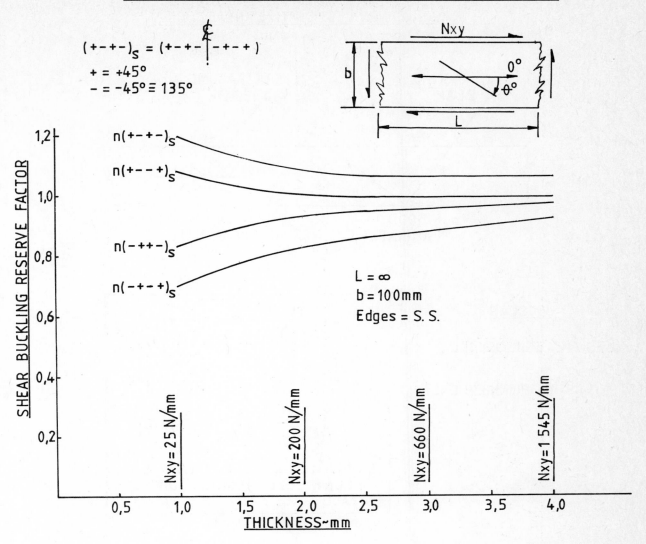

$$(+-+-)_S = (+-+-|-+-+)$$

+ = +45°

− = −45° ≡ 135°

$L = \infty$

$b = 100$ mm

Edges = S. S.

EXPLANATION.

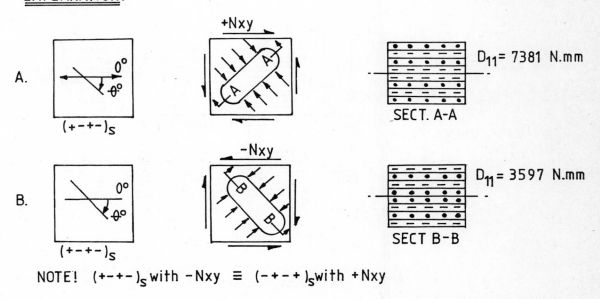

A.　$(+-+-)_S$　$+Nxy$　SECT. A-A　D_{11}= 7381 N.mm

B.　$(+-+-)_S$　$-Nxy$　SECT B-B　D_{11} = 3597 N.mm

NOTE!　$(+-+-)_S$ with $-Nxy$ ≡ $(-+-+)_S$ with $+Nxy$

Fig 9　Influence of stacking sequence on shear buckling

ULTRASONIC NON-DESTRUCTIVE INSPECTION

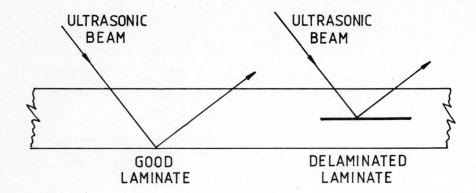

"A" SCAN

USES AN OSCILLOSCOPE

THROUGH THE THICKNESS ONLY

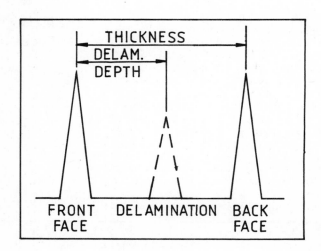

"C" SCAN

PLOTTED ON ELECTROSTATIC PAPER

PLAN VIEW ONLY

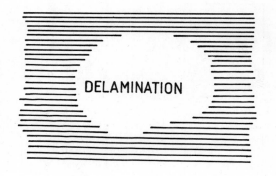

Fig 10   Ultrasonic non-destructive inspection

C387/016

Mechanical testing and the relevance of standards

F L MATTHEWS, BSc(Eng), ACGI, CEng, MRAeS, FPRI, **E W GODWIN**, BSc and **C RUEDA**, BSc(Chem), MSc, PhD, DIC
Centre for Composite Materials, Imperial College of Science and Technology, London

SYNOPSIS: A crucial step in designing any component is the acquisition of relevant mechanical properties. When using composite materials one is faced with a bewildering array of data and methods: there are national standards, company standards, textbooks, research papers, conference proceedings. The current paper reports on a series of tests on epoxy-based composites (reinforced with carbon, glass, or 'Kevlar' fibres) conducted to ASTM, BSI, and CRAG standards, in tension, compression, flexure, and shear. The differences in results emphasises the need for caution when using results obtained from such methods.

1 INTRODUCTION

A crucial step in designing any component is the acquisition of relevant mechanical properties. When using composite materials one is faced with a bewildering array of data; there are national standards, company standards, textbooks, research papers, conference proceedings. The situation is made worse by the fact that the constituents (fibres and matrix) of the composites are not always clearly stated, and the fact that, unlike metals, one cannot get 'off-the-shelf properties' since the material is usually formed in the process of making the component. A further shortcoming of much published information is that the data often refer to a non-standard test and relevant details are not given. A separate, but vital, issue is the relevance of the test method to the design being considered; it is not apparent that data are always meaningful for the proposed application.

National and international standards should play a key rôle in giving a consistent and reliable framework within which valid, design-useful, data can be obtained. However it is clear that there is some way to go in achieving a universal approach, particularly for impact, fatigue and creep testing (1). Even with some of the better established tests there is strong evidence that the methods are not always fit for their designated purpose (2).

Short-term tests for tension, compression, flexure and, to a lesser extent, shear are reasonably well defined. Even so there are many minor differences, for the same type of test, between major standards, which can, in some circumstances, lead to large differences between the results obtained. Current work at Imperial College is aimed at comparing methods defined by three, well known, standards organisations - American Society for Testing and Materials (ASTM), British Standards Institute (BSI) and Composites Research Advisory Group (CRAG). The current paper complements earlier publications (3,4) and summarises the results obtained for three fibre/matrix combinations from tensile, compressive, flexural and shear tests.

2 COMPARISON OF THE STANDARDS

A comparison of tensile, flexural and shear methods is given by Sottos (5) and Godwin (6), who also includes compression testing. Full details may be obtained by consulting the relevant standards (7-20). There are detailed differences between the recommendtions of the three organisations on almost every point although, because of the freedom allowed within each specification, overlap is frequently possible.

2.1 Tensile tests

The standards for tensile tests are ASTM D3039 (7), BS 2782 Part 3 (8), and CRAG (9).

The principal differences between testpieces are in end-tabbing detail and use of waisting. CRAG specifies a through-thickness waist if the specimens are to be used for generating design data, but allows the use of a full-thickness (unwaisted) specimens for quality control purposes. BS 2782 lists a variety of testpieces, some of which are waisted (BS2782 method 320F) and others simply relying on end tabs (method 320E).

ASTM specifies end tab material to be a balanced 0/90° nonwoven E-glass, and that it should be strain-compatible with the testpiece: the thickness should be between 1.5 and 4 times that of the testpiece. Care must be taken that the plies in the tab and specimen are well aligned at the interface: a high elongation (tough) adhesive should be used. The length of the tabs is 'determined by the shear strength of the adhesive, the tabs, and the testpiece'. The end tabs are tapered at the ends to reduce stress concentrations.

End tabs are not mandatory for tests to BS2782, depending on the material under test i.e. relatively weak materials such as SMC and DMC will not require tabs. Where tabs are used it is suggested that they be attached to a piece of material wide enough to produce several testpieces before final machining to width: a similar method is also allowed by ASTM.

CRAG requires the use of end tabs in addition to waisting, the recommendation being soft aluminium alloy for dry ambient conditions, or GRP (lay-up not specified) for hot or moist conditions.

CRAG specifies non-waisted specimen for multidirectional laminates thickness up to 3.0mm, the length being such as to allow a non-axial fibre to run the full width of the specimen and allow a half-width clearance before each end tab. The standard also states that testing without end tabs is permissible provided 'suitable grips are used'.

The width of the testpiece depends to some extent on the material under test. ASTM D3039 specifies 12.7mm for unidirectional material but requires a wider testpiece (25.4mm) if the laminate contains 90° fibres, in order to minimise edge effects. CRAG specifies a width of up to 30mm, dependent on thickness. BS2782 specifies 25 ±0.5mm for strength tests, 12.5 ±0.5mm if only modulus is required.

ASTM and BS2782 recommend the use of an extensometer (gauge length 50mm) in preference to strain gauges, which are recommended for use only if out-of-plane bending is suspected: in this case, ASTM specifies the use of three gauges. CRAG specifies strain gauges.

CRAG requires that failure occurs within 30-90 seconds. BSI specifies 1.0 to 5.0 mm/min. ASTM quotes a strain rate of 16.7 to 33.4 m/m/min. (or 0.01 to 0.02 in/in/min, values which conflict with the metric specification).

ASTM requires that failure should occur at least one specimen width away from the tab, and CRAG that failure should be in the waisted centre section. BS2782 does not specify a failure position.

2.2 Compression tests

The relevant standards are ASTM D695M (10), ASTM D3410 (11), and CRAG (9). BS2782: Part 3: Method 345A (12) also covers compression testing, using a testpiece similar to ASTM D695: this test has not been included in the present series.

The subject of compression testing is complicated by the requirement of avoiding premature failure by gross (Euler) buckling of the testpiece, whilst providing a gauge length sufficiently long to minimise end effects. It is difficult to reconcile these two requirements, particularly if angle plies are present in the composite. A further problem is that of introducing loads into the material. The conventional approach of simply bearing directly on the end of the material has the merit of simplicity, especially as many testing machines are not normally capable of gripping material whilst applying large compressive loads. Buckling in this case is prevented by the use of an anti-buckling support which permits the use of a reasonably long gauge length. The objection to this method is that the guides may over-constrain the gauge length. A more practical objection is that, unless the guides are of fairly elaborate design, a small amount of material is left unsupported at the ends: interlaminar weakness can lead to premature failure in this region, with the material becoming locally crushed ('brooming'). In the present series of tests the ASTM D695 anti-buckling guide was used. The standard actually specifies that a subsidiary loading rig should be used to ensure alignment during testing, although this was dispensed with in practice. Whereas the screws clamping the ASTM support together are tightened finger-tight, BSI requires a more massive anti-buckling system using a spring-loaded jig.

An alternative way of preventing buckling is to use a short gauge length, typically 10mm, in conjunction with accurately aligned grips in some form of subsidiary loading equipment consisting of wedge jaws designed to transfer compressive loads, together with guides of sufficiently massive construction, and built to sufficiently fine tolerances, to ensure non-eccentricity of the testpiece during loading. This is the method used in both ASTM D3410 and CRAG, the major difference between these methods being testpiece dimensions. The current tests employed the rig commonly known as the Celanese jig.

Strain is measured either using an extensometer, as recommended by ASTM D695 where a large gauge length is available and not obstructed by the anti-buckling guide or, where access to the specimen is restricted, as in the Celanese jig, strain gauges are used.

2.3 Flexural tests

The relevant standards are: ASTM D790M (13), BS2782 Part 10 (14), and CRAG (9).

Bending tests are simple and convenient to carry out, requiring equipment that is not elaborate and simple parallel sided specimens needing the minimum of preparation. They are thus well suited to quality control purposes: ASTM suggests that the three-point test is used for this purpose. However, there are still variations between the specifications for width, length, span, and support and loading roller diameters.

Clearly in a bending test accurate measurement of thickness is important: CRAG specifies the thickness as being as close to 2mm as can be conveniently moulded: ASTM D790 covers thicknesses up to 25mm and requires that it be measured to an accuracy of 'within 0.001mm', a remarkably high level of precision. Samples may be machined to a required thickness, material being removed from both faces, but this should be clearly stated in the report as results obtained may differ from results obtained from 'as-moulded' material. BS2782 (which covers a range of thicknesses up to 50mm) more realistically suggests a tolerance of 0.02mm, whilst CRAG simply calls for 'accurate measurement' which, with a standard (non-vernier) micrometer, might be taken as being within 0.02mm.

It is conventional to specify span (L) in terms of specimen thickness (or beam depth, d) of the material under test, the minimum generally being a ratio of 16/1, although ASTM D790 covers span/depth ratios of up to 60/1. This longer span is in order to minimise effects due to shear stresses. The CRAG specification requires a sufficient span to result in 'bending' failure, and specifies a minimum overhang beyond the rollers of 5.0mm. Other standards specify the overall length of the specimens, the values for overhang varying from 2d to 9d.

Whilst span is specified as a multiple of depth, width may either be tabulated or specified directly. Thus ASTM D790 specifies a width of 25mm for specimens of up to 3.0mm in thickness. Above this thickness, the specified width is reduced to 10mm, increasing with thickness until a thickness of 25mm is reached, when a width of 25mm is again specified. BS2782 gives widths which increase with thickness, the narrowest being 15mm and the greatest being 80mm. In the case of the present work, using material 2mm thick, ASTM D790 specifies 25mm width (w/d = 12.5) and BS2782 15mm (w/d = 7.5). CRAG simply specifies a width of 10mm, corresponding to a w/d ratio of 5.

There are also variations in the size of support and loading rollers, the smallest being 4mm and 5mm respectively (BSI). CRAG specifies 10mm and 25mm, with the option of 6mm and 10mm, but stresses that these smaller diameters may lead to local damage of the testpiece. ASTM D790 specifies diameters of >3d for the support rollers (but with a minimum of 6mm) and <8d, but greater than 6mm, for the loading roller: again there is reference to damage by indentation.

The testing speed required for tests to ASTM D790 can be calculated from the formula $V = ZL2/6d$, where V is testing machine speed and Z the desired strain rate. The strain rate specified is 0.01 mm/mm.min for materials failing at 'normal strains', or 0.1 mm/mm.min for materials failing at large strains. Testing speeds are also tabulated for various thicknesses and spans: for 2mm thick material (the results from which are reported here) the rate varied between 0.85 mm/min, for a 16/1 span/depth, up to 12.0 mm/min for the 60/1 ratio: the test is to be terminated when the strain in the surface fibres reaches 5%.

BS2782 calculates loading rate from the formula $V = d/2$, which gives a loading rate for the samples described here of 1 mm/min for 2mm thick specimens and 1.5 mm/min for 3.0mm samples. A speed of 10 mm/min is specified for 'routine' testing.

CRAG specifies that failure should occur within 30-180 seconds, and a test speed of 5 mm/min was found acceptable.

ASTM D790 also covers 4-point flexure. Testing conditions and testpiece requirements are similar to those specified for 3-point bending, and again dimensions of both specimens and supports are tabulated for a number of span/depth ratios, and for loading at 1/4 and 1/3 span points.

2.4 In-plane shear stress (IPSS) tests

In-plane shear properties are generally measured using a notched tensile test specimen, but ASTM D3846 (15) specifies a compressive test setup, utilising the D695 anti-buckling guide. The purpose of this appears to be to eliminate out-of-plane tensile stresses and it may be felt that this jig, or a similar one, should be employed using the tensile IPSS test methods. It should be noted that ASTM D3846 supersedes a similar standard, D2733 (16), in which tensile loading is used, and that the later version of D2733 refers to a support jig. D3846 also specifies that the sheared area should be measured after failure has occurred. Tensile loading is specified by the BSI, in the test method contained in BS4994 (17).

In-plane shear stress and strain data can be generated using longitudinal and transverse strain gauges on material laid up at $\pm45°$, as detailed in ASTM D3518 (18) and CRAG (9). It will be found that the material undergoes a very large extension, and that an excessively high strain rate would be necessary to cause failure within the recommended time limit.

2.5 Interlaminar shear stress (ILSS) tests

The interlaminar shear test is covered by ASTM D2344 (19), BS2782 (20), and CRAG (9). This is another test using a simple sample tested in bending, but in this case the span/depth ratio is sufficiently low to ensure that shear stresses predominate. Again, as with the flexural strength and stiffness tests, there are variations between standards. ASTM and BSI both describe the test as being for apparent interlaminar shear stress.

CRAG describes the test as being suitable for material having a flexural/shear strength ratio of >10/1, also specifying that the material must be axially orthotropic. ASTM D2344 suggests a thickness of <6.4mm, and specifies a span/depth ratio of 5. BSI specifies a thickness of 2 to 3mm, and CRAG a thickness of 2.0mm.

Again dimensions are related to depth and differences in geometry persist, thus: ASTM (span = 5d) length = 7d, width = 6.4mm; BSI (span = 5d) length = 6d, width = 10mm; and CRAG (span = 5d) length = 10d, using the preferred thickness of 2.0mm (or nearest mouldable thickness), the specified width of 10mm = 5d. The significance of differences in overhang resulting from variations in length will be seen to be reflected in the results.

3 CURRENT PROGRAMME

3.1 Specimens

Laminated plates were prepared by autoclaving, following the supplier's recommended curing schedule, from pre-impregnated material (prepreg). In all cases the matrix was Ciba Geigy 913 epoxy resin (120°C cure). XAS carbon and E-glass prepreg was available in unidirectional form whilst 'Kevlar' as prepreg was available only in the form of balanced, bi-directional, woven fabric. The plates were in 1 and 2mm thicknesses (8 and 16-ply), and made with a variety of lay-ups: carbon and glass in unidirectional, cross-ply (0/90°), $(0_2/\pm45°)$; quasi-isotropic (0/90/$\pm45°$), and angle-ply ($\pm45°$); 'Kevlar' in only cross-

ply and angle-ply. Coupons were cut from the laminates using a diamond impregnated cutting wheel and specimens prepared in accordance with the specifications in the three standards.

3.2 Results

In the current paper the results are compared in diagrammatic form. Other papers give more detailed results for the carbon (3) and glass (4,5) specimens. Future papers will present further results for compression of carbon and data for the $\pm45°$ 'Kevlar' materials. In the diagrams given below each vertical bar relates to a particular standard, the horizontal lines indicating the average and $\pm$ one standard deviation, from five tests.

3.3 Tension tests

As seen in Fig 1, no clear picture emerges from the results of the tensile tests, either for the relative magnitudes of stiffness and strength or for the scatter in the data. To assess the statistical significance of the differences would require the testing of larger samples (than suggested by the standards).

The relative positions of the three standards are different for stiffness and strength, and depend on the lay-up of the laminate. The CRAG method gives, in general, higher strengths than those of ASTM and BSI.

3.4 Compression tests

The results from the compression tests, which show much bigger differences as illustrated in Fig 2, serve to underline the problems associated with such tests; alignment of the specimen being a particular difficulty. It should also be noted that both CRAG and ASTM D3410 employ the Celanese test jig, whereas ASTM D695 uses a larger specimen with anti-buckling guides.

It is seen for the unidirectional materials that for carbon the tensile modulus and strength are higher than the corresponding compressive values, while for glass the moduli are effectively the same in tension and compression whereas the compressive strength tends to be higher than the tensile strength. Such observations are confirmed by other workers (e.g. Kretsis (21)).

3.5 Flexure tests

Although three-point bending is relatively simple to undertake, it could be inferred from Figs 3 and 4 that there is little else to recommend such tests. Clearly the results are strongly dependent on span-to-depth ratio, especially the modulus of unidirectional carbon and the strength of all forms of glass material.

It is to be expected that modulus will increase as span is increased since the shear stress contribution to deflection is reduced. However such trends are only valid for small deflections, which is certainly not the case for the glass materials. In the latter situation a correction should be applied to allow for the associated nonlinearity, although this has not been done for the results shown here.

Another point worth noting is that the moduli and strengths in flexure are not the same as, and are generally lower than, those in tension. Flexural behaviour can only be properly interpreted, particularly for multi-directional laminates, if the nonlinearities arising from geometric and the change in tensile and compressive moduli with strain (causing the neutral axis of the beam to move to the tensile surface) are properly accounted for (21).

3.6 Shear tests

The results for interlaminar shear strength (f

flexure tests) in Fig 5(a) show a large measure of agreement between the standards. The differences in magnitudes and scatter could well be related to the fact that each method specifies a different overhang length outside the support rollers.

Data for in-plane shear strength in Fig 5(b) show large differences between tensile loading of a notched bar (BSI and ASTM D2733) and compression loading of a similar specimen (ASTM D3846). In the former tests the specimen fails prematurely in 'peel' (such effects are suppressed in later versions of this test). The notched compression specimen and tensile ±45° plain specimen (ASTM D3518) give similar values to the short beam flexure specimens.

4 CONCLUSIONS

1.	The results presented in the current paper show that large differences can be obtained between properties obtained from mechanical tests according to ASTM, BSI and CRAG standards. This implies that one may be measuring specimen properties rather than material properties. It is not possible from the present series of tests to comment on the statistical significance of these differences. Neither is it possible to draw conclusions on the relevance of the data to design, although the CRAG methods are based on such relevance for CFRP.

2.	No clear picture emerges from the tensile tests. Differences in data are small but the relative positions of the three standards are not the same for stiffness and strength. For the latter, the CRAG method generally gives higher values than ASTM and BSI.

3.	For compression tests the differences between the results from the standards can be quite large. Such differences are thought to be a consequence of the sensitivity of the data to specimen and loading jig design.

4.	Results obtained from flexure tests are strongly dependent on span-to-depth ratio. For low stiffness specimens, giving large deflections, a correction should be made for nonlinear behaviour. The usefulness of such tests in obtaining design-relevant data should be questioned.

5.	The standards show best agreement in the results from interlaminar (short beam) shear tests.

6.	If a conservative approach is taken and the lowest values of the various properties are considered relevant then, for all the materials tested here (CFRP, GFRP and KFRP) in all the loading modes (except shear of GFRP), an ASTM method would, in general, be recommended. However, a method should be chosen which is most representative of the particular application.

7.	There is a clear case for harmonisation of standards.

REFERENCES

(1)	LOCKETT, F.J. The provision of adequate materials property data. Proc. Conf. ICCM-VI/ECCM-2, Imperial College, London, July 1987, Vol 1, 5-27 (Elsevier Applied Science).

(2)	HOGG, P.J. and TURNER, S. Mechanical testing of long fibre composites: standardization and harmonization in the U.K. Composites Research Group, Queen Mary College, London, 1988.

(3)	SOTTOS, N.R., HODGKINSON, J.M. and MATTHEWS, F.L. A practical comparison of standard test methods using carbon fibre-reinforced epoxy. Proc. Conf. ICCM-VI/ECCM-2, Imperial College, London, July 1987, Vol 1, 310-320 (Elsevier Applied Science).

(4)	GODWIN, E.W., HYON, T.C., HODGKINSON, J.M. and MATTHEWS, F.L. An experimental comparison of standard test methods used with GFRP. Paper 14, Proc. FRC'88, University of Liverpool, March 1988 (Plastics & Rubber Institute).

(5)	SOTTOS, N.R. A comparison of ASTM, BSI and CRAG standard test methods for the determination of tensile, shear and flexural properties in fibre-reinforced plastics. August 1986 (Centre for Composite Materials, Imperial College, London).

(6)	GODWIN, E.W. An experimental comparison of ASTM, BSI and CRAG standard test methods for the determination of tensile, shear and flexural properties. Part 2: Glass fibre-reinforced plastic. February 1988 (Centre for Composite Materials, Imperial College, London).

(7)	AMERICAN SOCIETY for TESTING and MATERIALS. ASTM D3039. Standard test methods for tensile properties of fibre-resin composites.

(8)	BRITISH STANDARDS INSTITUTION. BS2782, Part 3. Tensile strength, elongation, and elastic modulus.

(9)	CURTIS, P.T. CRAG test methods for the measurement of the engineering properties of fibre reinforced plastics. Royal Aircraft Establishment, Tech. Report 88012, February 1988.

(10)	ASTM D695M. Standard test method for compressive properties of rigid plastics.

(11)	ASTM D3410. Standard test method for compressive properties of unidirectional or cross-ply composites.

(12)	BSI BS2782, Part 3. Method 345A: Determination of compressive properties by deformation at a constant rate.

(13)	ASTM D790M. Standard test methods for flexural properties of unreinforced and reinforced plastics and electrical insulating materials (metric).

(14)	BSI BS2782. British standard methods of testing plastics, Part 10, Method 1005: Determination of flexural properties. Three point method.

(15)	ASTM D3846. Standard test method for in-plane shear strength of reinforced plastics.

(16)	ASTM D2733. Standard methods of test for interlaminar shear strength of structural reinforced plastics at elevated temperatures.

(17)	BSI BS4994. Vessels and tanks in reinforced plastics.

(18)	ASTM D3518. Standard recommended procedure for in-plane shear stress-strain response of unidirectional reinforced plastics.

(19)	ASTM D2344. Standard test method for apparent horizontal shear strength of reinforced plastics by short beam method.

(20)	BSI BS2782. Method 341A: Determination of apparent interlaminar shear strength of reinforced plastics.

(21)	KRETSIS, G. Mechanical characterisation of hybrid glass/carbon fibre-reinforced plastics. PhD Thesis, February 1987, University of London.

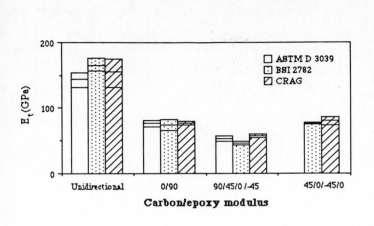

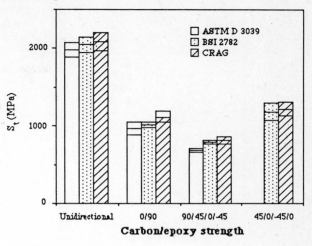

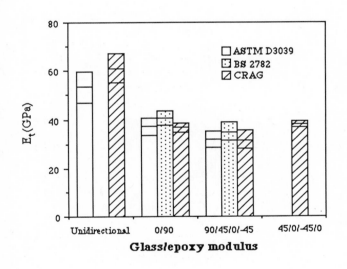

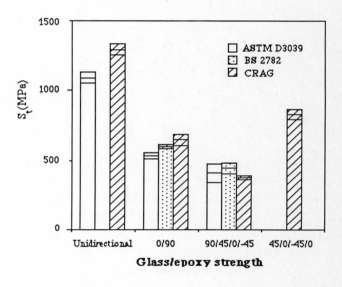

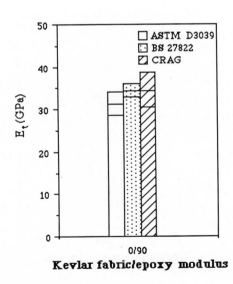

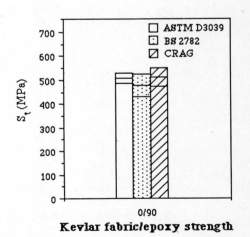

Fig 1   Tension test results

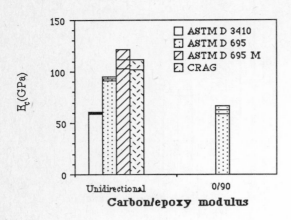

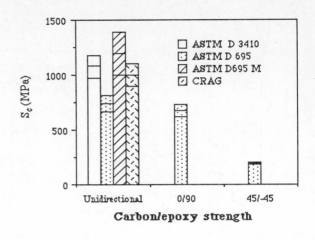

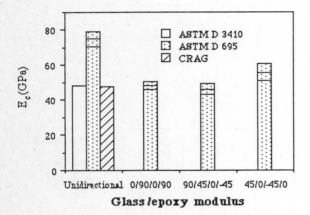

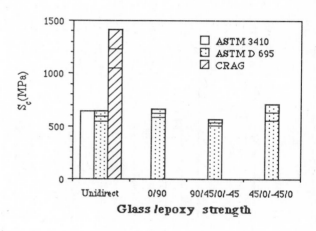

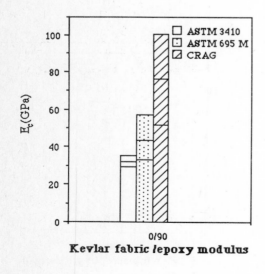

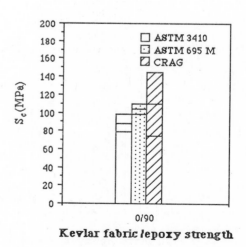

Fig 2   Compression test results

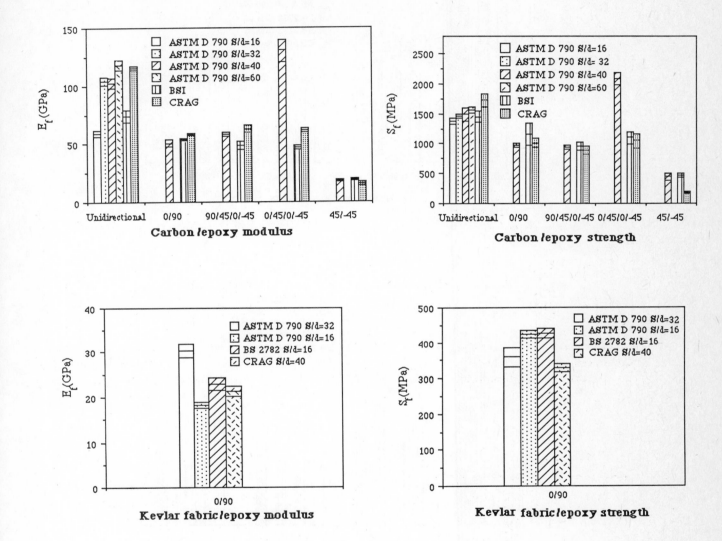

Fig 3   Three-point flexure test results for carbon and Kevlar

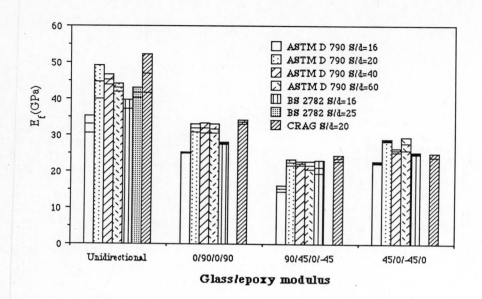

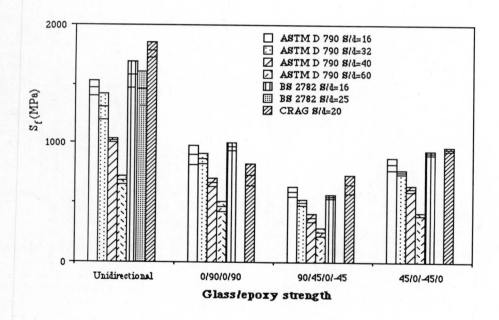

Fig 4   Three-point flexure test results for glass

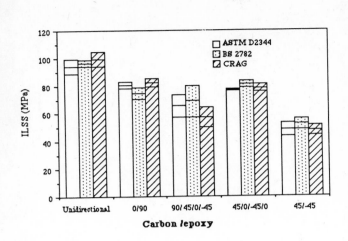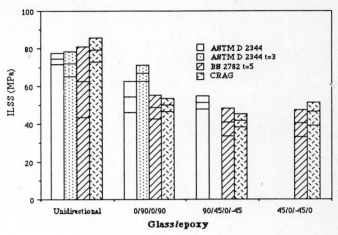

(a)   Interlaminar shear strength

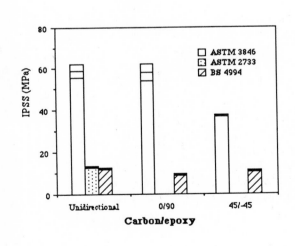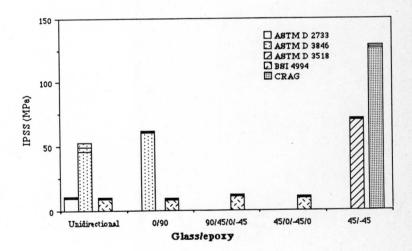

(b)   In-plane shear strength

Fig 5   Shear test results

C387/015

Panther Solo—the first production composite vehicle structure

D PARRY-WILLIAMS, BSc
The Panther Car Company, Harlow, Essex

SYNOPSIS The Panther Solo sportscar due to be launched in 1989, has a primary structure comprised of 3 major components: A steel underbody, a one-piece composite centre section and a one-piece composite roof inner moulding. These three components are adhesively bonded and riveted together. The resulting structure complies with all Federal and European structural requirements as well as fulfilling all normal demands of a modern production vehicle body.

1 INTRODUCTION

The manufacturing processes available to a small manufacturer wishing to build a high quality road vehicle body are limited on economic grounds but would probably include pressed and hand finished aluminium, resin transfer moulding, re-inforced reation injection moulding, wet lay-up moulding and possibly pre-preg composite moulding. Of these, resin transfer moulding, wet lay-up and pre-preg can all be used to produce structural repeatable complex body shapes with an acceptable suface finish. Pre-preg composite components can achieve very high specific strength and stiff-ness values from cheap easily produced tooling. This enables engineering development involving modifications to shape and structural properties of the components to be carried out at an early stage in the programme.

2 DESIGN CONCEPTS

Applying a novel material or collection of materials to an existing set of engineering prob-lems has resulted in some unusual solutions to these problems. Four design concepts are covered here, three of which were successful and the fourth was not and was subsequently re-engineered using more conventional methods. The reasons for this are dealt with in the appropriate section.

2.1 Three Piece Primary Structure

A major expense in vehicle production is in containing vehicle build tolerances to accept-able levels. In a conventional unitary con-struction steel bodyshell, effort is applied particularly to areas such as windscreen aper-tures and door apertures if they cannot be manu-factured as a single piece.

In a composite structure the shape of the Solo roof or roof 'spider' (see figure 2 a) it was considered to be undesirable to have any bonded joints across narrow sections because of the difficulty of controlling the quality of such critical structural joints.

For both of the reasons stated, every effort was made to keep the number of panels in the primary structure to a minimum and to incorpor-ate glass and door apertures in the same piece. The two piece roof structure has proved to be very resilient and provides a smooth load path under the various dynamic load cases exper-ienced under impact conditions (see figure 2.1b).

2.2 Door Design

In order to meet Federal road safety legislation, it is necessary to engineer a vehicle door that absorbs energy during a slow lateral crush test upto an intrusion of 18 inches. Since the door is restrained by the hinges and latch, a consid-erable amount of elongation is required. It was therefore necessary to include in the door a metal beam to perform this function. The metal beam is in fact a vacuum formed aluminium component bonded to the composite door inner panel and to which all mechanical components within the door attach, including the hinges and the latch. (See figure 2.2a).

Another requirement of the door design espec-ially on a vehicle like Solo, is the need to min-imise wind noise around the window frame at high speed. This is achieved by having adequate lateral stiffness of the window frame to resist the aero-dynamic forces on the door glass in addition to the force exerted from the inside by the weather seal. To maintain a homogeneous structure in the door, the door inner and outer panels both incorp-orate the window frame. Although these are bonded together, the glass frame stiffness would still be far from adequate without the inclusion of the glass run channel (see figure 2.2b). This comp-onent is made predominantly of uni-direction carbon fibre and performs a dual function; (a) it stiff-ens up the window frame by creating a closed cross section resisting bending and torsinal loads, and (b) it provides an accurate channel for the door glass run seal to locate into. The window frame is further stiffened by virtue of the lower ends of the glass run channel being bonded to the outer door skin.

2.3 Door Hinge Design

The door hinge pillar is one of the most repeatedly loaded areas of the upper body structure. Because of the leverage due to the length of the door, the loads fed into the structure via the hinge pillar in normal use are significant and under impact conditions the hinge will experience loads in excess of one ton (see figure 2.1b). In a steel unitary construction, the door hinge is usually welded to the hinge pillar and is in the form of two discrete hinges. This is obviously not appropriate to a composite vehicle and bolting a conventional hinge to the hinge pillar would induce high local stresses in the hinge pillar. It was therefore decided to manufacture a bespoke hinge designed to be bonded onto the vehicle (see figure 2.3). The principal of the design is that the hinge pivot falls on the two exterior surfaces of the pillar, the check arm is also mounted on this pivot and therefore the adhesive joint will only experience shear or compressive forces during normal use and abuse.

Under the extreme load case of the side door intrusion when the hinge and latch are pulled towards one another, the leading edge of the hinge pillar is subject to a peel force and therefore the steel retaining straps are included as peel stoppers.

2.4 Energy Management System (E.M.S.)

The E.M.S. was conceived as a replaceable front end composite structure based on the principle of a formula 1 racing car nose cone using aluminium honeycomb and glass reinforced skin construction. During slow crush tests in a laboratory, the construction proved to have excellent specific energy absorbtion. The problem is realising all of the potential energy absorbtion, given the confines of the packaging coastraints in a real vehicle. Because of the need for a useable boot space and for space around the front wheels, the frontal area available to mount a discrete composite crushable structure was insufficient to control the stability of that structure while it crushed end-on.

A fundamental difference between a metallic structure and a fibre reinforced composite one is that in the metal structure, energy is used up in yielding the metal and in the composite structure, the energy goes into breaking fibres and bonds within the laminate, therefore the composite structure will end up in many small pieces but the metal structure will still be one piece.

This does not preclude the use of composite crushable structures in the front of road vehicles but it does mean that a metal structure is more able to absorb a significant proportion of the energy it is capable of absorbing should it experience an impact in a direction different to that which is intended. This becomes important also since two similar vehicles will crush in a slightly different way in consecutive impacts under similar test conditions because the balance of strengths of the various parts of the structure is very sensitive. With a composite structure the difference in behaviour during two similar tests could make the difference between the structure crushing or large parts of it breaking off.

Finally, a hidden benefit of steel structures particularly, is their strain rate dependency; the harder you hit them, the stronger they get.

3 ENGINEERING OF MATERIALS

The major areas of concentrated development were the joining system and the lay-up of the composite panels with respect to structural requirements and cost effectiveness.

3.1 Joining System

The junction between underbody, centre section and roof spider was designed for ease of trimming, assembly and bonding and eliminating peel forces during the life of the vehicle. The bond line width was initially set a 20 mm with a 1 mm glue line thickness. The total bond line length between the three components is 22.5 metres. To ease assembly, the bond flanges are riveted every 150 mm. Once riveted, the assembly can be removed from its jig whilst the adhesive cures. The fasteners are left in to act as peel stoppers in the event of an impact.

Both toughened epoxy and polyurethane adhesives were evaluated. The two materials are entirely different. An interesting comparison is shown below:

	Toughened Epoxy 2 part	Polyurethane 2 part
Lap shear Strength (7 days)	40 MPa	5.6 MPa
Peel strength	9 KN/m	20 KN/m
Shear Modulus	400 MPa	3 MPa

Fig 1

It can be seen that while the epoxy material is over seven times stronger in lap shear tests, it is considerably more brittle, indeed the polyurethane material has an elongation of more than 750 per cent. This difference results in a failure mode under peel or cleavage conditions which is different for the two adhesives (see figure 3.1). Given the large bond area on the body structure, the polyurethane material is preferable because of its superior impact performance. In other words, the bond area is great enough for the ultimate strength of the adhesive not to be necessary, indeed because of the elongation charactistics of polyurethane, a greater separation between the adherends is tolerable before any failure is initiated. The body structure has a good torsional stiffness with polyurethane adhesive and therefore its superior peel strength and durability make it preferable to epoxy.

The requirements of the fasteners are that they are cheap, easy to install from one side only, provide a moderate clamping force and do not protrude on either side more than 2-3 mm.

This is because conventional automotive weather seals are used and they fit over the bond flanges and the rivets. Although conventional rivets cause local damage to the composite material, this is sufficiently localised and the stress levels in the structure sufficiently low for that not to present a problem. Since the rivets are not stressed significantly being buried within the bond line we do not anticipate durability problems with this method of fastening.

3.2 Composite Lay-up

The structural body components are low temperature moulded using vacuum only. The lay-up is comprised entirely of glass reinforcement in epoxy resin with aluminium honeycomb or P.V.C. foam core material. The only carbon fibre in the structure is the glass run channel inside the door frame.

The lay-up is modified in line with the specific load requirements of the structure, (see figure 2.1b). Where possible, the structural section was designed to feed the load into the structure but in the case of the upper shoulder anchorage, the styling and occupant packaging constraints resulted in a large point load being applied in the middle of a panel. The lay-up in this area varies from 1.5 mm at the bond flange to 6 mm in the middle of the panel where a steel threaded insert is moulded in to retain the seat belt anchorage (see figure 3.2). The honeycomb is deleted from the roof inner moulding and extensive use is made of uni-directional glass fibre both in the direction of normal torsional loads and the loads imposed by the seat belt anchorage in an impact.

Uni-directional fibres are used in strip form around all the apertures in the primary structure in an effort to save material while still retaining adequate stiffness and aluminium inserts are used where threaded holes are needed in the structure. These holes are all jig drilled and tapped for accurate assembly of the vehicle.

The early prototype vehicles incorporated carbon fibre in the 'A' posts and hinge pillars but it has been possible to remove the carbon fibre with careful use of uni-directional glass fibres. Another aspect of the lay-up which has undergone development is the core material; P.V.C. and P.U. foam core materials are more appropriate to a road car than aluminium or nomex honeycomb. The reason is that the weight saving offered by honeycomb is not necessary and the increased surface area of the foam results in a more reliable bond with the skins. This is particularly true in the case of Solo because we have used low viscosity resin systems in an effort to improve surface finish and this is not always consistent with a good bond between core and skin. With an aluminium honeycomb core it was necessary to use a film adhesive to assist this bonding, but this has not been necessary with a foam core material.

4 TESTING AND ANALYSIS

4.1 Sill/A-Post Junction

In order to assess the likely torsional stiffness of the bonded composite primary structure, and to investigate the failure mode of a critical junction in the structure, tests were carried out on a number of similar test pieces representing the door sill (or rocker panel) and hinge pillar junction. The inner panel here is a mild steel sheet and the remaining sides of the structural box section are part of the centre section moulding (see figure 2.1a). During excessive torsional loading of the structure or a frontal impact situation, this area will experience a bending moment in the plane of the door aperture causing the angle between sill and hinge pillar to change. The test was arranged as shown in figure 4.1a). By progressively loading the test piece until permanent deformation occured it became apparent that the limiting factor determining the stiffness of this area was the yield point of the steel inner panel. The steel inner panel was stiffened first with a mitred bulkhead through the corner and then with the addition of a shaped doubler after which the stiffness significantly improved. The results shown in figure 4.1 b) are related to a comparable steel section of similar size. It should be noted, however, that the steel piece weighed 7.5 kg and was a complex structure comprising 5 pieces. The weight of the composite and steel test piece was 5.5 kgs. The adhesive used was toughened epoxy with aluminium rivets. with the steel inner panel stiffened, permanent deformation occurs first with the inner bond flange and the doubler buckling simultaneously. The best compromise for the structure in this area is not the stiffest as can be seen from figure 4.1b), but it has the highest yield point. This means that provided that the overall stiffness is acceptable, the durability is improved because the stress experienced as a percentage of the yield point is lower for a given force.

4.2 Torsion Test

The torsion testing was carried out between the front and rear suspension anchorage points. The rear of the car was anchored and a torque applied about the front strut mounts. Deflections along the body structure were measured in ten placed at stations a,b,c,d and e (see figure 2.1a) and dimensions of screen and door apertures were recorded. The torque was applied to the structure in three stages: 500 Nm, 1052 Nm and 1552 Nm. The deflection in the door and screen apertures was recorded at the maximum level of 1552 Nm. Dial test indicator readings were taken at a distance of 750 mm from the vehicle centreline and are shown below. Dimensions are in millimetres.

POSITION   APPLIED TORQUE (Nm)

	0 RH	0 LH	500 RH	500 LH	1052 RH	1052 LH	1552 RH	1552 LH
a	0	0	+0,13	-0,03	+0,26	-0,06	+0,38	-0,10
b	0	0	+1,58	-0,42	+2,12	-0,85	+2,71	-1,30
c	0	0	+1,81	-0,61	+2,56	-1,19	+3,38	-1,83
d	0	0	+0,95	-0,75	+1,83	-1,15	+2,79	-1,24
e	0	0	+1,07	-0,75	+1,98	-1,42	+3,05	-2,13

The deflection in the door apertures and screen aperture was recorded from corner to corner. The door aperture deflection was within the limits of accuracy of the measuring method and the screen aperture deflection was 2.0 mm at the maximum applied torque.

The deflections measured correspond to an overall torsional stiffness of 7812.7 Nm/degree. The stiffness of the rear tubular structure is 10672 Nm/degree/metre.

The stiffness of the composite centre section is 20033 Nm/degree/metre.

With the front screen adhesively bonded in position the overall torsional stiffness rose to 9757 Nm/degree with the stiffness of the centre section being 22230 Nm/degree/metre.

In addition to the structural testing and adhesive bond testing the vehicle has passed European seat belt anchorage and North American roof crush tests. Both of these tests specify a maximum allowable intrusion into the vehicle of the roof pillars after the test. With the composite structure the deformation was minimal because the structure behaved elastically and under load the deflection was less than ten per cent of that allowable according to the legislation.

REFERENCES

1 Voy, Morsch
   Development of a Rigid Passenger Safety
   Compartment
   made of Composite Material
   SAE/860278

2 W.A. Lees
   Bonding Composites
   INT. J. adhesion and adhesives vol.6 no. 4.

3 Marwick, Sheasby
   Evaluation of Adhesives for Aluminium
   Structured Vehicles
   SAE/870151

4 Beerman, Thum, Tidbury
   The Prediction of the Energy Absorption
   of Composite
   Structural Materials
   1 Mech. E/C35/86

5 Joining Fibre - reinforced Plastics
   (ed. F.L. Matthew) Elsevier App. Science.

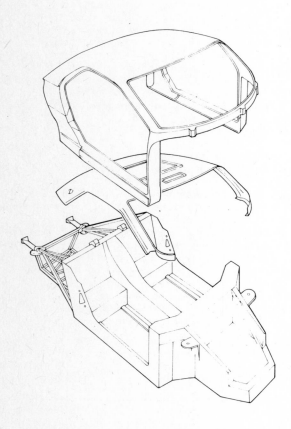

Fig 2.1a   Solo primary structure

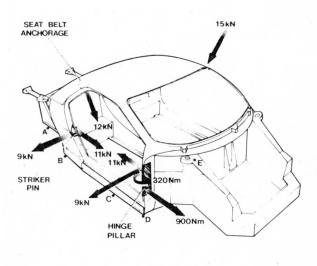

Fig 2.1b   Major loadings on structure

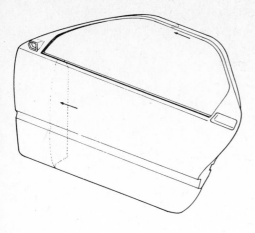

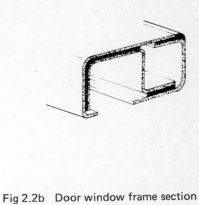

Fig 2.2b   Door window frame section

Fig 2.2a   Door construction

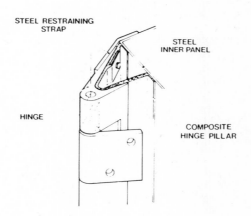

Fig 2.3   Section through hinge pillar

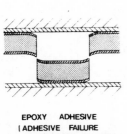

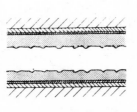

EPOXY   ADHESIVE
[ADHESIVE   FAILURE
&   ADHEREND   FAILURE]

POLYURETHANE   ADHESIVE
[100 %   COHESIVE   FAILURE]

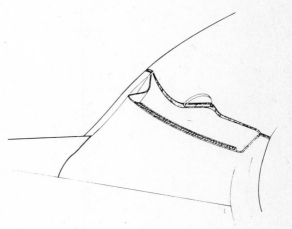

Fig 3.1   Typical bond failure

Fig 3.2   Section through seat belt anchorage

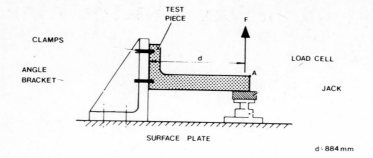

Fig 4.1a

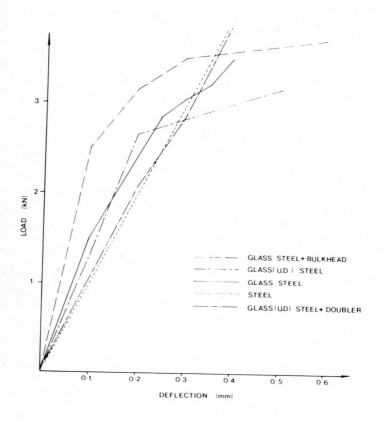

A POST SILL TEST PIECES (TO YIELD)

Fig 4.1b

Fig 4.1   'A' post/sill junction tests

Wood/epoxy composites for large wind turbine blades

M J PLATTS, CEng, MICE
Composite Technology Limited, Totton, Southampton

Modern wind turbines suffer very high fatigue loadings in the blades which catch the turbulent energy of the wind. While light weight is of some importance the paramount requirement for these blades is that they are cost-effective. As a primary structural material, wood surpasses all other composites on a fatigue performance/cost basis. This has lead to the use of wood in veneer form, used as a composite material with epoxy resin, laminated into moulds to form the blade shapes. This paper describes the laminating techniques and fixing details used, the quality control requirements and the mechanical performance and economic benefits achieved.

1 THE WIND ENERGY INDUSTRY

The fast-developing wind turbine industry has created a demand for a new combination of material properties, which has been met by an old/new material - wood, used in veneer form, laminated with epoxy.

Arising from the general interest in renewable sources of energy in the 1970's, the generation of electricity from wind has proved to be one of the most practical and economic options. The technology has developed apace with research turbines reaching 100m diameter, rated at several megawatts each, and smaller machines being installed in their thousands and operated reliably and economically. Some 2 per cent of California's electricity capacity is now provided by wind turbines (over 1500MW capacity, over $1 billion investment) and some countries in Northern Europe (Denmark, Holland) have commitments to achieve up to 10 per cent of their electricity capacity from wind energy by the end of the 1990's. In its preliminary submission to the Hinkley Point 'C' enquiry, the CEGB has stated that in the UK probably a Gigawatt of wind energy capacity could be installed in the UK at a generating cost (2.2p/kWhr) equivalent to the proposed nuclear station, with more capacity at higher cost. Wind energy is thus now a significant energy technology.

2 STRUCTURAL REQUIREMENT

Wind turbines present a particular structural problem to the designer. One of the main components in the turbine - the large rotating blades which catch the energy of the wind-see well over 10^8 duty cycles in a 20 year life, yet are also subject to the turbulent fluctuations of the wind in every cycle. No equivalent large structure is subject to such an extreme fatigue requirement. For instance aircraft wings only see a small number of duty cycles in a day. A wind turbine can see as many major load cycles in 5 minutes as an aircraft wing sees in a week. At the same time wind turbine blade design is driven by an acute requirement for cost-effectiveness. If this is not achieved there is no wind energy industry.

Weight is not of the same importance as it is in aircraft design, but it is still of some significance. Blades designed in steel suffer a significant fatigue load because of their own weight, which produces a gravity bending moment which reverses each cycle. Fibreglass can achieve reasonable weights but the associated low stiffness gives natural frequency problems, where the natural vibrational frequencies of the blades can be excited by the rotational speed of the machine. Advanced composites can achieve both the fatigue life and high natural frequencies required by wind turbines, but at a totally unacceptable cost.

Experience on both sides of the Atlantic has highlighted the benefits of wood, a naturally occurring 'fibre-reinforced composite' with very good fatigue properties, a good stiffness to weight ratio and an unbeatable performance to cost ratio (fig. 1).

3 MOULDING REQUIREMENT

At the same time as presenting a particular structural requirement, wind turbine blades also present a particular moulding requirement. Wind turbine blades are essentially cantilever beams of a rather sophisticated shape. The section has to be a carefully designed and very accurately reproduced aerofoil shape to give the rotor its energy capture performance. This shape tapers and twists along the blade. However, within these parameters a blade is an essentially linear structure, a cantilever beam loaded in bending and shear, with only secondary local aerodynamic pressure loads occurring within the cross-section.

A detail of the moulding requirement is that the centre of stiffness of the blade as a beam, and also the centre of weight of the blade cross-sections, should be located towards the leading edge of the aerofoil, to coincide with the centre of aerodynamic pressure acting in the blade. In this way no unwanted twisting of the blade occurs. This suggests a moulding in which a structural shell forms the front half of the aerofoil section while the rear half of the aerofoil is of relatively light seecondary structure. The structure is completed by a shear web, making a load carrying 'D' shape of the front half of the section (fig. 2).

This general moulding requirement has been very successfully met by using wood in veneer form, coated in epoxy resin and laid into female moulds, then vacuumed into place while the resin sets. The operation is very similar to a normal composites laminating technique using prepregs.

4 WOOD

Perhaps it is not a surprise that wood is a suitable material for this application, when the history of the technical use of wood is taken into account. No record of air operations during the second world war would be complete without mention of the all-wood De Havilland Mosquito, a fast and agile fighter/bomber, nor without the high speed laminated wood air/sea rescue launches. On the other side of the Atlantic, Howard Hughes built 'Spruce Goose'. - The largest plane ever flown was built entirely of wood.

Wood is in effect a low density composite, comprising cellulose fibres in a void-filled lignin matrix. The fibres are highly efficiently oriented in a 3D structure which would be the pride of any materials designer in a man-made composite (fig. 3). Wood has only been recently surpassed in technical merit by the higher performance composites using carbon and kevlar. It has never been surpassed on a performance/price basis.

Its major drawback in the past has been its moisture degredation. In the last decade this has been overcome, with the combining of wood with epoxy resin, enabling wood to take its proper place in the range of technical composites.

5 WOOD/EPOXY

To be a little more specific, epoxy brings two important advantages to the technical use of wood.

Moisture content stabilisation is one advantage, the other is in ease of construction.

The aircraft cited above as advanced examples of wood construction used glues which needed high clamping pressures to achieve a good bond - a common feature of wood glues. In contrast epoxy is a high strength, low shrinkage structural resin with excellent gap-filling qualities. Low cost, cold cure epoxy resins will flow in to cover and grip the open

cells on the surface of wood and provide a shear strength which is typically five times that of the wood it is holding, without requiring any clamping pressure at all. The vacuum bag technique used in wood/epoxy veneer lamination is for veneer location to achieve the shape required, rather than being essential to achieve a bond.

Depending on wood species the resin will be only 10 to 20 per cent of the finished weight of the wood/epoxy structure. Most of the resin is in fact absorbed into the cross-grain in the wood and very thin glue lines can be achieved between veneers. The result of this is that all the main strength and stiffness properties of the combined material are those of the wood, with the exception of an increase in density due to the absorbed resin. Because veneers are a high quality form of wood to begin with, this is a highly efficient way of using wood in structures, enabling high stresses to be used which would not be usable in bulk timber.

The moisture content stabilisation achieved by an all-over coating of epoxy is also an important factor in maintaining the high strength capacity of the wood. Wood used in the ordinary way is subject to moisture content changes with the ambient atmospheric moisture level. This causes moisture movement which can open up joints in structures and precipitate failure. Also high moisture content actively softens the wood itself and means that low stresses have to be used in design. In the process of manufacture, veneers are automatically dried to a low moisture content, which make its high strength immediately available. This can then be sealed in with a coating of epoxy resin, which acts as a high quality vapour barrier, restricting the exchange of moisture between the surrounding atmosphere and the wood so that the wood effectively remains permanently in its best condition. Tests show that such stability is achieved that the wood is ignorant of seasonal variations in external moisture and would only alter its moisture content to a small degree, over decades, due to gross changes of climatic environment (e.g. being used in jungle conditions). Wood/epoxy boats have shown no perceptible shift in properties after 15 years in the water.

6 LAMINATING TECHNIQUES

This form of construction using wood in veneer form, laid into moulds, is operationally a very cost-effective moulding operation. Wood veneers up to 4mm thick can be used (depending on the curvature required) cut with templates as a prepreg composite cloth would be cut, but without the special storage and warming requirements. Veneer preparation does however require carpenters' skills. Resin is rolled onto each side of the veneer as it is placed in the mould - a quick operation not requiring the rolling time associated with say wet layup composites. Cold cure resins are perfectly adequate to achieve the full strength of the wood. No bleed cloths or other expensive additional layers are necessary in the vacuuming process. Because the basic strength of the structure is the wood, there are no problems of early strength from a handling and storage point of view.

Thus rapid, efficient overall moulding cycles can be achieved on these large structures. Because the resin is in thin layers there is no exothermic limit to the thickness which can be laminated in one operation.

7 QUALITY CONTROL

The normal procedural controls of any laminating operation of course apply to wood/epoxy. However there is a specific inspection requirement for the incoming veneers. Wood, being a natural material, has a significant natural density variation which takes with it variations in strength and stiffness (a Standard Deviation of 10% is typical). If these properties are important in the application concerned, it is essential to batch incoming veneers according to density. This can be done at the same time as visually inspecting each sheet for flaws. Normal statistical sampling can then follow for stiffness and strength checks.

8 WIND TURBINE BLADE ROOT FIXINGS

The high fatigue duty of a wood/epoxy wind turbine blade has generated a requirement for a high fatigue performance connection detail, enabling the wood/epoxy material to be joined to a metal hub by a normal bolt-type mechanical engineering fixing detail.

A highly efficient stud insert has been developed to achieve this, consisting of tapered steel studs inserted into holes drilled axially into the wood/epoxy laminate and bonded in with a filled epoxy grout (fig. 4) For this, the holes are drilled from an accurate drilling jig. The studs are all inserted, mounted on an accurately faced plate so that the shoulders of the studs themselves form an accurate mating face. This mating face, plus the steel studs protruding from it, gives an excellent and entirely conventional metal to metal connection.

The steel stud tapering into the wood gives a steady transition of stiffness and a smooth transfer of stress from the metal to the wood. Stress concentrations cannot be entirely removed in practice, but this form of detail nevertheless surpasses any other, such that connections of this sort have to be tested back to back in order to be able to fatigue test them at all. The tapered stud develops a high proportion (over 60%) of the available shear capacity of the surrounding wood. The joint does not fail at either the stud/resin interface or the resin/wood interface but in the wood, the stud pulling out a cone of attached wood with it, when it fails.

9 FATIGUE PROPERTIES

Because it is a combination of high strength fibres in a (low density) matrix, wood is a genuine composite material and can be considered as such. All the design methods for multi-directional laminates can be applied to wood.

More correctly, wood is a whole range of composite materials, because different species offer a very wide range of properties.

General work on fatigue behaviour in wood suggests that to a first order, fatigue performance varies directly with static strength. Particularly detailed work in fatigue testing of wood/epoxy has been carried out in the UK at Bath University (ref. 1) using Khaya Ivorensis (African Mahogany). A Goodman diagram for this wood is shown in fig. 5. This demonstrates wood's natural high tensile strength compared to its compressive strength, with a particularly interesting dip at the ratios where fatigue damage which is essentially compressive, is accelerated by being brought into slight tension. This is directly attributable to the failure mechanism in wood, where compression damage occurs by buckling and crushing of the cell walls and tension then actively breaks the damaged interface apart. A typical S-N curve for fully reversed loading is shown in fig. 6.

10 COSTS

Wind turbine blades are sophisticated composites structures, with many detailed requirements that would add cost to any moulding operation. Wood/epoxy is used for the main structural material, but this only accounts for some two-thirds of the blade weight and one-third of the blade material cost. Typically, the cost per kg of finished blades falls with blade size, reflecting the diminishingly proportionate cost of details as against the simple bulk of the structure. Here, 'larger' blades represent mouldings weighing perhaps 8 tonnes each, whereas 'small' blades are still of the order of half a tonne. Over this range, finished item costs can be achieved in the £8-£15/kg range, given suitable production runs. Given the low weights achieved for wood/epoxy composite wind turbine blades, this gives them a cost-effectiveness unachievable using any other main structural material.

The development of this technology over the last decade has introduced a further material into the already wide range of composite materials. It will be interesting to see if this new material - this renewed 'old' material - finds further application in the future, in other areas of engineering.

REFERENCES

(1) TSAI, K.T. and ANSELL, M.P. Fatigue testing of wood composites for aerogenerator rotor blades, Part II, Effect of moisture and R-ratio, in Wind Energy Conversion 1985, ed. A. Garrad, Mechanical Engineering Publications Ltd, pp.285-292, 1985.

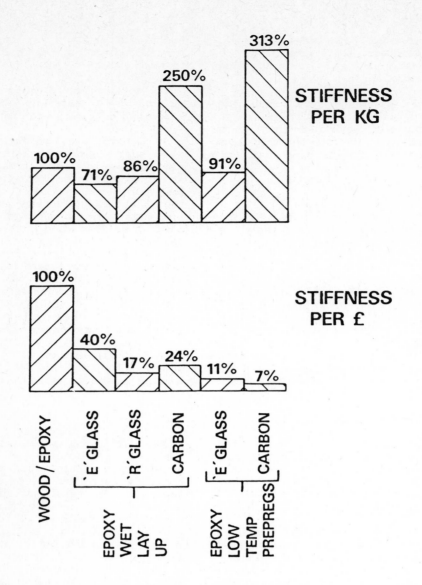

Fig 1   Stiffness comparison of wood/epoxy and UD glass/epoxy

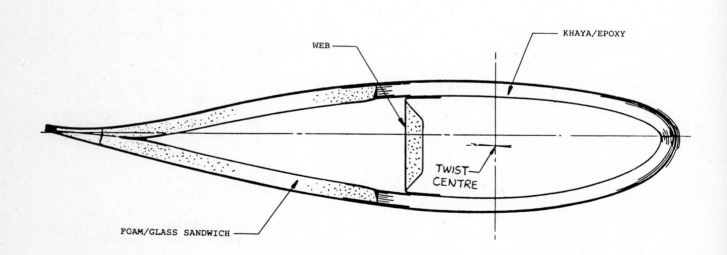

Fig 2   Typical aerofoil section

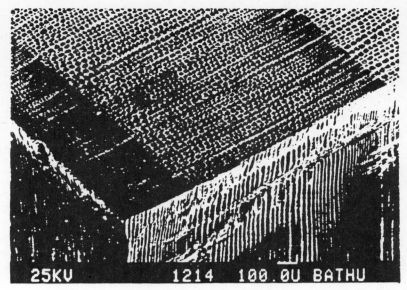

.Transverse (TS),tangential longitudinal (TLS) and radial
longitudinal (RLS) sections through Scots Pine (Pinus
sylvestris) wood.

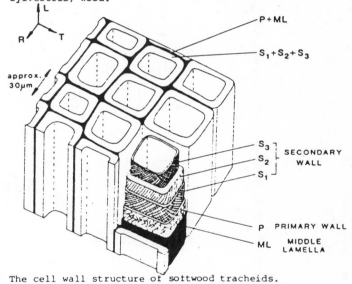

The cell wall structure of softwood tracheids.

Fig 3   Cell wall structure of softwood

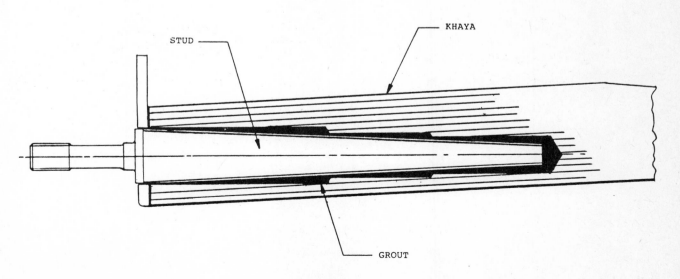

Fig 4   Typical stud in blade root

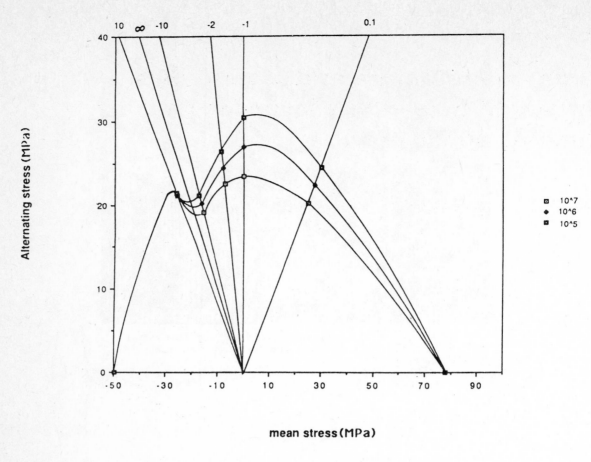

Fig 5   Constant life diagram for axially tested khaya

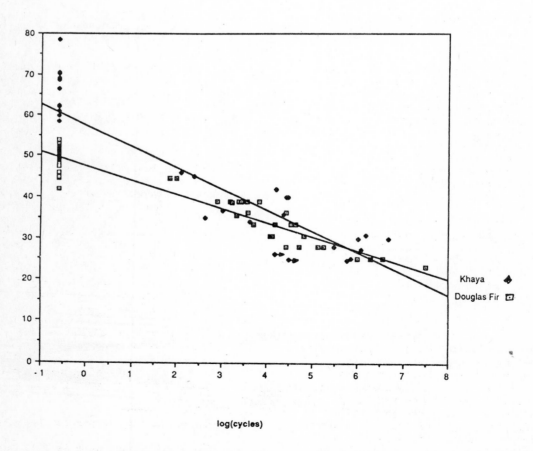

Fig 6   S—N curve for khaya and douglas fir at R=−1

C387/024

Design, manufacture and testing of a lightweight heavy duty lever for an industrial application

D C CORBET, MA, AMIMechE and **G S BOYCE**, BSc, MSc, MPRI
PERA (Production Engineering Research Association), Melton Mowbray, Leicestershire

Introduction

Reciprocating mechanisms constructed from steel and aluminium alloys are commonplace in industrial machinery. These components are often critical to the performance of the equipment and machinery in which they are used. The quest for increased production rates and energy efficiency are two reasons why design engineers continually examine ways of reducing the mass of these components. Weight saving measures, however, are usually based on either optimizing the design of the existing structure or on the use of lower density metals such as aluminium alloy.

Composite materials are rarely considered technically or economically viable for these applications and it has only been in light engineering industries such as the textile industry that composite materials have been truly accepted and the benefits appreciated.

The cost savings, generated by increased production rates and energy efficiency, through the introduction of light weight advanced composite materials in the area of reciprocating mechanisms are potentially huge and equivalent to those witnessed by the saving of weight on aircraft. Additional technical benefits are also obtained including reduced vibration and noise, increased fatigue life coupled with ease of handling and installation.

In order to support innovation in this field of light weight composite reciprocating mechanisms for heavy duty applications, the DTI, PERA and three UK companies embarked on a research programme to establish the technical and economic viability of these materials in this critical area.

Around the time that this programme was being established PERA was approached by a UK company producing high speed press forming machinery. Their problem was noise and vibration levels created by the reciprocated mechanism in the machinery. PERA was asked to examine the possibility of reducing the weight of the mechanism, possibly by the use of advanced composites. This work was subsequently incorporated into the DTI/PERA research programme.

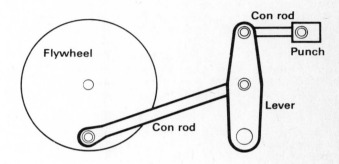

Fig 1   A schematic diagram of the reciprocating mechanism

After reviewing the reciprocating mechanism it was decided to replace the steel lever shown in figure 1.

As will be observed from figure 1 the lever in this case study is responsible for transferring the forces from the flywheel to the punch. Loads up to 20 tonnes are exerted on the lever during operation which reciprocates at 160 strokes per minute.

Existing Design and Associated Problems

The existing lever was a welded steel fabrication weighing over 160 kg. Loads are transferred to the connecting rods via solid bearings bolted to the lever. With this all steel assembly, continuous cycle speeds are limited to 180 strokes per minute. For brief periods this can be increased to 270 strokes but the elastic strain associated with the very large moment then gives rise to severe vibrations which increase the bearing wear rates unacceptably. The desired cycle speed is 350 strokes per minute and the limiting factor is the moving mass of the lever and connecting rods. This low cycle rate and high power consumption necessitated the re-design of the assembly.

Design Considerations for Replacement Lever

The requirements were as follows:

1. Low reciprocating mass and hence reduced vibration.
2. Very high stiffness to enable rapid reciprocation with minimal elastic strain.
3. Very good fatigue resistance.
4. Very high compression strength and bearing strength for longevity of the bearing/lever interfaces.
5. Resistance to elevated temperatures caused by bearing friction and hot machine oil.
6. Damage free survival of a press jamming situation.

Materials Selection

The use of aluminium had been considered previously but had been ruled out owing to high fabrication cost, insufficient weight saving and poor fatigue resistance. A suitable composite system had therefore to be selected.

A wide range of matrix resin types, fibres and processing techniques are used in the multitude of products manufactured under the general description of fibre reinforced plastics.

The principal raw materials are based on unidirectional or woven fabrics of glass, aramid or carbon fibre (or mixture thereof) in an epoxy resin matrix. The choice of fibre depends upon the particular balance of properties required whilst the resin principally ensures that the loads are transferred to the fibres adequately as well as providing environmental resistance. Processing techniques currently used are based on autoclave moulding, press moulding or vacuum bag moulding.

Selection of the optimum materials, for the fabrication and use of any given item, can only be made satisfactorily after considering the nature of the part to be produced, the mechanical performance required, equipment available for fabrication and cost.

Fibre Reinforcement

The three principal fibre reinforcements are those based on glass, aramid (Kevlar) and carbon. Table I lists typical properties of these various fibre reinforcements. The main disadvantages of the glassfibre reinforcements for this application are their inherent poor stiffness characterized by specific tensile modulus values of 28–34 GPa.

Although it can be shown that the maximum forces experienced by the con rods and swing lever are tensile, there are still large compressive forces experienced by these components during the processing cycle. These large compressive forces limit the use of Kevlar fibres in the structure because of its poor compressive strength property, typically one third of its tensile properties.

Carbon fibre, on the other hand, although expensive, has the inherent advantage of high specific properties in both tension and compression and was therefore considered the most suitable material for this application. In certain areas, where low forces are experienced, cost savings could be made by replacing some of the carbon fibre with E-glass. The degree to which E-glass could be substituted for carbon fibre would be determined by balancing the degree of weight saving required, the mechanical performance and cost.

Matrix Selection

The environmental conditions of working temperature up to 70°C in the presence of 5% oil/water emulsions should not cause any difficulty to an epoxy resin system. However, prospective resins were screened by subjecting the materials to certain tests including immersion ageing with and without pre-stressing in a solution of oil/water, and then measuring essential mechanical properties over a period of time.

Epoxy resin systems are available which can be cured at room temperature and have the capability to operate up to 130°C. Upon curing the resin forms a rigid cross-linked structure which provides good dimensional stability coupled with excellent chemical resistance to most solvents, oils and greases.

Developments in epoxy resin technology have led over the years to the manufacture of resins which can be used to pre-impregnate uni-directional or woven fibre cloths. This enables a component to be built more easily with accurate control over the resin content. These types of pre-impregnated reinforced materials do, however, require curing temperatures up to 170° and pressure (15–75 psi) to totally consolidate the fibres so their processing is restricted to press-moulding and autoclave moulding operations.

To fulfil the mass, stiffness and bearing strength requirements, high strength carbon fibre was selected. To fulfil the temperature and bearing strength requirements, a high temperature cure epoxy resin was selected. This choice is not ideal from a fatigue viewpoint since these resins are more notch sensitive than lower cure temperature types, however this is a stiffness critical component possibly operating at high temperatures due to the poor heat dissipation of the carbon/epoxy material and frictional heat generated at the bearings.

Design

The basic design of the carbon fibre component has been based on the current dimensions of the original steel component, so a direct substitution would be possible. Furthermore, the maximum forces exerted on the individual steel component were used during the stress analysis of the composite component, even though it has been calculated that for a given crank speed the resultant forces would be smaller due to a lower component mass.

The optimum design of the lever was found to be a monolithic or solid laminate consisting of uni-directional and woven carbon fibres. The majority of the uni-directional fibres were oriented along the length of the lever for high bend strength, with woven cloth laid at $\pm$ 45° for the shear loads. A lower proportion of uni-directional fibres were positioned in the transverse direction to provide delamination resistance. The laminate configuration (i.e. No. of plies/orientation) was specified using computer aided laminate stress analysis software such that under the critical loading conditions the strain in any direction did not exceed the design allowable strain of 0.002%. The design allowable strain limit was determined after taking into account the type, and magnitude of loads, fatigue (i.e. number of expected life cycles), environmental conditions (temperature, oils, greases etc) and safety factors.

Figure 2 illustrates the carbon fibre lever showing the two carbon fibre/epoxy side cheeks and the metal bush inserts which carry the bearings.

Fig 2   Carbon fibre lever showing the two carbon fibre/epoxy side cheeks and the metal bush inserts which carry the bearings

Processing Method

Since the component is flat and of very high thickness, for a composite pre-preg laminate, it was decided to use the press moulding process. This allows the use of simple tooling and can provide the high moulding pressures required.

Due to the component being subjected to very high flexural loadings, the quality of the laminate edges is critical since crack

excellent consolidation through the thickness of the laminate but owing to the bleed direction, edges can become resin rich. Consequently, it was decided to mould the laminate over size and subsequently machine the lever's profile and holes for bushes to remove the resin rich edges.

Matched die tools were used with a suitable clearance between the mould halves to enable excess resin to bleed out. Mould stops were positioned to prevent over consolidation and to control the laminate thickness.

The individual layers of pre-preg were stacked in the desired configuration in the female half of the mould tool. The layers were regularly debulked to assist with the removal of air.

Thermocouples were positioned through the thickness of the initial laminates to determine the temperature difference between the inner and outer layers during moulding. This ensured that the outside layers had not gelled preventing resin bleed out from the inner layers.

Additional work was carried out to determine the optimum temperature and pressure conditions as a function of time. It was found from these experiments that it was necessary to increase the temperature of the material gradually until the temperature was reached at which the resin was at its lowest viscosity. Once this temperature was reached a pressure in excess of 280 psi was applied for a period of 30 minutes.

After this period the laminate was cured at a higher temperature for a period typically in excess of two hours. Only after the mould had cooled to under 50°C was the pressure released and the part ejected.

The laminate profile was cut using a template and conventional machining practices. The bearing holes were rough cut to approximately 1 mm undersize followed by precision jig boring.

Carbon fibre laminates are notch sensitive so for high cycle loading conditions, bolting of components should be avoided. Bonding the metal bushes into place was also considered but no adhesive was capable of withstanding the high compressive loads. An interference fit was therefore used by freeze fitting the inserts into position.

Initial Trials

To determine the load bearing capability of laminate and the component strains at critical points on the lever, static tests were conducted at loads over 2½ times those obtained during normal running condition.

It was observed that under these conditions the interference fit of the centre bearing was maintained. Furthermore, strain gauges attached to the lever established that the maximum strains reached at normal running loads were considerably lower than the critical strains for fatigue degradation. The maximum strain region was at the lever edge adjacent to the centre bearing.

Preliminary dynamic tests were also conducted on the lever at 35 cycles per minute for a total of 20,000 cycles. The centre bush was removed and the composite bearing surface examined for wear. No evidence of matrix or fibre failure was observed.

In Service Performance Testing

Several levers have been installed in production environments at various plants for a period of over a year. These have been running as near continuously as possible to assess the long term viability of the components. The most severe of these has been operating at speeds of up to 300 cycles per minute for nearly 10 million cycles at the time of writing. Measurements of strain levels in the lever have indicated that speeds of up to 350 cycles per minute should be achievable. A noticeable decrease in the amount of vibration generated by the press has also been observed.

Economics

Although the carbon fibre lever costs three times as much as the original steel lever, the additional cost represents less than 1% of the total cost of the machine.
The increased production capability of ultimately 350 cycles per minute with the composite lever, has suggested that companies operating machines with this increased capability will save up to £0.5 million per machine per year.

The company involved have now incorporated the carbon fibre lever as a standard item in their press machinery due to the strong demand for faster, quieter and more cost-effective equipment from their customers. This has resulted in a further six levers being ordered and a total of 20 levers are expected to be produced during 1989.

This project is an example of a high cost, high performance material being used in a very competitive, heavy industrial application and bringing benefits in terms of cost-effectiveness, greater productivity and reduced environmental noise. The project should provide an impetus to other companies involved in the manufacture of high speed industrial machinery to move forward and to gain the benefits of advanced composite materials.

Acknowledgements

The assistance of The Department of Trade and Industry and the following companies is gratefully acknowledged: Advanced Composites Developments Ltd, Ciba-Geigy (Bonded Structures) Division Ltd.

Table 1 - Typical Properties of Various Types of Fibre Reinforcement

Reinforcement	Specific Gravity	Tensile Strength lbf/in^2 (MPa)	Tensile Modulus lbf/in^2 (GPa)	% Elongation to Break	Specific* Tensile Strength lbf/in^2 (MPa)	Specific* Tensile Modulus lbf/in^2 (GPa)
E-Glass	2.54	3.2×10^5 (2200)	10.4×10^6 (72)	4.8	12.5×10^4 (866)	4×10^6 (28)
S-Glass	2.49	4×10^5 (2800)	11.6×10^6 (80)	5.3	16.3×10^4 (1124)	4.6×10^6 (32)
R-Glass	2.53	6.4×10^5 (4400)	12.3×10^6 (85)	5.2	25.2×10^4 (1740)	4.9×10^6 (34)
Kevlar 49	1.45	4.2×10^5 (2900)	18.8×10^6 (130)	2.0	29.0×10^4 (2000)	12.9×10^6 (89)
XAS-Carbon	1.76	4.4×10^5 (3000)	33.3×10^6 (230)	1.0	24.6×10^4 (1700)	18.8×10^6 (130)

Specific tensile values indicated are defined as the $\dfrac{\text{tensile property}}{\text{specific gravity}}$

C387/025

The uses of composite materials in the design and manufacture of Formula 1 racing cars

B P O'ROURKE, BSc, CEng, MRAeS
Williams Grand Prix Engineering Limited, Didcot, Oxfordshire

SYNOPSIS In recent years a new application for advanced composite materials has been in the construction of load-bearing components for Formula 1 racing cars. Their use has been progressively extended and they currently comprise a major part of the vehicle assembly for all competing Formula 1 designs. Here the experiences gained with these materials at Williams Grand Prix Engineering are described. The initial interest in this technology was for optimisation of structural efficiency. A wide range of component design criteria are covered and advantages have also been found in the areas of strength, impact performance, geometric accuracy and speed of manufacture.

1   INTRODUCTION

Formula 1 World Championship motor racing has for many years provided a public arena in which to demonstrate the benefits of advancing technology. One of the more recent examples of this has been the introduction of advanced composite materials to the manufacture of load-bearing structures.

Williams Grand Prix Engineering Limited, as one of the leading organisations competing in Formula 1 racing, has always been alert to the potential of any new technological development that may provide a performance advantage over opposing entrants. Advanced composite materials appeared to offer opportunities to enhance structural performance and so effort was directed to acquire the skills required to design and manufacture components by this method within our own facilities. The use of these materials grew from simple beginnings to the present state where this technology forms a major part of our manufacturing capability.

1.1 Progression to composite materials

In order to gain an understanding of the reasons for our interest in composite materials it is necessary to examine the 'anatomy' of the current Grand Prix car. The configuration of vehicle depicted in Fig. 1 is that which has become the standard for the last 20 years. It comprises a central component of semi-monocoque construction which accommodates the driver cell, fuel tank and front suspension elements.
The engine is attached directly to the back of this unit and, thereafter, is connected to the gearbox casing. This, in turn, is supported by the rear suspension components. These units-chassis, engine and gearbox - therefore form a 'box-beam' structure through which are carried all of the inertial and aerodynamic loads generated whilst the car is in motion. To this central unit are attached the wing structures, underbodies, cooler ducting and the bodywork which clads the engine. The entire car assembly must not, by regulation, exceed a mass of 500 kg

It may be appreciated that the chassis or 'monocoque' component is of major structural importance. The efficiency of its design is reflected in the total assembly and, ultimately, in the handling characteristics of the car. The search for better solutions has resulted, over the years, in a succession of different manufacturing technologies. Initially, tubular 'space frame' structures were used until replaced by folded and rivetted aluminium shell structures. More recently bonded aluminium skinned honeycomb sandwich panels replaced the fabricated ones. It was a logical progression, therefore, that advanced composite materials should replace the aluminium used as the sandwich panel face sheets.

1.2 Reasons for using composite materials

As with many other design applications, the attractions to the Formula 1 engineer of composite materials relate to structural efficiency. These are derived, principally, in two ways. Firstly, they are inherently of greater specific modulus than most engineering metals and, secondly, the ability to directionally tailor the mechanical properties of a component can lead to a more effective design solution. The weight restrictions imposed by regulation mean that a gain in component stiffness may be made without increasing its mass. Alternatively, weight savings, if needed, could be made without sacrificing stiffness.

With a greater section of material being used, strength margins may be improved upon simultaneously.

Table 1 Design constraints

Component	Function	Criteria
Chassis	Primary vehicle structure, driver, fuel and suspension accommodation, aerodynamic fairing.	Torsional and bending stiffness, impact performance, geometric accuracy, minimum mass.
Wing structures	Aerodynamic downforce generation.	Stiffness, geometric accuracy, minimum mass.
Underbodies	Protection of structure underside, downforce generation.	Damage tolerance, temperature resistance, vibration tolerance, bending stiffness, minimum mass.
Nosebox	Impact energy absorption, front wing support	Impact performance, stiffness, geometric accuracy, minimum mass.
Cooler ducting	Maintain airflow to coolers	Stiffness, geometric accuracy, minimum mass.
Bodywork	Aerodynamic fairing, engine and systems covering	Geometric accuracy, handleability, stiffness, minimum mass.

2 DESIGN CRITERIA

The case for using advanced composites in the primary structure of the vehicle having been accepted, attention was then turned to other possible components. It was found that their use could be extended to a range of applications. An examination of the FW12 car of 1988 depicted in Fig. 2 will reveal how for the process has been taken. It will also illustrate that a wide variety of design criteria are encompassed.

The components, their functions and major design constraints are summarised in Table 1.

3 DESIGN PROCESSES

Vehicle design begins with concept studies. From these a definitive layout of the major components is chosen and around this a geometric envelope is built. The Computer Aided Engineering facilities available within the company allow us to build a 3-D surfaced model of the shape envelope and this is used to generate data for wind-tunnel model construction.

Aerodynamic testing provides information which is used to refine the computer-modelled shape. This process continues in an iterative manner until the level of performance required is achieved. The definitive geometric data is then released and full-scale patternwork begun. At the same time the geometry is broken down into assemblies and component design initiated.

3.1 Chassis Structure

The chassis assembly, being central to the overall function of the vehicle, is apportioned the major design effort. The design tasks may be divided into groups:-

i) Structure geometry and configuration definition

ii) Structural analysis and laminate design

iii) Ply geometry and junction detailing

iv) Attachment position details

The structural configuration of the chassis (fig.3) is determined by the positions of the front suspension components, the size of the fuel tank, the driver envelope and the engine mounting method. The outer shell structure is reduced to the minimum possible number of parts. In our case this consists of two, a separate, largely flat, floor panel being joined to the remainder at the bottom level. Bulkheads are positioned so as to feed suspension point loads into the structure and to enclose the cockpit bay.

The complexity of its geometry and the material used in its construction result in this structure not being a simple one to analyse. This is an area where optimisation is clearly some distance in the future since we have much yet to learn about the subject. Analysis done to date has been based upon simple idealisations of structural behaviour and a desire to improve upon the section properties of the aluminium forerunning designs. We now have at our disposal, however, composites-capable finite element analysis software packages which are enabling us to understand and predict structure performance. These, we hope, will greatly help us with future designs although we appreciate that the time when the process is truly interactive is some way off.

Loading data is generated by the experience of previous track testing using strain-gauged components in conjunction with on-board recording equipment. Additionally, assumed standard load cases are examined to cover the entire predicted performance envelope. Currently drivers of Formula 1 cars experience up to 4.5 'g' lateral loading, as much as 8 'g' in 'bump' condition and 3 'g' deceleration.

Loads are applied to, or reacted by, the chassis at the suspension attachment points and engine mounting positions (fig 4). The effects of the inertia forces generated by 200l of fuel must be accounted for in the tank bay design as must those associated with the driver be at the seat-belt attachment points. The technical regulations defined by the FISA, the governing body for international motorsport, state load cases for the compulsory roll-over protection structures situated above and in front of the driver. These must withstand 7.5 'g' downward, 5.5 'g' rearward and 1.5 'g' sideways without collapsing in the event of the car overturning.

It is, perhaps, unnecessary to add that as well as those already discussed, there are always other, more difficult to quantify, load cases that may occur when a driver deviates from the prescribed route around a circuit. Recently, however, test requirements have been introduced which provide values for impact loads that must be accommodated. These are now major factors influencing the final structural details. Detailed descriptions of these tests are presented in section 6.

3.2 Other Components

The design processes relating to the remaining components follow those described for the chassis assembly but may vary in priority depending upon the function of the particular part. In the case of wing structures the stiffness criteria and aerofoil accuracy are of paramount importance and so determine the configuration and method of manufacture. Bodywork and other secondary or non-structural components are more influenced in their design by geometry, moulding details, feasibility and economy of production methods.

4 PRODUCTION PROCESSES

The range and number of components manufactured from composite materials that are currently used on a Formula 1 car neccesitates the allocation of sizeable manufacturing resources both in terms of manpower and facilities. In common with most of the other leading teams, Williams Grand Prix Engineering Limited first gained experience of the material in the late 1970's. In our case, the usage of composites increased steadily, if slowly, over the next few years. A threshold was reached, however, when the decision was made to change to a full composite chassis structure, and simultaneously, to replace the outdated wet lay-up polyester/glass bodywork with prepreg bonded sandwich components. This occurred over a short space of time in the interval between the seasons 1984 and 1985, and somewhat later than our major competitors. As a consequence of this much had to be learnt in a short space of time and the quantities of pre-preg material used increased from the one year to the other by some 500%.

4.1 Production Facilities

Once the commitment to composite materials had been made, it was necessary to provide additional facilities for their processing. A purpose-built area was commissioned to accommodate the work and improved equipment procured. Our facilities presently comprise:-

Total floor area	:	700 m^2 (7500 ft^2)
Clean Room	:	230 m^2 (2500 ft^2)
Curing facilities	:	Autoclave 1.8m (6') dia x 4.6m (15') length, 200 DegC x 7 bar.
	:	Autoclave 1.1m (3' 7") dia x 2.4m (8') length, 250 DegC x, 10 bar.
	:	Air-circulating ovens : 2
Total Manpower	:	15 nom. (Pattern + Production)

4.2 Patterns and Tooling

The geometry of the car exterior, having been generated using the C.A.D. system is transmitted (in drawing form at the time of writing) to the pattern making department. Full size male patterns are hand built in an appropriate material - mostly CIBA-Geigy Ureol 450 - and finished with a high gloss sealer.

Moulds for components are entirely manufactured in epoxy resin reinforced with carbon fibre and are all made in-house. Considerable experience has now been gained with the wet lay-up CIBA-Geigy resin systems LY568 and XD893 which, impregnating carbon cloth, have become our standard moulding processes. Recently, however, much has been learnt about prepreg tooling systems, principally ICI Fiberite's Toolrite. The newer lower temperature systems now available also have attractions and are being evaluated with a view to future use.

In addition to the materials used in moulding, expertise has been gained in the field of mould design. Good and bad design practices for composite details are fairly well understood and accounted for in determining the best configuration for a component and hence for its mould and patternwork. Attention is also given to the requirements for quantity production of a component. Whilst we may only build, perhaps, eight chassis assemblies in a year it may be necessary to produce up to eighty undertrays. A part that has been designed to be simple in production terms is of little time advantage if too long is spent in disassembling its mould for ejection and in turn-around.

Conventional composites consummable materials are used throughout manufacture except in the case of certain components where the time factor is significant and so resort has been made to tailored, re-usable rubber vacuum bags. The reductions in bagging time and effort resulting from this have been greatly appreciated by the production personnel and consistent results have been obtained.

4.3 Production Materials

The composite materials used in components manufactured at Williams Grand Prix Engineering Limited comprise a range of carbon fibre and kevlar reinforced epoxy resin prepregs, aluminium and Nomex honeycomb core materials and epoxy adhesives and fillers in film and paste forms.

The majority of components are manufactured from a 125 Deg. C-curing, high toughness epoxy prepreg; typically Fiberite type 7714B or CIBA-Geigy 920 system. Where mechanical property retention at temperature is important, however, we have standardised on Fiberite type 984. Carbon fibre, mostly Toray T300-3K, is used in both uni-directional and woven forms, the latter comprised of a 285 g/m^2, 5 harness satin form. Kevlar is used in woven form only; the majority being of a 170 g/m^2, 4 harness satin style.

Honeycomb materials are used in almost all of the forms commercially available. The complex geometries of some of the components, particularly the chassis, have resulted in some combinations of types being chosen for purely manufacturing reasons. Aluminium honeycomb is used in both hexagonal cell and 'flex-core' forms whereas Nomex material is procured in standard hexagonal and over-expanded types. The latter is most useful in areas where curvature is in one direction only while 'flex-core' will cope with regions of complex double curvature.

4.4 Lay-up Procedures

Prepreg lay-up for our composite parts is accomplished by hand and follows accepted practices and procedures. Detail drawings and laminate stacking sequence documents received from the design engineer are used to generate prepreg ply templates. A precise, repeatable method of template use has been evolved for the cutting and positioning of prepreg, honeycomb core and core inserts. Plies are laminated to the orientations specified in an appropriately configured mould, a vacuum bag is applied and curing takes place in an autoclave to the recommended cycle.

5   COMPONENT MANUFACTURE

The design solutions to the criteria described in section 2 are translated into final component form for manufacture. Brief descriptions of their construction and assembly techniques are presented below.

5.1 Chassis Assembly

The FW12 chassis consists of six principal components. The most major of these, the outer shell, includes the front and rear bulkheads, the top, sides and integral roll-over hoop base. Since the car uses its outer shape as working structure, this component is inherently of complex geometry being largely comprised of compound curvatures, attachment details and the cockpit opening. It is also necessary that it be produced in a female tool. Sandwich construction is employed throughout and it is moulded in two stages; the first skin being cured at full autoclave pressure (7 bar or 100 lbf/in^2) and the subsequent film adhesives, honeycomb core, inserts and inner skin cured at a pressure safe for the core, typically 3.5 bar (50 lbf/in^2). The skins are primarily of woven carbon/epoxy prepreg due to the constraints of curvature and laminates are modified with uni-directional material where necessary. Every effort is made at the design stage to eliminate unwanted tailoring and thickness accumulations by careful study, and accurate definition, of all areas of ply overlaps and drop-offs.

The other chassis main components, the four bulkheads and floor panel, are produced using similar sandwich construction techniques and cure schedules. The whole is then jigged, assembled and bonded using a cold-set paste adhesive. There is no mechanical fastening of these components. Finally, the assembly is trimmed and drilled to accept attachment fasteners. Manufacture time is, typically, two weeks. The finished assembly weight is approximately 50% of that of an average Formula 1 driver.

5.2 Underbodies

Two components form the underside of the car. Their construction is similar and consists of thin skins of carbon/epoxy and kevlar/epoxy prepreg either side of 6mm honeycomb core. Since these are vulnerable components and may have a relatively short life, emphasis has been placed upon ease and speed of production. Both skins and the skin/core bonds are formed in one curing operation. By making extensive use of edge moulding and synthetic rubber slave skins, trimming is eliminated resulting in components that may be laminated by one man, cured and finished in one working day.

The rearmost of these two panels is situated underneath the engine and is subjected to heating both radiantly and by entrained exhaust gases issuing adjacent to its lower surface. Because of this a higher temperature epoxy prepreg is used throughout and, at times, this has been augmented by a phenolic-based separate heat shield.

5.3 Bodywork

The bodywork, or external covering of the rear part of the car, consists of three main components. They are identical in construction being made up of single kevlar/epoxy plies forming skins on each side of 3mm Nomex honeycomb. A higher resin content prepreg is used in these cases to allow the deletion of a separate adhesive film. This results in a very lightweight component. Again, these parts are cured in a single process giving a fast production time.

5.4 Wing Structures

There have been several methods employed in building racing car wings, most involving wrapping carbon/epoxy prepreg skins around some form of foam core. Currently, however, increased aerodynamic loading and the need for greater aerofoil profile accuracy have provoked the adoption of a different solution entirely.

The present design utilises two separate skins moulded in female tools and subsequently paste-adhesive bonded together and to a substructure consisting of ribs and spars. In some cases the skins may be of sandwich construction, in others monolithic. The result is a component embodying a more effective section and a smooth, accurate surface profile.

6 STRUCTURAL TESTING

It has always been the custom at Williams Grand Prix Engineering Limited that newly designed structural components are subjected to an appropriate kind of proof load test before any initial circuit trials. In recent years, however, the emphasis upon structural testing has been intensified as a result of new regulations issued by the governing body, the FISA. Specifically, they have imposed two compulsory tests aimed at improving vehicle impact performance. These must be carried out successfully, and witnessed, before that design of car is allowed to compete in any of the Grands Prix.

6.1 Frontal Impact Test

The first test pertains to frontal impact performance. A fully representative chassis front section and nosebox, as illustrated in Fig.5 must be subjected to a mass of 780 kg impacting it at a velocity of 10 m/s; this equating to an energy of 39 KJ. This must be absorbed by the structure and contain the damage to the area ahead of the driver's feet whilst the average deceleration must not exceed a level of 25 'g'.

The introduction of this regulation for the 1985 Grand Prix season caused considerable effort to be put into the design of the nosebox, a component that, hitherto, had been regarded largely as a piece of bodywork although some attempt had been made to provide driver protection in the chassis foot-box region. Initial testing at the end of 1984 demonstrated fairly comprehensively, however, that the sort of structures used until that date - which many people regarded as being very effective - were completely inadequate in terms of meeting the new regulation.

All of the impact testing undertaken by Williams Grand Prix Engineering Limited has been done using the facilities of Cranfield Impact Centre. Frontal crash testing is performed on their Large Pendulum rig.

A specimen is manufactured comprising a nosebox and the front 1/3 of a chassis built and equipped to a standard identical to that to be entered for the Grand Prix. This is mounted on a fixed, ridid support structure and the 780 kg pendulum allowed to drop and impact it horizontally.

The design of nose and chassis structures has progressed to the level where, in 1988, damage can be entirely confined to the nosebox and the resulting average deceleration is kept below 50% of the 25 'g' permitted. Whilst most people appreciate that a 90 degree frontal impact is a very rare occurrence, there can be little doubt that the amount learnt about chassis design that has come about as a consequence of having to carry out this test has improved the overall integrity of the product.

6.2 Lateral Crush Test

A second obligatory test was introduced at the beginning of 1988 concerning the lateral crush strength of the chassis. The intention of this regulation was to ensure that all designs for Formula 1 chassis satisfy at least a specified minimum level of side impact performance. The test, however, is not an impact one in the same sense as in the nosebox case previously described but rather a statically-equivalent fixed load application.

A load of 2000 kg must be applied on a solid pad measuring 300 mm x 100 mm and reacted on an identical area as shown in Fig. 6. There are two specified positions of application at longitudinal stations equivalent to:-

i)   the cockpit level with the driver's hips

ii)   the centroid of the fuel tank

Under the action of this load there must be no detectable damage to the inner skin of the sandwich shell structure and a maximum deflection of 20 mm must not be exceeded.

The chassis built for the 1988 season, the FW12, was successfully tested to these criteria, no damage in any area being found.

7 PROJECT MANAGEMENT AND TIMESCALES

The processes and procedures described so far differ little from those encountered by any other concern engaged in the business of design and manufacture using advanced composite materials. There is one respect, however, in which the motor racing industry, and Formula 1 in particular, are subjected to special disciplines - timescales.

Examining the assembly of components that comprise a Grand Prix car it is possible to isolate, perhaps, twenty examples that could be described as major projects in their own right, given the effort required to design, tool and manufacture them. Considering also that work has to be done on all of them simultaneously the magnitude of the task assumes significant proportions. This is compounded by the time allocated to do the job.

The FW12 of 1988 illustrates the difficulties in this respect rather aptly. The car configuration and specification were finalised in the last week of October, 1 9 8 7 . The resulting vehicle was circuit testing in the last week of February, 1988 - a time difference of only 4 months.

Given these constraints and the necessity to produce a sufficient quantity of components prior to the commencement of the racing season less than one month later, it becomes clear that careful plannining is essential to avoid any embarrassment. The addition to the schedule of the impact testing has emphasised its importance since specimens must also be manufactured and successfully tested as well. It need not be added that, with no time margin for error, the necessity to produce good parts - and the corresponding pressure on the design and production teams - is very great.

The successful completion of a series of these projects has provided us with much useful management information. As work progresses, careful records are made of the time duration for each particular task. This data has been vital in the planning of future programmes.

8 CONCLUSIONS

Now that advanced composites have become regarded as the standard materials of which high performance competition cars are built, it is worth examining exactly what has been achieved by their use and what might be the direction of future development.

8.1 Structural Stiffness

The initial reason for using composite materials in the field of Formula 1 car design was that gains were hoped to be made in respect of stiffness and/or weight of component. Since the absolute weight of the complete vehicle has always been close to the allowable minimum, decisions were made to keep the chassis structure weight constant and seek improved performance. This goal was achieved immediately and has been improved upon with each subsequent design. The situation today is that measured chassis torsional stiffness is more than 100% greater than that of the final aluminium structure built.

8.2 Impact Performance

There is little doubt that the general crashworthiness of the whole package is considerably enhanced relative to that which was considered to be adequate prior to 1985. Physical impact testing of structures has demonstrated results that would once have been regarded as difficult to achieve. Additionally, unscheduled in-service impact testing has reinforced this belief. The example of the FW11B driven by Nelson Piquet at the 1987 San Marino Grand Prix at the Imola circuit has been held up as an outstanding example of the survivability of the modern Grand Prix car.

8.3 Production Efficiency

One area in which advantages have been seen against the expectations of most people is that of production time-saving. Considering the labour-intensive nature of composite component manufacture by hand lay-up methods this may appear surprising. Compared with the fabrication of an aluminium structure, however, the number of parts is much reduced and the fastening task removed. The minimum time achieved for a metal chassis assembly was some 300 man-hours whereas the composite designs have reach as few as 250 man-hours.

8.3 Geometric Accuracy

The ability to accurately mould a shape has provided new opportunities for the manufacture of aerodynamically 'clean' components. Good examples of this are wing surfaces where the accuracy, finish and repeatability of the components made in composite materials are a major advance on their metallic forerunners produced by hand forming and rivetting. Bodywork fitting is also much more consistent than before and parts can now be regarded as truly interchangeable.

8.4 Component Durability

There has been a general observation that the service life and durability of the composite assemblies is also an improvement upon that of the aluminium structures. The absence of mechanical fasteners and complex panel junctions has removed the cracking problems found in thin metal parts when used in a high vibration environment.

8.5 Future areas of Development

A rational examination of what has been achieved with composite materials at Williams Grand Prix Engineering Limited leads to the general statement that major lessons have been learnt in the fields of detail design, tooling and component production skills whilst under considerable timescale pressures. Building upon these, other areas must receive equal emphasis from now on. Amongst these are the subjects of new material development, inspection procedures, structural analysis and testing. The development of design analysis tools and test instrumentation will enable us to gain more confidence in the prediction of structural performance and, therefore, help us towards our goal of greater component optimisation.

Fig 1   Williams FW12 (1988)

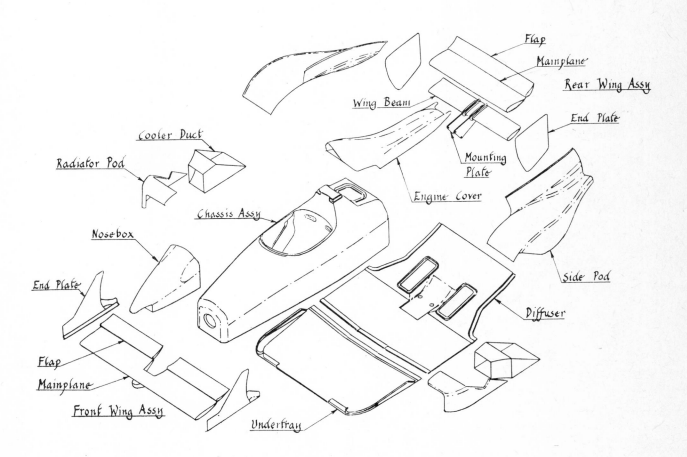

Fig 2   Components manufactured from composite materials

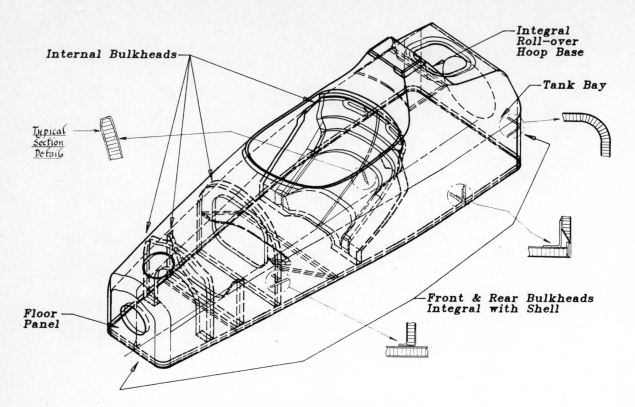

Fig 3   Chassis structure assembly

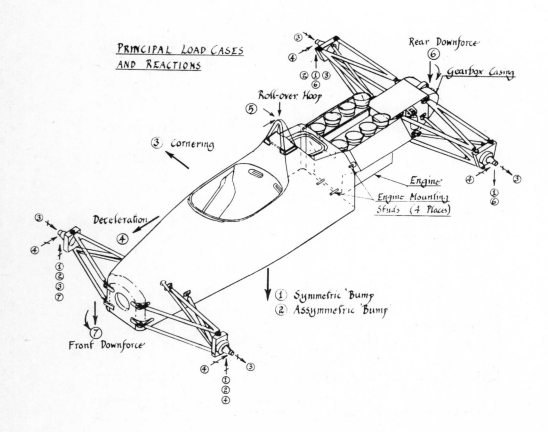

Fig 4   Structure idealization

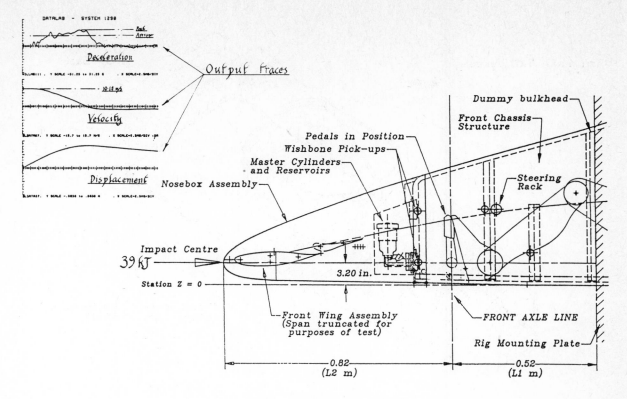

Fig 5   Frontal impact test

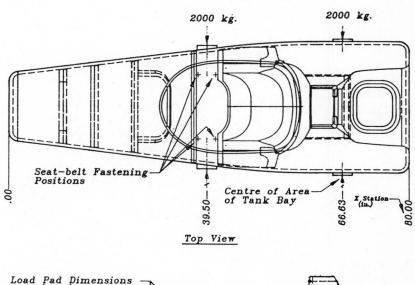

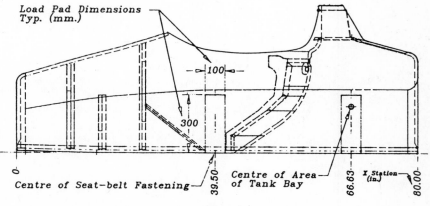

Fig 6   Lateral load test

C387/004

Optimum design of laminated structural members

S J HARDY, BSc, PhD, CEng, MIMechE, FIED and **N H MALIK**, BSc, MSc
Department of Mechanical Engineering, University College of Swansea

SYNOPSIS Developments in computational capability have resulted in advances in the field of design optimization. In particular, the finite element method has emerged as the most powerful technique for solving a wide range of continuum and structural analysis problems. The optimal design of composite structures depends on criteria such as stiffness, strength and stability. The finite element method provides such information for given properties, which depend on the 'make-up' of the material.

The paper describes an attempt to automate the design process using an optimization loop around a standard, commercially available, finite element package.

NOTATION

h – square box sectional dimension

m – total number of design variables with explicit constraints

n – total number of variables including implicitly constrained variables

r_i – ith psuedo-random number of value between 0 and 1

t – thickness of material

x_e – element longitudinal axis

x_m – material longitudinal axis

y_e – element transverse axis

y_m – material transverse axis

D – outer diameter of tube

E_x – Young's modulus for a ply in the longitudinal direction x_m

E_y – Young's modulus for a ply in the transverse direction y_m

F – objective function

G_{xy} – shear modulus associated with the x_m – y_m plane

G_i – lower constraint on the ith-design variable

H_i – upper constraint on ith-design variable

V_f – volume-fraction of fibre in the material

X_i – ith design variable

α – reflection factor used in optimiser

β – included angle between sections of two-section cantilever

θ – fibre-orientation angle

ν_{xy} – Poisson's ratio for a ply associated with x_m – y_m plane

ρ – density of composite material

1. INTRODUCTION

Current trends towards more efficient and cost-effective component design and manufacture have resulted in an increasing interest and emphasis on the use of advanced composite materials as a viable alternative to traditional engineering materials. Such materials have major benefits in terms of their strength, stiffness and fatigue performance. Significant weight reductions can be achieved. There is now a wide choice of general purpose and more sophisticated materials for both the fibres and the matrix.

The analysis of component designs which utilise composite materials is not straight-forward in view of the complexity of the material behaviour. Material properties are highly dependent on the 'set-up' of the composite. Simple approximations (in order to develop a material model which can be used in an analysis) are unlikely to be of any value, particularly in view of the need for greater cost-effectiveness. One approach still used extensively is to simply replace the existing component with a geometrically identical design made from a suitable composite material. Although the choice of new material may well be based on sound engineering judgement coupled with extensive 'in-service' testing and may provide a satisfactory solution, it does not utilise the full potential of the material. Further weight savings, still maintaining the function of the component, are likely to be attainable. The only way to realise that full potential is to re-design the component in order to optimise on material and geometric characterisics of the design while still meeting the mechanical specification.

Some structural optimization algorithms have been developed which are used in conjunction with design analysis techniques in an attempt to meet this need, particularly in the U.S.A. for the aerospace industry. These developments are discussed in more detail in section 2. From this review, there are a number of observations which were taken into consideration when the objectives of the project (described in this paper) were defined:-

1) many procedures are designed around single parameter optimization, usually weight;

2) although complex procedures have been developed for the high-tech aerospace industry, they are application-specific and are not generally available;

3) there is little evidence of the coupling of design analysis techniques and optimization algorithms for use in general engineering design.

A need for general-purpose advanced design analysis procedures, with multi-point constraint optimization capability, has been identified.

Finite element analysis (FEA) is an extremely powerful aid in the design process for complex components and loading conditions and is widely used in industry. There are numerous general purpose programs available and many of these include composite element formulations. The method is approximate and highly numerical and can be very costly in terms of computer usage. However, if the finite element model is created effectively, then the predictions can be very accurate and considerable savings can be made in terms of component design, manufacture and testing. Parametric design studies can be performed economically so that variations in material and geometry can be studied at the conceptual design stage.

Optimizational feedback would appear to provide a major enhancement to FEA technology with extreme flexibility so that structured parametric studies can be performed. One obvious application is in the use of composite materials.

The paper gives details of a project being carried out in the Department of Mechanical Engineering at University College, Swansea. The aim is to develop a multi-parameter optimization program, 'bolted-on'

to a standard commercial finite element package, which can be used to investigate the optimum design of laminated structural members. The main application to be studied is in the field of robotics where the use of light-weight structural elements made from a composite material would be beneficial. This is particularly true for the long-reach multi-axial arms used for probing, inspection, welding, painting etc. Clearly such a program will have wide-ranging applications in the field of structural design.

Relevant background information on composite design and optimization techniques is given in section 2. The development of the finite element/optimization package is discussed in section 3 and examples of its use are given in sections 4 and 5. A discussion of the progress to date and details of the next stages of the project are given in section 6. Conclusions are drawn in section 7.

2 BACKGROUND

2.1 Composite structure design

The design of any structure using fibre-reinforced materials is basically made up of two interdependent studies; one centred on the choice of material and the other on the static and dynamic behaviour of the structure. The optimized result is generally a compromise based on set targets of cost, performance and weight. The method of fabrication is also included at this stage of the design cycle since it has a direct bearing on the cost and feasibility of the product.

After an initial design study, general requirements for the material or set of materials can be established. The standard building block of advanced composites is the lamina structure. Micromechanic formulations, such as the Tsai-Halpin equations (1), can be used to predict the elastic properties of the lamina from fundamental fibre and matrix data. The determination of the mechanical behaviour of a laminated material is not so precise. Some simple models have been developed (e.g. 2). These models assume perfect bonding between fibre and matrix and no fibre-matrix interactions. The individual laminae are stacked into a laminate, mechanical properties are mathematically calculated using conventional laminate theory.

When the selected laminate or laminates satisfy the requirements of a preliminary structural analysis, a detailed investigation can be carried out using more advanced and accurate techniques such as FEA. Many general purpose finite element packages now contain a composite material model for which they require the macromechanical material properties (see section 2.3).

2.2 Optimization methods

While engineers move towards analysing more complex structures, design optimization allows them to save on material cost/weight and can be used in sensitivity studies to further improve the integrity of the product.

Engineering design optimization and engineering analysis are fundamentally different in nature. In analysis, one is generally assured that a solution exists and numerical methods are 'stable'. In optimal design, the existence of even a basic design which satisfies the constraints (or conditions) is not assured and the probability reduces as the number of constraints is increased.

The normal procedure is to define a set of conditions for an optimum solution and then systematically generate a solution which satisfies these conditions. Inevitably, more than one solution will exist and the question 'what is the optimum of all such optimums?' has to be addressed. This uncertainty about the nature of the absolute optimum has created interest in the development of optimization algorithms.

The rapid growth in computational capability over the last two or three decades has provided the necessary stimulus to the development of sophisticated design optimization schemes in all disciplines of engineering. Numerical methods for the determination of an optimum solution are quite sensitive to the initial estimates and complex iterative convergence techniques have also become necessary. Venkayya (3) has produced a useful review of the structural optimization literature and methods. However, his basic design approach and prototype example problems give a generalized overview of structural optimization favouring optimality criteria methods.

In general, optimization methods are used to optimize a particular feature of the design for a given set of design variables. This particular feature, known as the objective function, will be some criteria against which the design is evaluated. Weight is an obvious example, but more realistic objective functions are likely to be linked with structural integrity e.g. stiffness, stability etc. The design variables are the range of geometric and functional requirements which dictate the bounds of the design and from which the ideas are developed. These optimization methods can be grouped into three general categories (4):-

1) Parametric studies

Used to select combinations of design variables from contour plots of the objective function to yield the optimum value. Parametric studies are generally extensive pieces of work in which all possible combinations of the variables are analysed.

2) Structural index method

The structural index relates the structural efficiency (degree of conformity) of a member to the loading conditions and the design variables.

Mathematical relationships are used to generate contour plots and then design parameters are selected for efficient component utilization.

3) Structural synthesis

The objective function is optimized using a structured approach in order to achieve the best compromise for the given variables.

The latter category is the most relevant to this project since these methods are essentially computer-based numerical optimization techniques where the best compromise is reached by an iterative process. Structural synthesis methods are being used in many optimization programs developed for composite materials, as discussed in the following section.

2.3 Optimization with fibre-reinforced materials

By using the directional properties of these materials to suit the mechanical requirements, promising engineering designs are possible. The only problem, however, is the lack of pertinent data available to the designer in this field, except for basic studies and uniaxial behaviour (e.g. 5). Basic laminate treatment and micromechanical behaviour are discussed in (6).

There are a number of design variables to be considered when designing a composite panel. These include:-

a) micromechanical properties - fibre material constants, matrix material constants, fibre volume fractions, fibre array type.

b) macromechanical properties - fibre orientation, thickness of plies, number of plies, stacking sequence.

and many more. A number of constraints have to be formed which include any constraints on each of the above variables plus geometrical and manufacturing constraints and failure criteria. All of these make the task of producing an optimal design extremely difficult, if not impossible.

The optimization of the component design combines the requirements above with mechanical constraints such as impact resistance, bending and torsional stiffness, material damping, cost, weight, geometry and many other influencing factors. Besides being a complex non-linear problem, the design requirements such as strength and stiffness are stated as inequality constraints (e.g. lower limit on structural stiffness).

To approach the design problem, the optimization is treated as a problem of mathematical extremization of the objective function in an 'n' dimensional design space constrained by behavioural functions (7). The search for the optimum is carried out by a variety of linear and non-linear programming methods, such as gradient projection, steepest decent, feasible directions and penalty unconstrained techniques (7). Others include optimality criteria approaches, optimal control theory and dynamic programming. Emphasis and importance have been given to one or more of these methods depending on the size and nature of the particular optimization problem.

A number of research papers have been published which illustrate and identify design criteria for composites. Schmit and Farshi (8) present a method of minimum weight design for symmetric fibre-laminates in which ply thickness is a design variable and ply orientation is pre-assigned to reduce complications and to avoid local optimums. Liao et al (9) consider the design of symmetric laminated beams with optimal damping. Ply angle and thickness are the design variables and quadratic programming was employed. The dynamic behaviour of laminated flexural members has been investigated by Adams and Bacon (10) together with experimental investigations into mechanical properties of angle-ply laminates. Thompson, Sung and others (11-13) have presented a series of models covering different aspects in composite-design. Although providing a useful insight, these are all rather application specific models.

Computer programs, mostly for the aerospace field, have been written in this context. Examples include COMAND (14), OPTCOMP (15), OPTIM (16), ASOP (17) and DESAP (18). Many of these use discrete optimality criteria with bounds on strength, stiffness, static stability and aeroelastic behaviour. Flanagan and Palazotto (2) have written a series of weight-optimization programs for use on microcomputers. Although some programs are large and employ finite elements methods (e.g. 15), they have been written for particular applications and are not suitable for general-purpose analysis.

The optimization of both the material and the structure is complicated and expensive in computer resources. Furthermore, it is an area of development in which limited information has been published and hence is the subject of this investigation.

2.4 Future developments

The availability of a wide variety of literature on optimization methods gives an indication of the interest and activity in this field. However, the pursuit for more diverse and powerful techniques is still on (7). With advancements in materials technology, fabrication techniques and the nature of the applications, even more sophisticated optimization techniques will be required in the future.

The applications of advanced composites is no longer restricted to the aerospace field. The use of composite materials in everyday products such as washing machines and fishing rods is becoming increasingly more popular for a number of well founded reasons.

The need for general-purpose analysis methods, such as FEA, which include composite material formulations together with optimization capabilities is self-evident. Cost-effective design and manufacture will be the motivation for these future developments.

3 THE PROGRAM

3.1 Procedure

The optimization routine has been designed to operate in conjunction with the general-purpose finite element package PAFEC (19). An outline flowchart is shown in Fig. 1 from which it can be seen that PAFEC is an integral part of the optimization loop.

The data input to the program is a combination of fixed values, design variables and optimization control data. The fixed values are defined as those pre-determined finite element model parameters :-

structure geometry in the form of nodal coordinates

choice of element type(s) and topology

structural boundary conditions or constraints

loading type(s) and values

At this stage in the development of the program, the design variables are the micro- and macromechanical material properties referred to in section 2.3, some of which are to be the subject of optimization investigations. Other design variables will be included in future versions of the program (see Note below). Depending on the nature of the investigation, the values given for each material property will be either fixed or variable (if being optimized). In the latter case, a range and an initial guess are required.

Optimization control data includes the objective function and the convergence criteria.

Note

It is proposed that a future version of the program will include the facility to optimize on certain aspects of structural geometry as well as material configuration (see section 6).

With reference to Fig. 1, the form of the iterative loop is as follows :-

1. Data input;

2. Micromechanical material constants are evaluated. These are essentially the terms of the Compliance matrix (19), obtained from the material modulii and the respective Poisson's ratios. These are referred to various lamina, if multi-layer laminae with different properties are present.

3. The data is compiled in a form acceptable to PAFEC.

4. The finite element code is executed. It is unlikely that the material symmetry axes coincide with the axes of the element for all elements in a given idealization. If the element axes are orientated at an angle θ to the material symmetry axes, as shown in Fig. 2., then the Compliance matrix is transformed to give the modified compliances associated with the element axes. The stiffness matrices of all the elements are found and put onto backing store. The system equations are then solved for the primary unknowns in the problem. In the case of static loading, nodal displacements are given for all degrees of freedom. In the dynamic case, PAFEC optionally uses a limited number of dynamic freedoms to find out natural frequencies and mode shapes.

5. The PAFEC output routines have been modified so that nodal displacements are stored in a separate file and the usual output phase is omitted (until an optimum solution has been achieved). For a dynamic analysis, natural frequencies are also stored in this file.

6. The objective function to be optimized is extracted from the data file and the optimization model (see section 3.2) used to assess convergence and provide new values for the design variables, if necessary.

7. If the convergence criteria is violated, then this new data is used in the next iteration (i.e. return to item 2).

8. If convergence is successful, then the analysis is complete and the finite element results are printed.

The optimization loop has been designed so that the necessary modifications to the commercial finite element program are minimised. In this way, such a loop could be adapted for any commercial package, the PAFEC-specific parts being only :-

a) the pre-processing routine to prepare the input data in the required form;

b) the way in which the finite element output file is modified (see item 5 above).

The optimization model itself is contained in a stand-alone routine with input from the newly created PAFEC output file and output to the pre-processor. All coding is written in FORTRAN 77.

3.2 Optimization model

The optimization the algorithm currently used is a modified form of "Complex" method by Box (20). The minimum or maximum of a multi-variable nonlinear function is sought which has the form:-

$$F(X_1, X_2, X_3, \ldots X_m)$$

for 'm' design variables, subject to the conditions :-

$$G_k < X_k < H_k, \quad k = 1, 2, \ldots n$$

where implicit variables $X_{m+1} \ldots X_n$ are also allowed and are dependent functions of the explicit independent variables $X_1, X_2 \ldots X_m$. The upper and lower constraints H_k and G_k are either constants or functions of the independent variables.

The algorithm proceeds as follows:-

1. A 'complex' is generated consisting of m+1 sets of values for the design variables. The first set contains the feasible starting points selected by the user within the constraints and there are a further m sets of values generated from random numbers :-

$$X_{ij} = G_i + r_{ij} (H_i - G_i), \quad i = 1, 2, \ldots m$$

and $j = 1, 2, \ldots k - 1$,

(where r_{ij} are random numbers between 0 and 1)

and verified against the constraints.

2. The objective function is evaluated by PAFEC for each set of design variables.

3. The set of design variables which produces the least acceptable value for the objective function (for example, the highest objective function where the function is to be minimised) is replaced by a set of design variables located as follows :-

$$X_i (new) = \alpha(X_i' - X_i' (old)) + X_i',$$

$i = 1, 2, \ldots . m.$

where X_i' is the mean of the remaining values for each design variable. The best value of α used is 1.3 for most rapid convergence.

4. If an explicit constraint is violated, the new value for the design variable is modified to be just within the constraint. If an implicit constraint is violated, the value is adjusted so that the point is halfway between the present and centroidal values.

$$X_i (new) = (X_i (old) + X_i')/2 , \quad i=1, 2, \ldots m$$

This process is repeated until all implicit constraints are satisfied.

5. This new set of design variables is used as the input to the next iteration of the finite element program to find a new objective function. The revised m+1

objective functions are the input to the optimization process (i.e. back to item 3).

6. If the least acceptable value for an objective function is repeated, the corresponding design variables are re-located mid-way between the current and centroidal values.

7. Convergence is achieved when the objective functions are within the specified criteria for a specified number of iterations.

The flow chart for this procedure is given in Fig. 3.

3.3 Optimization analyses

Two sample problems are presented to illustrate the operation of the program. The first, given in section 4, shows how :-

a) bending and torsional stiffness and
b) natural frequencies

are optimized in a simple straight hollow cantilever with the design variable being ply angle. In section 5, a similar analysis is carried out on a two-section cantilever with a number of configurations in order to simulate a simple two-section robot arm. At this stage in the development of the program, multi-parameter optimization has not been considered. The examples are intended to show the potential of the program using single design variable type optimization (see section 6.2).

4 CASE 1 - STATIC AND DYNAMIC ANALYSIS OF A SIMPLE CANTILEVER

The problem is shown diagramatically in Fig 4. Square and circular hollow cross-sections have been analysed. A number of assumptions have been made in order to simplify this first analysis :-

a) fibre and matrix are homogeneous and linear elastic;

b) regular spacing in the matrix;

c) optimization on a single design variable type - ply angle;

d) for a given laminate, ply angle is constant along the length of the cantilever.

In addition, the following details complete the definition of the optimization problem :-

e) 8 laminates through the thickness;

f) ply thickness is constant and equal to 0.18 mm;

g) balanced angle-ply laminate topology;

h) laminates assumed to be made from T300/5208 Graphite Epoxy and having the following properties (6):-

E_x = 153 GPa , E_y = 10.9 GPa

ν_{xy} = 0.3 , G_{xy} = 5.6 GPa

V_f = 0.7 , ρ = 1691 Kg/m^3;

i) constraints on ply angle are:-

$-90 < \theta_i < 90$ for each ply;

j) sixteen 8-noded shell finite elements (4 along length, 4 around section) are used to model the structure;

k) for bending and torsional stiffness optimization, the objective function is maximum nodal displacement which is to be minimised;

l) for natural frequency optimization, the objective function is lowest natural frequency and this is to be maximised.

m) for the analyses of equivalent aluminium structures, standard PAFEC material data is used (19).

n) the laminate topology is:-

$$(\theta_i/-\theta_1/\theta_2/-\theta_2...)_8$$

and an initial value of $\theta_i = 45^{\circ}$ is used for all i.

The results are presented in Tables 1 and 2 for the box and circular sections respectively. For static loading, optimal ply angles in the 8 laminates together with stiffness/weight ratios are given for the bending, torsion and combined cases. The stiffness/weight ratios are derived from the maximum linear displacements. The optimal ply angles, initial and optimal first natural frequencies obtained from the dynamic analyses are also presented. The equivalent results for a geometrically identical aluminium structure are given for comparison.

For the box section, the bending stiffness is maximised (i.e. minimum nodal displacements) when the fibres are aligned axially (within numerical accuracy), as one might expect. For torsional stiffness, the optimal ply angles are laminate dependent with outer laminates 1, 2, 3 and 4 towards the transverse direction and inner laminates 5, 6, 7 and 8 in the mid-range. For the combined case of bending and torsional loads, it would appear that the bending effect is dominant since the alignment is generally towards the axial direction.

In most cases, there is a significant improvement in the stiffness/weight ratio between the initial and optimal conditions. The only exception is a reduction in the torsional stiffness for the combined loading case, but since the results are dominated by the bending stiffness this reduction has no overall significance. The optimal stiffness/

54

values for aluminium although it would appear that this would not necessarily be true for $\beta < 120^{\circ}$.

As with the simple cantilever analyses, the rate of convergence is slow (up to 27 iterations) and improvements are deemed necessary.

6   DISCUSSION

6.1 Overview of the results

In all the cases analysed, the optimal stiffness/weight ratios are significantly greater than the values with the initial selection of ply angles. More importantly, the results indicate that improvements in the stiffness can be achieved when T300/5208 graphite epoxy is used in preference to aluminium. Because the initial ply angles are arbitrary and do not necessarily correspond to the worst conditions, it is interesting to note that unconditional replacement by graphite epoxy would not always result in improved static and dynamic characteristics. For example, the bending stiffness/weight ratio for the simple cantilever made from aluminium is greater than the unoptimized composite value. Similarly, the results indicate that the use of the graphite epoxy can have a detrimental effect on vibration characteristics. In every case, the first natural frequency reduces when the material is changed from aluminium to unoptimized graphite epoxy.

The optimal ply angles obtained in the analyses are loading, cross-section and configuration dependent. One obvious result is that optimal alignment for bending (and therefore first natural frequency) is axial. Also for pure torsion of the uniform hollow tube section, the greatest stiffness is achieved when the fibres are at 45 degrees to the axis. The results for the hollow box section in torsion and all the results when bending and torsion act together are more difficult to justify.

6.2 Project and program development

The project and program are still at an early stage of development but already the potential of such an analysis package is being realized. A number of areas of project and program enhancement have been identified:-

1.   Multi-parameter optimization - this is a fundamental aim of the project and investigative analyses are underway. The main concern is the method by which two or more design variables can be linked in order to define a realistic objective function.

2.   Geometrical optimization - in addition to optimizing on the basis of material properties, an ability to consider geometrical design variables, in particular overall thickness, should be included. This will require further interaction with the finite element

weight ratios are between 119 and 171% higher than the equivalent values for aluminium. There is a 120% increase in the lowest natural frequency between the initial and optimal solutions. The optimal alignment is axial. This to be expected because the first mode of vibration is a simple bending mode. The optimal first natural frequency is 71% higher than the equivalent value for aluminium.

For the circular section, the trends are similar to those already identified. For torsional loading, optimal conditions clearly occur with all the fibres at around 45 degrees. Also, this particular cross-section is very stiff in torsion when compared with the box section. Again, bending effects appear to dominate the combined loading case. The optimal stiffness/weight ratios are up to 188% higher than the equivalent values for aluminium. From the dynamic analysis, optimal alignment is axial and the first natural frequency is 113% higher and 59% higher than the initial value and the equivalent value for aluminium respectively.

One important point to note is that the optimal results were obtained only after a significant number of iterations, in some cases in excess of 20. Improvements in the solution procedure are currently being investigated, as discussed in section 6.2.

5   CASE 2 - STATIC AND DYNAMIC ANALYSIS OF A SIMPLE TWO-SECTION ROBOT ARM

The problem is shown diagrammatically in Fig. 5. The two parts have a hollow circular cross-section. The assumptions made in the previous analysis are repeated here with the exception of d). In this example, the ply angle is constant along each section but variation between sections is permitted. The sections have equal lengths and three configurations have been analysed; $\beta = 180^{\circ}$, 150° and 120°.

The results are presented in Table 3 for the combined case of bending and torsion due to a normal offset tip load. The optimal ply angles in both sections and the calculated stiffness/weight ratio are given. Optimum ply angles and first natural frequencies obtained from the dynamic analyses are also shown. The equivalent results for an aluminium structure are given for comparison.

The optimal ply angles in each section are configuration and lamina dependent with no apparent general trends. This is probably because the stiffness/weight ratio has a minimum value, due to the nature of the loading, for a configuration somewhere between 120 and 180 degrees. Optimal bending stiffness/weight ratios are significantly higher than initial values and at least 107% higher than the equivalent values for aluminium. Again, there is a deterioration in torsional stiffness. For optimal dynamic behaviour, alignment of the plys is towards the axial direction as for the simple beams. In all cases, the optimal first natural frequencies are greater than the equivalent analysis data and objective functions which combine weight and strength requirements.

3. Programming techniques – the current optimization process, which is based on random search, is slow and needs to be made more efficient (although it is versatile, easy to implement and probably takes less iterations when compared to gradient methods). This will be achieved by improvements in the programming technique.

4. Strength constraints – an important, yet relatively simple future development will be to introduce limiting stress constraints to the optimization process.

5. Experimental verification – work is in progress to design and manufacture a simple two-section robot arm with interchangeable steel and composite sections which can be used to verify the program results.

7 CONCLUSIONS

A need for a multi-parameter optimization program, incorporating sophisticated analysis techniques, has been identified. Such a program has wide ranging applications in the design and analysis of structural components made from composite materials. Such a program is being developed at Swansea using an optimization algorithm which is linked to a commercially available finite element package.

The current version of the program has been used to provide some data for relatively simple components with a number of simplifying assumptions being made. The results are encouraging and future developments for the project and program are planned.

The analyses described in this paper have identified a number of advantages of using composite materials in preference to a typical structural material such as aluminium. In most cases, there are significant improvements in two important structural requirements, stiffness and natural frequency, for geometrically equivalent composite and aluminium structures. Further improvements could be achieved since reductions in material section may be appropriate. This aspect of re-design is to be considered in the future.

REFERENCES

(1) TSAI, S.W. and HAHN, H.T. Introduction to composite materials. Technomic Publishing Co., 1980.

(2) FLANAGAN, G. and PALAZOTTO, A.N. Composite laminate optimization program suitable for microcomputers. Computers and Structures, Feb. 1986, 995–1009.

(3) VENKAYYA, V.B. Structural optimization: A review and some recommendations. International Journal of Numerical Methods in Engineering, 1978, 13, 203–228.

(4) BROUTMAN, L.J. and KROCK, R.H. Composite materials, structural design and analysis – Vol. 7 & 8. Academic Press, 1975.

(5) Advanced composite design guide. A.F.M.L., Wright-Patterson Air Force Base, Ohio, 1968.

(6) VINSON, J.R. and SEIRAKOWSKI, R.L. The behaviour of structures composed of composite materials. Martinus Nijhoff Publishers, 1986.

(7) HAUG, E.J. and AURORA, J.S. Applied optimal design. J. Wiley and Sons, 1979.

(8) SCHMIT, L.A. and FARSHI, B. Optimal laminate design for strength and stiffness. International Journal of Numerical Methods in Engineering, 1973, 7, 519–536.

(9) LIAO, D.X. SUNG, C.K. and THOMPSON, B.S. The optimal design of symmetric laminated beams considering damping. Journal of Composite Materials, 1986, 20, 485–502.

(10) ADAMS, R.D. and BACON, D.G.C. Effects of fibre orientation and laminate geometry on the dynamic properties of CFRP. Carbon Reinforced Epoxy Systems, Volume 1. Technomic Publishing Co., 1974.

(11) SUNG, C.K. and THOMPSON, B.S. A methodology for synthesizing symmetric laminated beams with optimal elasto-dynamic response characteristics. Int. Journal of Mechanical Sciences. 1987, Vol. 29, 12, 821–830.

(12) SUNG, C.K. and THOMPSON, B.S., A methodology for synthesizing high-performance robots fabricated with optimally tailored composite laminates. Transactions of ASME-Journal of Mechanisms, Transmissions, and Automation in Design. March 1987, 109, 74–86.

(13) SUNG, C.K. and THOMPSON, B.S., The design of robots and intelligent manipulators using modern composite materials. Mechanism and Machine Theory, 1985, 20, 471–482.

(14) VANDEPLAATS, G.N. COMAND – A fortran program for simplified composite analysis and design. NASA TM X-73, 104, Feb. 1976.

(15) KHOT, N.S. Computer program (OPTCOMP) for optimization of composite structures for minimum weight design. AFFDL-TR-76-149, Wright-Patterson Air Force Base, Ohio, 1977.

(16) GELLATLY, R.A. DUPREE, D.M. and BERKE, L. OPTIM-II, A magic compatible large scale, automated minimum-weight design program. AFFDL-TR-74-97, Wright-Patterson Air Force Base, Ohio, 1974.

(17) ISAAKSON, G. and PARDO, H. ASOP-3, A program for the minimum weight design of structures subjected to strength and deflection constraints. Grumman Aerospace Corp., Bethpage, N.Y. AFFDL-TR-76-157, 1976.

(18) KIUSALAAS, J. and REDDY, G.B. DESAP-2, A structural design program with stress and buckling constraints. NASA CR-2797 to 2799, NASA, Washington, 1977.

(19) PAFEC Level 6.1, data preparation manual. PAFEC Limited, Nottingham.

(20) KUESTER, J.L. and MIZE, J.H. Optimization techniques with fortran. McGraw Hill Book Company, 1973.

Table 1 Hollow-box cantilever with different loading conditions.
Values in brackets are for equivalent geometry Aluminium member.

	STATIC LOADING								DYNAMIC ANALYSIS					
Loading type	Optimal ply-angle (degrees)				Bending Stiff./Wt ratio		Torsional Stiff/Wt ratio		Optimal ply-angle (degrees)				First mode freq. (Hz)	
	θ_1	θ_2	θ_3	θ_4	Unopt.	Opt.	Unopt.	Opt.	θ_1	θ_2	θ_3	θ_4	Unopt.	Opt.
Bending	+5	+2	−3	−5	48.2 (59.6)	161.6								
Torsion	+75	+70	−56	−47			4669.1 (2185.7)	4780.8	+10	+8	+11	+10	224.8	494.2
Combined	+23	+16	−11	−19	33.1 (58.8)	149.3	5257.8 (2136.1)	1866.5					(288.3)	

Table 2 Tube cantilever with different loading conditions.
Values in brackets are for equivalent geometry Aluminium member.

	STATIC LOADING								DYNAMIC ANALYSIS					
Loading type	Optimal ply-angle (degrees)				Bending Stiff./Wt ratio		Torsional Stiff/Wt ratio		Optimal ply-angle (degrees)				First mode freq. (Hz)	
	θ_1	θ_2	θ_3	θ_4	Unopt.	Opt.	Unopt.	Opt.	θ_1	θ_2	θ_3	θ_4	Unopt.	Opt.
Bending	0	0	0	0	60.5 (88.2)	254.1								
Torsion	+43	+39	−41	−42			38595 (17249)	38750	0	0	0	0	302.7	644.6
Combined	−34	+3	+11	+10	70.3 (86.5)	219.3	29613 (20294)	19585					(405.7)	

Table 3 Tube bent at angle β at mid-span, combined load normal to Section 2.
Values in brackets are for equivalent geometry Aluminium member.
* – Angles are with respect to the axial direction for each section.

		STATIC LOADING								DYNAMIC ANALYSIS					
		Optimal ply-angle (degrees)*				Bending Stiff./Wt ratio		Torsional Stiff/Wt ratio		Optimal ply-angle (degrees)*				First mode freq. (Hz)	
β		θ_1	θ_2	θ_3	θ_4	Unopt.	Opt.	Unopt.	Opt.	θ_1	θ_2	θ_3	θ_4	Unopt.	Opt.
180°		−34	+3	+11	+10	70.3 (86.5)	219.3	29613 (20294)	19585	0	0	0	0	302.7 (405.7)	644.6
150°	#1	+23	+14	−45	−51	80.2 (67.3)	139.4	19366 (16350)	14198	0	+2	−1	+1	335.1 (416.9)	504.0
	#2	+31	−76	+84	+59					+6	−8	+5	+3		
120°	#1	+17	+22	+27	−31	190.0 (75.1)	247.8	14562 (12288)	9558	+8	+11	−3	−13	360.9 (440.3)	455.6
	#2	+60	−54	+86	+59					−16	+6	−9	−11		

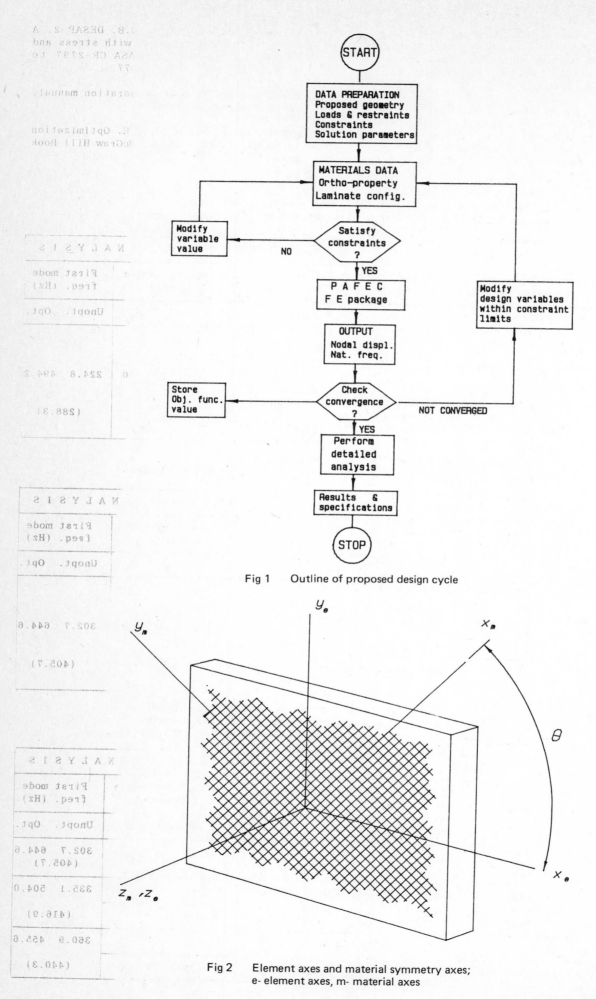

Fig 1   Outline of proposed design cycle

Fig 2   Element axes and material symmetry axes;
e- element axes, m- material axes

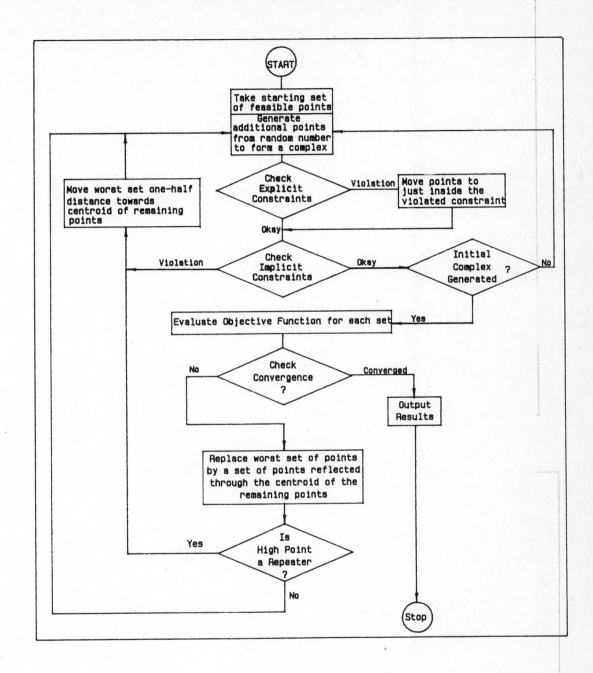

Fig 3   Optimization procedure flowchart

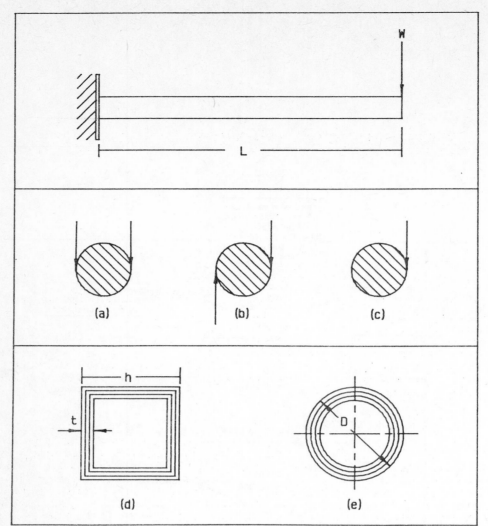

Fig 4   Cantilever beam with different loads and cross-sections;
         (a) bending, (b) torsion, (c) combined loads at free end,
         (d) hollow box and (e) tube cross-sections with L/h =
         L/D = 10, and H/t = D/t = 16

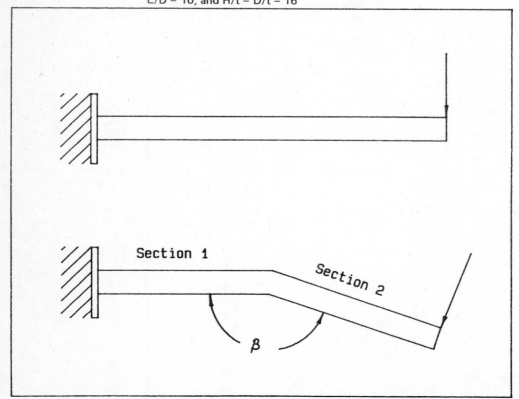

Fig 5   Cantilever tube in different configurations; (1) straight,
         (2) bent at midspan

Carbon fibre composite bolted joints

L A BURNET, BSc
British Aerospace plc, Warton, Lancashire

SYNOPSIS

This paper aims to give an introduction to the design of composite bolted joints at British Aerospace.
Basic failure modes and the effects of geometric and lay-up variations are discussed. Codes of design practice to ensure optimum joint design are presented.
The most common joint occurring in aircraft structures is a countersunk fastener in single shear. Results from programmes investigating the static and fatigue response of such joints as a function of laminate thickness and fastener type are presented.
Finally the two methods of stressing bolted joints under combined loading are discussed. The first method is applied to relatively lightly loaded joints using small fasteners e.g. wing skin/spar bolting. The second is applied to highly loaded joints using large fasteners e.g. wing/fuselage attachment.

1. INTRODUCTION

Carbon fibre composites (CFC) materials are used extensively on military aircraft structures due to their high specific strength and stiffness resulting in minimum mass structures, hence increased agility and a greater payload. Structural joints whether bolted or bonded are necessary. This paper gives an introduction to design of bolted joints for aircraft structures.

2. DESIGN CONSIDERATIONS

A typical aircraft wing is shown in Fig.1. The lay-up of a wing skin would range from 10-65% 0° from tip to root to cater for wing bending, ±45° plies to cater for shear and tension and 90° plies for pressure bending and local load inputs from flaps, etc.

The following factors must be considered in the design phase:

a) In hot humid climates, the matrix resin absorbs moisture.

b) Wing skin temperatures can be up to 120°C depending on the aircraft and flight conditions.

c) Allowance must be made for the presence of stress concentrations.

All of these degrade the strength of CFC.

Allowance can be made for temperature and moisture in strength predictions by testing in the relevant conditions. A typical compression strength carpet plot is shown in Fig.2 for 120°C/1% moisture content (by weight), laminate strengths being presented as % ±45° and % 0°, the remainder being implicitly % 90°. Fibre dominated laminates have higher strengths than matrix dominated laminates and are less affected by the effects of temperature and moisture.

Notch factors for a 6mm diameter unloaded hole, this hole diameter being very common on aircraft structures in an infinite plate shown in Fig.3, have been derived empirically by comparison of plain and notched coupon results. Theoretical notch factors are much higher than achieved on test as small holes exhibit notch blunting, arresting damage propagation and hence the effective notch factor is small. Theoretical notch factors are exhibited when the hole size approaches 25mm.

In compression, the notch factor associated with a filled hole is less than that with an open hole since the load can be transferred across the fastener. In tension, the difference is not as pronounced although in high % 0° laminates, the presence of a filled hole restricts Poisson's contractions, resulting in shear failures parallel to 0° fibres.

In practice, finite widths exist and strengths are reduced at narrow sections; for example, for a width of four times the hole diameter, the correction would be 8% in comparison to the infinite plate. Also, when larger bolt diameters than 6mm are used, the stress concentration factor approaches the theoretical value and the hole size corrections must be made. Corrections must be made to the notch factors for a 6mm diameter hole. For example, the correction for a 10mm diameter hole is approximately 15% and for a 25mm diameter hole, approximately 40%.

3. BOLTED JOINTS - FAILURE MODES

Three basic failure modes occur in CFC bolted joints as shown in Fig.4 - net tension, bearing and shear-out depending on the joint and laminate configuration.

Net section failures occur when the effective width is too low. Laminates with a low percentage of 0° fibres in the load direction require large widths to preclude net section failures, whereas those with higher percentages of 0° fibres require smaller effective widths.

Shear-out failures occur when edge distances are low, laminates with a low percentage of ±45° fibres being generally more sensitive to shear-out failures.

For most structural laminates, the bearing strength is practically constant with lay-up, bearing failures occurring when the geometry excludes net section or shear-out failures.

4 CODES OF DESIGN PRACTICE

As a guidance to design, edge distances of 3d are preferred although a minimum of 2,5d is acceptable, provided the associated 10% drop in bearing strength is permissible. In fuel sealed areas, a staggered pitch of 4.5d as a maximum is required. Away from fuel sealed areas, a pitch of 6d is typical or as dictated by the loading.

When using countersunk fasteners in thin laminates, care must be taken to avoid a feather edge. Wherever possible at least one third of the laminate should be plain shank and two thirds the countersunk head.

5. FASTENER TYPES

Generally, standard fasteners used in metallic structures are also used in CFC structures. Titanium bolts plus anchor nuts and blind fasteners constitute the largest proportion of fasteners on a structure. Care must be taken to separate the aluminium alloy on the anchor nuts or collars of the blind fasteners from the CFC by the addition of a barrier, e.g. pre-sealant to avoid corrosion.

Special fasteners have been developed for composites offering:

i)   galvanic compatibility

ii)   prevention of damage to CFC during assembly.

iii) increased performance.

At present, these fasteners are cost prohibitive. On Tornado, approximately 30,000 blind fasteners and a similar quantity of titanium bolts are used costing 50p each for the quantities purchased. A "special" CFC fastener currently costs £3-£6 each, again depending on the quantity purchased, therefore, the design must certainly justify the use of these fasteners!

6. SINGLE SHEAR JOINTS WITH COUNTERSUNK FASTENERS

The vast majority of attachments on aircraft structures are single shear joints using countersunk fasteners to maintain a smooth aerodynamic profile. Using a titanium countersunk fastener, the load carrying capability of the CFC joint is limited by the bolt strength.

Fig.5 shows the design allowable bolt load as a function of substrate thickness derived for a 6mm diameter 100° countersunk titanium fastener in aluminium alloy substrate. Test work supports this design curve for composite substrates. For thin laminates, the "knife edge" is damaged easily and allows bolt tipping. This eventually results in a shear/tension failure of the bolt at the base of the countersink, which is already weakened by the presence of the recess for assembling and torque tightening the fastener. As the laminate thickness increases there is more resistance to tipping and the bolt will fail in shear.

Superimposed on Fig.5 are test results for the same titanium fastener in 3mm thick CFC, the countersink head depth being 2.6mm. Also shown are results for a "special" titanium fastener of the same diameter, but in this case the countersink depth is only 1.5mm. The failure mode of the standard titanium fastener joint was one of bolt failure whereas laminate failures occurred with the "special" fasteners.

The conclusion from this work is that higher joint strengths both statically and in fatigue can be achieved using a fastener with a small countersink depth. However, penalties of cost and possible installation problems would have to be paid.

7. BOLT GROUPS - STRESSING METHODS

7.1 Lightly Loaded Joints

For lightly loaded joints with small fasteners typically 6 or 8mm in diameter, e.g. wing/spar joint or access panel landings, a relatively simple stressing method can be applied.

Using the carpet plots for tension, compression and bearing strength and notch factors, design charts can be drawn up relating the tension or compression passing strains to the allowable bolt load (hence bearing stress). A typical design chart for a 25% 0° 50% ±45° 25% 90° laminates under 120°/1% moisture conditions is given in Fig.7. Under high applied field strains the allowable bolt load represents only a small percentage of design ultimate bearing stress and conversely, at the design ultimate bearing stress, only low field strains can be permitted.

For shear loading, a pessimistic assumption that only the ±45° plies carry shear can be made. The laminate can then be considered as 100% ±45° under pure shear loading with a thickness equal to the number of ±45° plies in the original laminate. This in turn reduces to a 50% 0° 50% 90° laminate under tensile and compressive loads, allowing a design chart similar to Fig.7 to be used.

7.2 Highly Loaded Joints

For highly loaded joints with large fasteners typically 16-25mm diameter, e.g. wing/fuselage joint, the theory developed previously is less accurate. In this case, finite element methods are used.

A fine mesh NASTRAN model of an isolated critical bolt hole can be set up. The bolt is represented by springs sized to represent the bolted joint shear stiffness. The bolt load is applied as nodal loads representing a sinusoidal normal pressure around the edge of the hole.

From this model edge strains can be determined which can be compared with allowable fibre strains for plain laminates.

8. CONCLUSIONS

This paper has presented some problems associated with bolted CFC joints. Design methods allowing for these limitations have been presented.

BAe experience is that structurally efficient joints can still be produced using CFC.

REFERENCES

1. British Aerospace Stress Data Handbook

2. ROBINSON, BURNET

   "Laminate Thickness Comparison For a CFC Countersunk Bolted Joint.

   BAe Report SOR(P)174 July 1987

3. SIMMONS

   "Fastener Performance Comparison for a CFC Bolted Joint"

   BAe Report SON(P)563 October 1986.

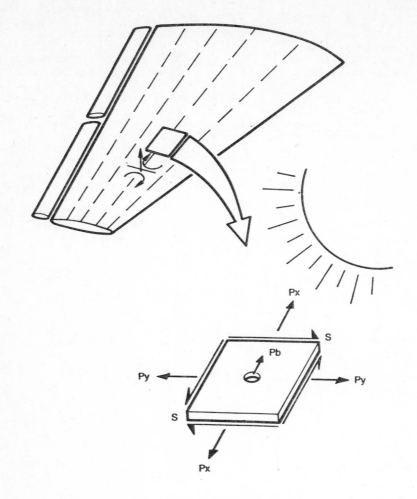

Fig 1   Typical aircraft wing

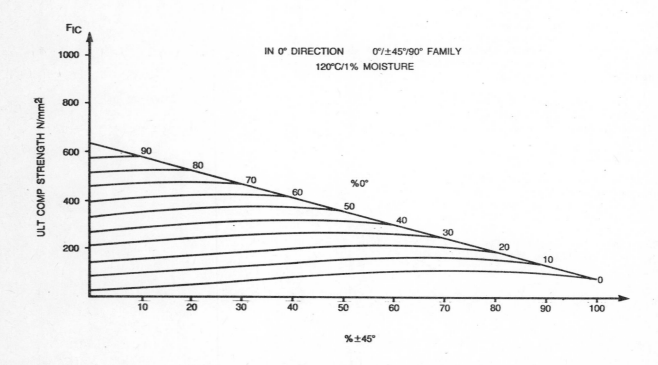

IN 0° DIRECTION   0°/±45°/90° FAMILY
120°C/1% MOISTURE

Fig 2   Compression strength

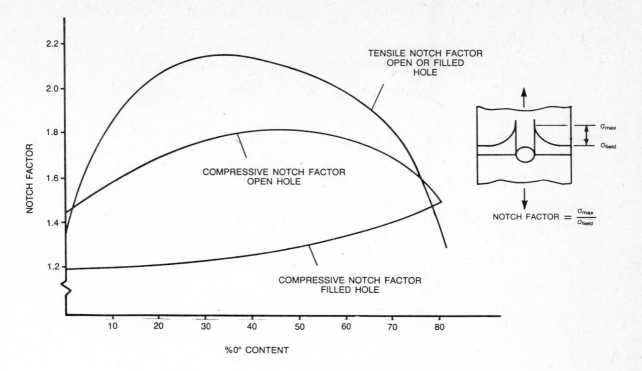

NOTCH FACTOR $= \dfrac{\sigma_{max}}{\sigma_{field}}$

Fig 3   Typical notch factor (6mm hole, ∞ plate)

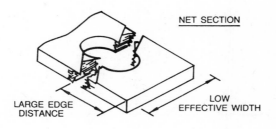

NET SECTION

LARGE EDGE
DISTANCE

LOW
EFFECTIVE WIDTH

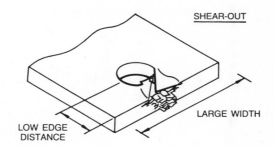

SHEAR-OUT

LOW EDGE
DISTANCE

LARGE WIDTH

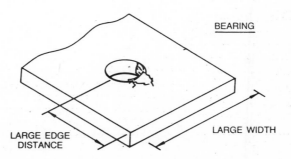

BEARING

LARGE EDGE
DISTANCE

LARGE WIDTH

Fig 4   Bolted joint failure modes

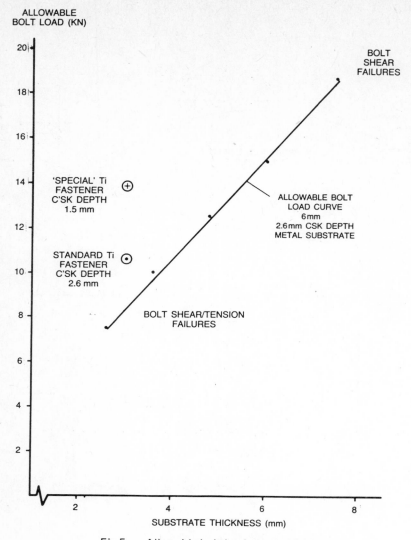

Fig 5   Allowable bolt load versus thickness

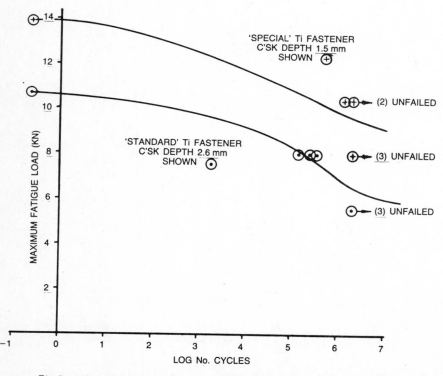

Fig 6   Comparison of c'sk head depth under constant amplitude fatigue

CFC/EPOXY 25%0° 50% ± 45° 25%90°

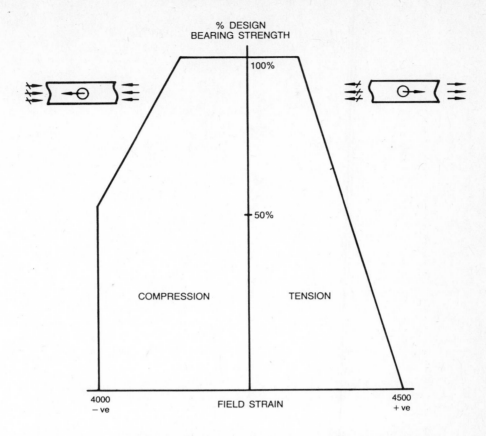

Fig 7   Lightly loaded joints: interaction of bolt load and passing stress

C387/022

Experimental study on the buckling and postbuckling of carbon fibre composite panels with and without interply disbonds

G B CHAI, BSc, **W M BANKS**, BSc, MSc, PhD, CEng, FIMechE and **J RHODES**, BSc, PhD, CEng, MIMechE
Division of Mechanics of Materials, University of Strathclyde, Glasgow

SYNOPSIS An extensive experimental investigation is extended from the work of Rajan[1] and Banks et al[2] on the effect of prescribed interply delaminations on the postbuckling strength of carbon fibre (Grafil XAS/914C Fibredux) composite panels. The test set-up gave simply-supported boundary conditions on the unloaded edges and fully fixed conditions on the loaded ends. The work was completed with a view to the possible structural exploitation of the postbuckling strength of carbon fibre composite panels and to investigate the possible structural degradation due to the adverse effect of interply delaminations. The details of the experimental tests and their results are presented, and the significance of the work is emphasised.

1 INTRODUCTION

Though the study of the initial instability of composite panels has been well researched – Jones[3] Harris[4] and Leissa[5] are a few of the authors from the vast amount of literature available – very little attention has been focussed on the postbuckling behaviour of composite panels in compression. Panels with a large breadth to thickness ratio range of 15–50 are common in current civil aircraft designs. In panels of these dimensions there is a considerable postbuckling strength waiting to be exploited. In this study eight carbon fibre composite (CFC) panels with a breadth to thickness ratio (b/t) of approximately 70 and twelve CFC panels with a b/t of about 50 are tested to investigate the effect of geometry and delaminations on the postbuckling behaviour.

The existence of delaminations (disbonds between layers) may have a detrimental effect on the stiffness and strength of the overall structure. Delaminations can come about due to either manufacturing faults, such as inclusions and voids, or impact of foreign objects such as bird strikes. They are undesirable and in many cases inevitable. The understanding of the effect they have on the structural behaviour is thus crucial. There is a dearth of published work on the experimental studies of the effect of interply disbonds on the overall behaviour of these panels.

The aim of this paper is to supplement the few existing publications on the experimental study of composite panels with interply delaminations in the postbuckling range. The panels were fabricated from 14 layers of unidirectional carbon fibre prepreg using an autoclave process. The delaminations are in the form of penny shaped layers of peelply. These are placed at various locations on the plate surface and at selected positions through the thickness.

2 DESCRIPTION OF THE TEST PANELS

There was a total of 20 test panels manufactured in five separate batches. The results of the tests for the first batch of 6 test panels were published by Rajan(1) and Banks et al(2). The first four batches of the test panels were manufactured by British Aerospace plc at Woodford and the fifth batch was manufactured by the Aeronautical Department at Imperial College.

2.1 Panel lamination, geometry and material properties

Each test panel was nominally 1.75 mm thick with 57.1% of the layers at 0°, 14.3% at 90°, and 28.6% at +45°. The geometries of the panels are given in Table 1 and all test panels have the detailed stacking sequence of [+45/0/0/90/0/−45/0]s. The reinforcing material was manufactured by CIBA-GEIGY, Grafil XA-S unidirectional carbon fibre in 914C Fibredux epoxy resin. The prepreg standard was BAe Spec BACM 372 and CFC1-1170 cure cycle. Thickness variation was very small being 1.75 ± 0.05 mm. It should be noted however that test panels SCB3-1 to SCB3-4 have nominal measured thicknesses of 1.83 mm.

Each built-in delamination was simulated by using 2 thicknesses of A4000 release film cut to the appropriate shape and interleaved between the plies during the impregnation process. The nominal material properties of the test panels are:

Longitudinal Modulus, E_{11} 130 GPa
Transverse Modulus, E_{22} 9 GPa
Shear Modulus, G_{12} 4.8 GPa
Poisson's Ratio, ν_{12} 0.28

3. PRESCRIBING THE DELAMINATIONS

A preliminary simple theoretical analysis

based on the strain energy approach was carried out to predict the critical buckling load and modal shape of the test panels. This simple approach, assuming that the ends and the edges are simply-supported was used as a basis for determining the buckle crest and inflection point position and was also used to confirm the analysis performed by British Aerospace plc using COMPLAN developed by Dr D J Allman of RAE (see Rajan[2]). COMPLAN confirmed the authors' analytical model shape and critical buckling load.

In addition COMPLAN also predicted the areas of maximum direct stress and areas of maximum interlaminar shear stress. Based on these predictions, delaminations were prescribed to coincide with these critical areas of stresses. Table 2 gives a summarised description of the positions of the delaminations for each panel and these positions were chosen to coincide with the following conditions:

1) The position of highest interlaminar shear stress at edges of buckle nodal line. (Panels SCB1-2, SCB2-4, SCB2-4A, SCB3-3 and SCB3-4).

2) A position of low interlaminar shear stresses but with high direct strain. (Panel SCB1-3).

3) The central buckle peak. (Panel SCB1-4).

4) The edges of buckle peak. (Panels SCB2-3, SCB2-3A).

5) The central buckle node where the lengthwise component of the interlaminar shear stress τ_{xx} is a maximum. (Panels SCB1-5, SCB1-6. SCB3-2 and SCB3-2).

The last batch of test panels SCB3-1 to SCB3-4 have delaminations placed taking into account among others the findings of Buskell et al(6). They concluded that regardless of the stacking sequence delaminations were always found to occur near the middle surface of the laminate and at the edges of the buckle nodal line. These areas are known to have the highest interlaminar shear stress.

4. TESTING EQUIPMENT AND INSTRUMENTATION

An illustration of the testing equipment used in the experimental investigation is shown in Fig 1. The loading machine, a Tinius Olsen, induced the loading increments on the test specimens. The strain gauges on the surface of the test specimens were linked to the datalogger, an Intercole Spectra, which processed the readings. In addition, a horizontal transducer was incorporated with a vertical transducer and connected to an X-Y plotter to plot the out of plane deflection at each load increment.

The test panels were extensively strain gauged at strategic locations to permit a rigorous and thorough evaluation of the strain and stress distributions in the test panels.

5. TESTING PROCEDURE

The panels were fitted into aluminium end blocks using araldite and loads were applied at this end. For the last batch of test panels these end supports were modified to screwable clamped ends to allow easy removal of the test panels at any time during the loading process for an ultrasonic evaluation (the ultrasonic results will not be presented in this paper as the Dry Scanning method has not been fully developed). A small load was then applied on the end blocks before tightening the screws in order to eliminate any non-uniform loading caused by maladjustment of the end blocks. These two methods simulated fully fixed end conditions.

The long edges were supported on adjustable knife edges which simulated simply supported conditions. The test panel overhung the knife edges by 6.5 mm and this narrow strip is assumed not to influence the buckling behaviour. During testing these knife edges were coated with grease to reduce any friction effect and thus ensure that the sides of the panel were 'free to wave' in plane and also remain stress free.

The assembled rig was then placed onto a structural frame which allowed the displacement transducers to be fixed integrally. This set-up permitted the deflection profiles to be plotted onto an X-Y plotter at any loading step. The whole integrated unit was then placed onto the loading machine fixed bottom platen. A dial gauge was used to measure the in plane movement of the end platen of the rig. This was used to confirm the results obtained from the loading machine drum plotter.

During the test the test panel was subjected to a very small load to allow it to settle into the test rig and take up any movement between the components of the rig. This load was then removed, the dial gauge reading zeroed and the strain gauges balanced for the zero reading. The load was applied in incremental steps, step size was reduced in the critical buckling region and in the critical failure stage. Each load step was held for a short period of time to enable the required readings to be recorded before the next load increment.

The load was applied within the elastic range and removed to allow the panel to further settle into the rig, and also to check for any irregularities in the readings especially the strain gauge readings. After the checking, and several loading and unloading tests, the panel was then tested to failure. Since the Tinius Olsen machine is a displacement controlled machine, collapse of the panel was denoted as a sudden reduction in load.

Using this approach a series of preliminary tests were conducted to give a feel for the problem. Finally a series of 14 test panels were tested to try and establish the instability behaviour of the laminated panels and the effects the prescribed delaminations had on their postbuckling behaviour.

6. TEST RESULTS

Some typical results of the tests are presented in Figs 2 and 3 for the load versus end shortening behaviour, and in Figs 4 and 5 for the load versus maximum out-of-plane deflection behaviour. Figs 6(a) and (b) depict the plotted deflection profiles along the length of one perfect panel and one delaminated panel respectively. Figs 7(a) and (b) are the deflection profiles for two other delaminated panels where delaminations are prescribed near and at the centre of the panel respectively.

Figs 8(a,b) and Figs 9(a,b) compare the load versus strain behaviour at the same location between the perfect panel and the delaminated panel respectively. The load–strain distribution of Fig 9(b) indicates some local interaction at a load of 294 N/mm. The layouts of the strain gauge locations on these test panels are illustrated in Figs 10 and 11.

Tables 3 to 7 summarise the overall behaviour of the test panels. All the experimental buckling loads in these tables are obtained from the membrane strain reversal curves near or at a buckle peak. These tables show the buckling loads, the load to first audible cracking, failure load, maximum lateral deflection at failure, maximum end displacement at failure and the highest strain recorded in each of the test panels. Theoretical buckling loads predicted by the simple energy approach and by COMPLAN finite element analysis are included for comparison. The maximum strain recorded compared to the maximum permissible strain of −9350 microstrains, commonly used in industry is also included.

Detailed illustrations of the failure behaviour and apparent fracture lines are shown in Figs 12 to 16.

7. DISCUSSION AND CONCLUSIONS

To the authors' knowledge only a limited number of experimental results have been published on the postbuckling behaviour of laminated panels and an even more limited number on the effect of interply delaminations on the behaviour of the composite panels.

7.1 Relative Stiffness

From Figs 2 and 3 the relative stiffness, the ratio of the postbuckling stiffness to the prebuckling stiffness, is found to be between 0.4 to 0.5 in all the test panels. The detrimental effect of the existence of interply delaminations was only observed in test panel SCB2-4A (Fig 5). In this case the delamination was near the edge of the buckle node (see Fig 17) i.e, at the point of highest interlaminar shear stress. The effect on the postbuckling behaviour was obvious there being a considerable reduction in the postbuckling stiffness. Figs 4 and 5 show a stiffening effect on the maximum central deflection in the far postbuckling range, possibly a 'flattening' of the buckle waveform in this region.

7.2 Failure

Some interesting observations on failure can be made from the results. In Figs 6(a) and (b) failure is clearly shown to occur at a buckle node for the panels SCB2-2A and SCB-4A. The test panel SCB-2A however (not delaminated) shows a significantly higher failure load than test panel SCB-4A (delaminated at the edge of a buckle node). The values are 554 N/mm as against 405 N/mm respectively (see Table 6).

In Figs 7(a) and (b) the position where failure will occur is shown to be influenced by delamination. The test panel SCB-3A is delaminated near but not at the panel centre and test panel SCB-3 is delaminated at the panel centre. It appears that failure has occurred at the delamination and spread across the centre of the panel (see Fig 14 and 16).

Comparing Figs 8(a) and (b) with Figs 9(a) and (b), similar load-strain behaviour in both test panels SCB2-2A and SCB-4A is observed until at a load of around 294 N/mm some local interaction disturbs this similarity in Fig 9(b). This probably indicates a hint of local instability of the delaminated area at that particular load, the local buckling may be so small that visual observations fail to identify it. A similar interaction was found on gauges G2/G3/G4 on test panel SCB2-4A but they showed a disturbance at a load of about 230 N/mm.

7.3 Critical delamination area

The conclusion from Figs 12 to 16 is that the critical area for delamination is at or near the buckle nodal line, though some edge problems at the loaded ends causing a premature failure are also indicated.

Tables 3 to 7 show the failure load is about 4 to 5 times the critical buckling load in all the test panels indicating a considerable postbuckling range to be exploited. The experimental buckling load more or less confirms the theoretical predictions. The results also indicate that if the commercially used maximum permissible strain of −9350 microstrain is employed then the failure load in half of the test panels is over estimated.

7.4 The concluding observations

From the above discussions and conclusions it is clear that a considerable postbuckling strength of carbon fibre composite panels can be exploited. Rigorous theoretical approaches using the combination of the Rayleigh-Ritz method, the von Karman large deflection equations and the strain energy method are in progress to model the instability of carbon fibre composite panels subjected to in-plane compression.

The possible adverse effect of the existence of interply delaminations should be borne in mind at the design stage. An analytical approach to study their effect has been undertaken based on the instability of the delaminated area.

A failure criterion based on a maximum permissible strain of −9350 microstrain is inadequate in these applications. A realistic failure criterion is thus required to adequately describe the failure modes of laminated panels in compression.

8. ACKNOWLEDGEMENTS

The authors wish to acknowledge the support of the MoD and the European Space Agency. British Aerospace plc personnel also contributed with helpful discussions.

9. REFERENCES

(1) RAJAN, A. A. J. Buckling and postbuckling of Carbon Fibre Composite Compression Panels with Deliberately Built-in Delaminations. MSc. Thesis of the University of Strathclyde, (June 1985).

(2) BANKS, W. M., RHODES, J. AND CHAI, G. B. Assessing the Effects of Delaminations on the Postbuckling Strength of CFRP Panels. Proceedings of a Workshop: "Composites design for Space Applications", ESTEC. Noordwijk, ESA SP-243, February 1986, pp 197-203.

(3) JONES, R. M. Mechanics of Composite Materials, McGraw Hill 1975.

(4) HARRIS, G. Z. Instability of Laminated Composite Plates. Agard Conf Proc No 112, Paper 14 (1973).

(5) LEISSA, A. W. An Overview of Composite Plate Buckling. Composite Structures 4, Vol 1 (1987), pp 1.1-1.29.

(6) BUSKELL N., DAVIES, G. A. O. and STEVENS, K. A. Postbuckling Failure of Composite Panels. Composite Structures 3 (1985), pp 290-314.

Table 1   The dimensions of the test specimens.

Specimen No	Width	Length	Thickness	b/t
SCB1-1 SCB1-2 SCB1-3 SCB1-4 SCB1-5 SCB1-6	120	458	1.75	68.57
SCB1-1A SCB1-2A	120	458	1.75	68.57
*SCB2-1 SCB2-2 SCB2-3 SCB2-4	90	458	1.75	51.43
SCB2-1A SCB2-2A SCB2-3A SCB2-4A	90	458	1.75	51.43
SCB3-1 SCB3-2 SCB3-3	90	458	1.83	49.18

*Experimental results for this test panel were not presented due to errors encountered during the testing. All dimensions are in millimetres, and the thicknesses are nominal. The length and width are measurements between supports.

1.   Panels SCB1-6 were tested by Rajan(1).

2.   Panels SCB3-1 to SCB3-4 were manufactured by Imperial College: all others by BAe (see text).

Table 2   Description of the locations of prescribed interply delaminations in the test panels.

Specimen No	Location of Prescribed Delaminations
SCB1-2	Between the 7/8th ply near the edges of buckle node.
SCB1-4	Bet. the 3/4th ply, and bet. the 11/12th ply near the centre of buckle node.
SCB1-5	Between the 7/8th ply near the centre of buckle node at panel centre.
SCB1-6	Bet. the 3/4th ply, and bet. the 11/12th ply near the centre of buckle node.
SCB2-3 SCB2-3A	Bet. the 3rd/4th ply, and bet. the 11th/12th ply near edges of buckle peak.
SCB1-3 SCB2-4 SCB2-4A	Bet. the 3rd/4th ply, and bet. the 11th/12th ply near edges of buckle node.
SCB3-1	Between the 6/7th ply near the centre of buckle node.
SCB3-2	Between the 6/7th ply near the centre of buckle node at panel centre.
SCB3-3	Between the 6/7th ply near the edges of buckle node at panel centre.
SCB3-4	Between the 6/7th ply near the edges of buckle node.

All other test panels not listed here are without prescribed delaminations.

Table 3   Summary of results of test panels SCB1-1 and SCB1-6.

Test Panel	Buckling Load (N/mm) *66.42 ‡60.93	Load to first audible cracking (N/mm)	Failure Load (N/mm)	Max Lateral Deflection (mm)	End Displ. at Failure (mm)	Highest Strain Reading Registered (μ-strain) ·-9350
SCB1-1	60.93	253.17	319.50	7.45	2.38	-7208
SCB1-2	57.88	174.25	297.25	6.60	2.66	-9167
SCB1-3	56.66	196.08	346.58	7.40	3.21	-13039
SCB1-4	61.54	271.33	370.67	7.75	3.82	-5769
SCB1-5	61.54	296.33	324.33	6.60	2.54	-7145
SCB1-6	56.66	333.58	370.67	7.30	2.67	-10773

* Theoretical buckling load (COMPLAN Finite Element Analysis).
‡Theoretical buckling load (Author's analysis).
· Theoretical strain criterion commonly used in industry.

Table 4   Summary of results of test panels SCB1-1A and SCB1-2A.

Test Panel	Buckling Load (N/mm) ·60.93	Load to first audible cracking (N/mm)	Failure Load (N/mm)	Max Lateral Deflection (mm)	End Displ. at Failure (mm)	Highest Strain Reading Registered (μ-strain) ·9350
SCB1-1A	63.50	166.50	296.67	6.18	2.21	-6875
SCB1-2A	60.50	163.66	304.08	6.47	2.29	-9212

·Theoretical buckling load.
· Theoretical strain criterion commonly used in industry.

Table 5   Summary of results of test panels SCB2-2 to SCB2-4.

Test Panel	Buckling Load (N/mm) ·108.32	Load to first audible cracking (N/mm)	Failure Load (N/mm)	Max Lateral Deflection (mm)	End Displ. at Failure (mm)	Highest Strain Reading Registered (μ-strain) ·-9350
SCB2-2	108.00	338.67	425.67	4.90	3.32	-14132
SCB2-3	106.90	277.44	445.56	5.00	3.31	-7151
SCB2-4	116.00	311.56	489.44	4.55	3.61	-8976

·Theoretical buckling load.
· Theoretical strain criterion commonly used in industry.

Table 6   Summary of results of test panels SCB2-2A to SCB2-4A.

Test Panel	Buckling Load (N/mm) *108.32	Load to first audible cracking (N/mm)	Failure Load (N/mm)	Max Lateral Deflection (mm)	End Displ. at Failure (mm)	Highest Strain Reading Registered (μ-strain) *-9350
SCB2-1A	108.50	296.66	496.92	6.18	3.42	-7769
SCB2-2A	120.00	311.56	553.78	5.95	3.86	-15795
SCB2-3A	112.50	286.78	474.67	5.44	3.21	-13640
SCB2-4A	105.00	247.22	405.44	5.88	3.11	-13535

* Theoretical buckling load.
* Theoretical strain criterion commonly used in industry.

Table 7   Summary of results of test panels SCB3-1 to SCB3-4.

Test Panel	Buckling Load (N/mm) *123.91	Load to first audible cracking (N/mm)	Failure Load (N/mm)	Max Lateral Deflection (mm)	End Displ. at Failure (mm)	Highest Strain Reading Registered (μ-strain) *-9350
SCB3-1	124.00	370.78	474.67	5.15	2.83	-5318
SCB3-2	119.75	385.56	474.67	5.29	2.92	-13420
SCB3-3	133.00	370.78	427.22	5.00	2.56	-12187
SCB3-4	116.25	375.78	448.44	5.44	2.59	-14831

* Theoretical buckling load.
* Theoretical strain criterion commonly used in industry.

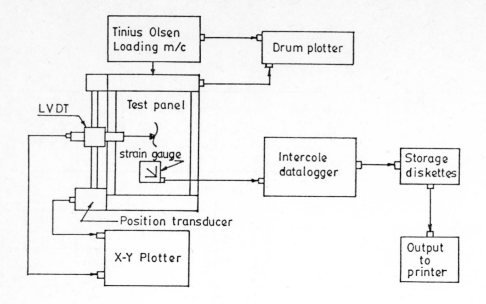

Fig 1   A schematic drawing of the overall layout of the equipment and
instrumentation used in test

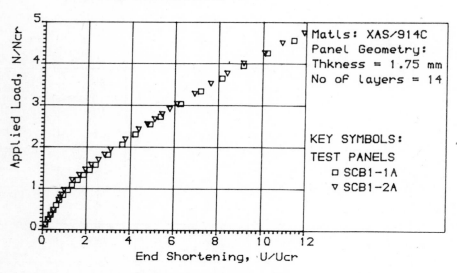

Fig 2   The experimental results of test panels SCB1-1A and SCB1-2A

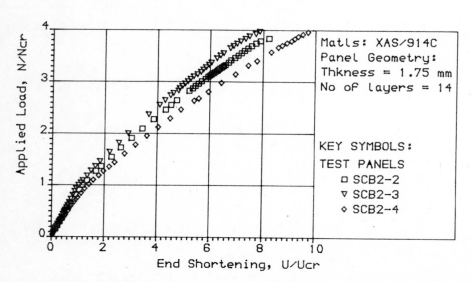

Fig 3   The experimental results of test panels SCB2-2 to SCB2-4

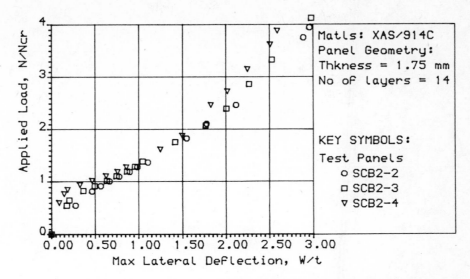

Fig 4   The experimental results of test panels SCB2-2 to SCB2-4

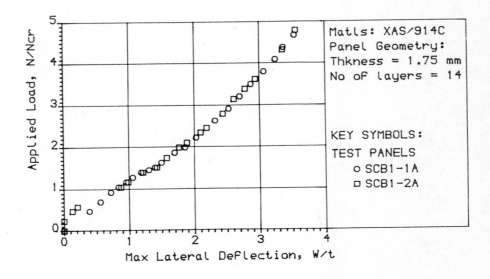

Fig 5   The experimental results of test panels SCB1-1A and SCB1-2A

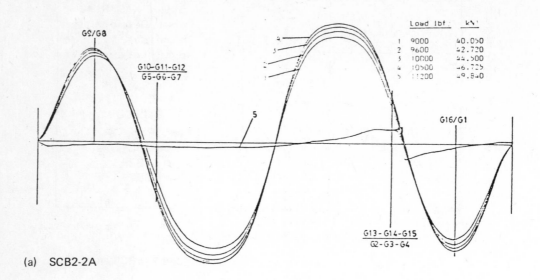

(a) SCB2-2A

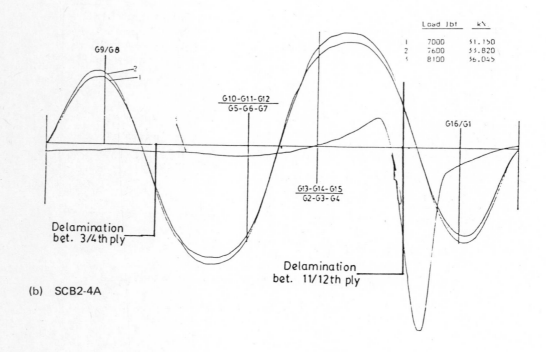

(b) SCB2-4A

Fig 6   The out-of-plane deflection plots for test specimen No SCB2-2A
         and SCB2-4A

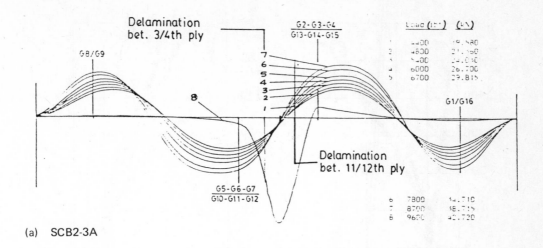

(a) SCB2-3A

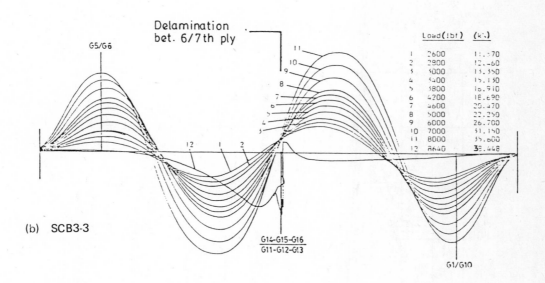

(b) SCB3-3

Fig 7 The out-of-plane deflection plots for test specimen No SCB2-3A and SCB3-3

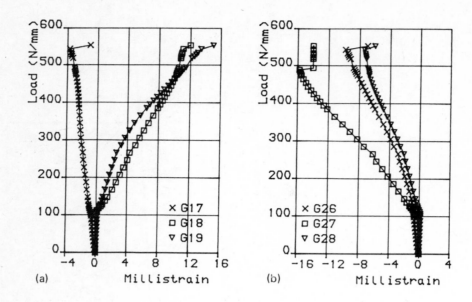

Fig 8   Load–strain plots for specimen SCB2-2A

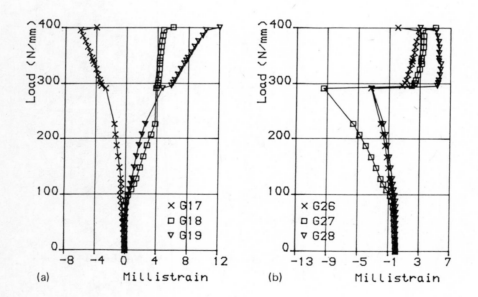

Fig 9   Load–strain plots for specimen SCB2-4A

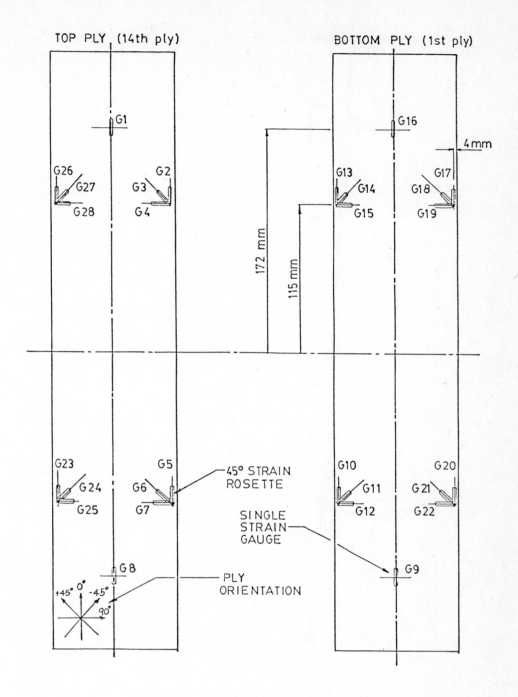

Fig 10   Layout of strain gauges on test panel No SCB2-2A

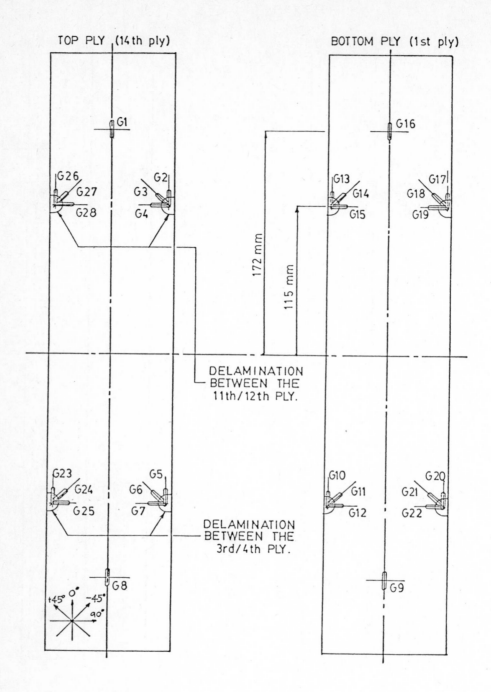

Fig 11   Layout of strain gauges on test panel No SCB2-4A

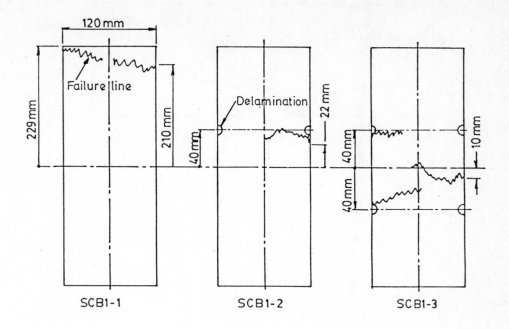

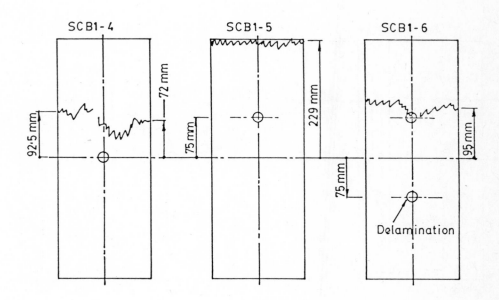

Fig 12 Position of delaminations and lines of apparent fracture

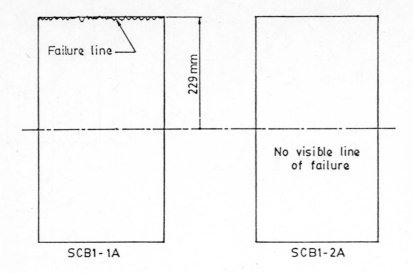

Fig 13   Position of lines of apparent fracture

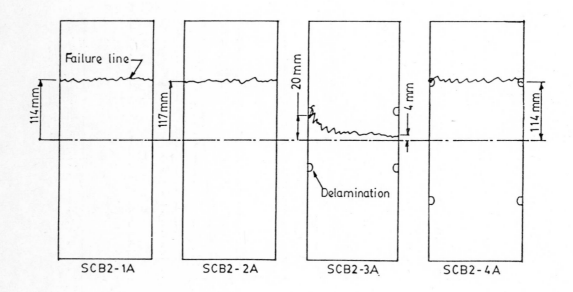

Fig 14   Position of delaminations and lines of apparent fracture

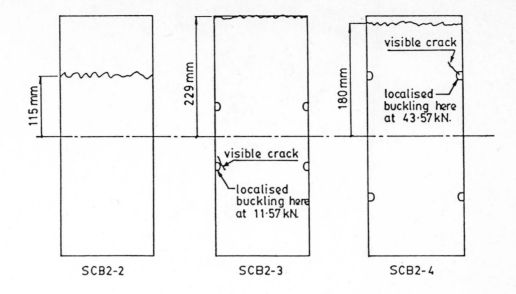

Fig 15   Position of delaminations and lines of apparent fracture

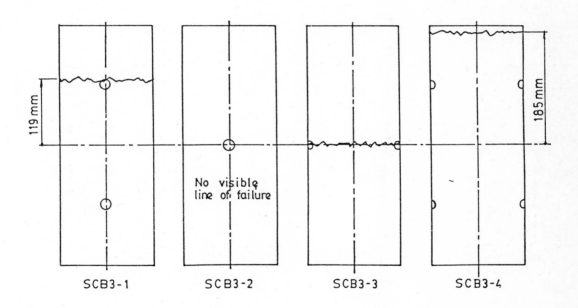

Fig 16   Position of delaminations and lines of apparent fracture

C387/005

Shear effects between the layers of laminated beams under impact loading

Y XIA, BEng and C RUIZ, Dr-Ing, CEng, MIMechE, MASME
Department of Engineering Science, University of Oxford

SYNOPSIS   Laminated beams under impact loading are investigated by dynamic photoelastic tests, finite element method and theoretical analysis. The three methods show good agreement. The stress wave propagation and transmission, the high interlayer shear strain and the energy absorption are studied for layers in simple frictional contact, joined with a compliant adhesive and joined with a rigid adhesive.

1   INTRODUCTION

In the case of impact, multilayer composites consisting of a number of laminae, that may be bonded or not, are found to be advantageous as they can alter the damage mode or increase the damage resistance capability of the structure [1,2,3].

The adhesive may be as rigid as the matrix of the laminae, or even more. It may also be extremely compliant. The situation when adjacent laminae are just held together under frictional contact when the adhesive breaks down, may be regarded as a limiting case when the adhesive is infinitely compliant. Under static loading, shear stresses in the adhesive result from the need to satisfy the equilibrium conditions and the compatibility of displacements. These stresses, in the case of a cantilever beam, are maximum along the neutral axis. A simplified model, designed to study the relative importance of shear and tensile (bending) stress can therefore be taken as a beam consisting of two bonded layers. Under dynamic loading the equilibrium conditions are considerably complicated. The waves are generated and reflected or diffracted at the joint between the two layers which effectively act as waveguides. The ratio between the maximum shear stress at the interface and the maximum tensile stress on the two layers is important in characterising the modes of failure. The interlayer shear or slip would also influence the overall structural responses such as the impact force, the impact duration and the energy absorption of the structure.

2   EXPERIMENTAL PROCEDURE AND RESULTS

Aradite CT-200 models of one and two layer cantilever beam specimens with different adhesives or without bonding between layers, were subjected to impact loading by a falling weight. The beam was 100mm long and each layer was 10mm thick. The resultant dynamic photoelastic patterns were captured using a spark source which was fired at different times. A sequential series of photographs was built up.

Strain gauges were used to measure the stress level in the impactor. The transient loading profiles are displayed in Fig. 1 and these curves clearly exhibit the characteristics of the dynamic response of the laminated structures. The vertical axis represents the strain gauge signal in millivolts, proportional to the impact force.

It is seen that the joining method has not much influence until about 30μs after the impact. The impact force decreases as the stiffness of the bonding is relaxed. The second impact time for the rigidly bonded specimen is about 600μs, for the flexibly bonded specimen it is about 900μs and for the frictional contact case 1100μs (not shown in the figure).

The most significant effect of the adhesive is on the wave transmission and propagation. Fig. 2 shows the dynamic photoelastic fringes for three different conditions when the cantilever is impacted at its tip. In the case of a rigid cyanoacrylate adhesive, the wave initiated at the tip travels both along as well as across the beam. The wave pattern is almost the same as for the case of a single layer beam. The zero order fringe travels along the interface of the two layers. In the case of a flexible silicone rubber bonding, there is a time delay when the wave is transmitted from the upper layer to the lower layer. The two layers tend to behave like two independent layers but the two zero order fringes still meet with each other when Fig. 2(b) is considered. The fringe pattern is almost the same as two independent layers as can be seen from Fig. 2(c).

The wave propagation and transmission is affected by the stiffness of the joint. The impact force is reduced and more energy is absorbed at the expense of large interfacial shear strain (slip).

3.   NUMERICAL ANALYSIS

3.1 COMPARISON WITH THE PHOTOELASTIC ANALYSIS

The finite element package ABAQUS is first used to analyse the same specimen as used in the photoelastic test. The materials of the layers are chosen to have Young's modulus 3.26GPa and Poisson ration 0.38. The adhesive has a Young's modulus of 75MPa and Poisson ratio 0.4. For frictional slide, the friction coefficient is taken as 0.3. Fig. 3 illustrates the contours of the Tresca equivalent stresses in the two layered beam. The Tresca contours correspond to the photoelastic fringes.

The qualitative agreement between the ABAQUS and the photoelastic results can be seen. The differences in the wave pattern caused by the stiffness of the joint show the same tendency as the dynamic photoelastic analysis.

The verification of the ABAQUS results, espcially when the contact line or the very thin layer of adhesive layer is introduced, is done by comparison with a theoretical analysis. This will be described later.

3.2 FAILURE MODES OF LAMINATED COMPOSITES

As mentioned in the previous section, there are large shear strains along the adhesive region. It is the dynamic loading that generates the high interlayer shear stresses and increases the delamination sensitivity of a composite material.

A laminate composed of two layers of quasi-isotropic composite material is considered. Typical values of E_l, E_t, G and ν for a T300/5208 quasi-isotropic laminate are taken as [4,5]: E_l=53.3GPa, E_t=14.3GPa, G=7.1GPa and ν=0.28. The density of the composites is 1300.Kg/m^3. The bonding adhesive is an epoxy (E_a=3.0GPa, ν_a =0.4, ρ_a = 1000.0Kg/m^3). The two layers are assumed to be identical. The beam length is 0.1m and its overall thickness is 0.02m. The adhesive layer is assumed 0.1mm thick. A detailed finite element mesh design and analysis can be found in [6].

The laminated beam is clamped at its end. Different dynamic and static loads are applied on the other end. Since the deformation is kept small, the analysis is geometrically linear. Under transverse loading at one end, the maximum tensile stresses appear at the upper fiber of the upper layer. In the static case, it is at the clamped end while in the dynamic case, it strongly depends on the wave propagation. The location of the maximum tensile stress moves from near the impact point to the clamped end and may then stay at the clamped end or shift to the region near the clamped end. The maximum shear stress, on the other hand, remains near the loading point for the static case, and moves and oscillates all along the beam in the dynamic case. The dynamic shear stress is found to exceed the static case. The ratio between the maximum tensile stress to the maximum interlayer shear stress, therefore, determines the failure mode, whether it is tensile break of the layer or delamination.

Fig. 4 shows the ratio σ_T/τ for various impact loading profiles. The pulse shapes are step, triangular, linear ascending and linear descending. Since the analysis is linear, the ratio is independent of the loading amplitude. Therefore, it is the shape of the pulse which has an important role in determining the failure mode. When static loading is considered, the ratio is about 20.0 while the ratio fluctuates and remains lower than the static one when the transient analysis is introduced. The sudden change in the slope of the pulse curve makes the ratio oscillate. This is due to the sudden change of the shear stress in the adhesive region. The building up of tensile stress (at the clamped end) is much slower than the interlayer shear stress, normally delayed until multiple wave reflection occurs.

The fact that the ratio is lower in the dynamic cases than in the static case means that, if the maximum tensile stresses are the same for both dynamic and static cases, the dynamic interlaminar shear stress is much greater than the static shear stress. Take the linear ascending load for example, assuming the load is increased from zero initally to 10KN at 200μs, the ratio σ_T/τ is calculated at each time step (2μs a step). In the mean time, static loads are applied to the laminate, and the ratio as well as the strain energy of the structure are obtained. Table.1 lists the static analysis of the beam including the maximum tensile stresses and maximum interlayer shear stresses. p is the applied load and E_p is the external work. In contrast, Table.2 gives the dynamic results for the linear ascending load.

Table. 1. Static loading results

p(KN)	E_p(J)	σ_T(MPa)	τ(MPa)	$\frac{\sigma_T}{\tau}$
2.0	0.021	3.273	0.170	19.253
3.0	0.047	4.910	0.255	19.254
4.0	0.084	6.546	0.340	19.253
5.0	0.131	8.183	0.425	19.254

Table. 2. Dynamic loading results

t(μs)	E_p(J)	σ_T(MPa)	τ(MPa)	$\frac{\sigma_T}{\tau}$
74	0.020	1.702	0.280	6.079
98	0.049	2.251	0.370	6.084
116	0.085	2.698	0.430	6.274
132	0.133	3.411	0.507	6.728

4 ANALYTICAL MODELS

The analytical model based on the method of characteristics makes the quantitative check of the ABAQUS results possible. It is also used in cases when the finite element method requires large computing capability.

The analytical model that copes with the two layered beam with interlayer slip [u] is developed in [6]. The governing equations are:

$$b(\rho_1 h_1 + \rho_2 h_2)\ddot{u} + b\frac{h_1 h_2}{2}(\rho_1 - \rho_2)\ddot{\psi} - \frac{\partial N}{\partial x} = 0$$

$$b(\rho_1 h_1 + \rho_2 h_2)\ddot{v} - \frac{\partial Q}{\partial x} + p = 0$$

$$b\Gamma\ddot{\psi} + b\frac{h_1 h_2}{2}(\rho_1 - \rho_2)\ddot{u} - \frac{\rho_1 h_1^3 + \rho_2 h_2^3}{6h}[\ddot{u}]$$

$$- \frac{\partial M}{\partial x} - Q = 0 \quad (1)$$

$$b\frac{\rho_1 h_1^3 + \rho_2 h_2^3}{3h^2}[\ddot{u}] - b\frac{\rho_1 h_1^3 + \rho_2 h_2^3}{6h}\ddot{\psi} + \frac{2}{h}\frac{\partial M*}{\partial x} - \frac{2}{h}$$

$$Q + T = 0$$

where

$$\Gamma = \frac{1}{12}[\rho_1 h_1(h_1^2 + 3h_2^2) + \rho_2 h_2(h_2^2 + 3h_1^2)]$$

$\rho_{1,2}$ is the density, and b is the width of the layer. The accompanying constitutive equations are found to be

$$N = b(E_1 h_1 + E_2 h_2)\frac{\partial u}{\partial x} + b\frac{h_1 h_2}{2}(E_1 - E_2)\frac{\partial \psi}{\partial x}$$

$$M = b\frac{E_1 h_2}{2}(E_1 - E_2)\frac{\partial u}{\partial x} + \Lambda\frac{\partial \psi}{\partial x} - \frac{E_1 h_1^3 + E_2 h_2^3}{6h}\frac{\partial [u]}{\partial x}$$

$$M* = b\frac{E_1 h_1^3 + E_2 h_2^3}{12}\frac{\partial \psi}{\partial x} - b\frac{E_1 h_1^3 + E_2 h_2^3}{6h}\frac{\partial [u]}{\partial x} \quad (2)$$

$$Q = \kappa b(G_1 h_1 + G_2 h_2)(\psi + \frac{\partial v}{\partial x} - \frac{2}{h}[u])$$

$$T = G_a b\frac{[u]}{\eta}$$

where

$$\Lambda = \frac{1}{12}[E_1 h_1(h_1^2 + 3h_2^2) + E_2 h_2(h_2^2 + 3h_1^2)],$$

N and Q are the axial and shear forces respectively. M is the moment with respect to the central line x = 0. M* is the sum of moments with respect to the central axis of each layer. T is the interfacial shear force, G_a the adhesive shear modulus, η the adhesive thickness, and κ the shear correction factor of the beam. The subscripts 1 and 2 represent the two layers.

Excellent agreement between the analytical and the ABAQUS results is reached as reported in [6]. The interlayer slip histories, the interlayer shear stresses show a very close match between the two methods. This also supports the ABAQUS results described in the previous section.

Also of interest is the dynamic response of composite laminates subject to the impact of a rigid sphere. In order to simplify the analysis, the composites are again taken as quasi-isotropic (T300/5208). The adhesives between the two composite layers can be considered as an interleave. The transverse normal stresses are ignored. This is acceptable for the beam analysis since the attention is focused on the influence of the different interface conditions. Hertzian contact is assumed thoughout the course of impact. The Hertzian law for planar isotropic composit es is taken from [4].

Two 4mm thick layers of composites bonded with different adhesives are impacted by a 8mm diameter steel ball. The beam has 80mm span and is clamped at both ends. The strength of bonding is characterised by the shear modulus of the designated adhesives. Multiple impact occurs because of the flexibility of the beam. The whole impact event lasts about 140μs. The first impact occurs when the beam has not acquired sufficient velocity. This is followed by a period of loss of contact. As the beam reaches the maximum deflection and returns, it hits the ball again causing a second impact. It is observed that when the adhesive shear modulus is about 200MPa or less, there is a third impact thus increasing the rebound velocity of the impactor. The second and third impact merge with each other as the adhesive becomes even softer. It takes longer for the second impact to occur for the compliant adhesive than for the relatively rigid adhesive. This is physically correlated with Fig. 1 from the dynamic photoelastic test. Table 3 shows the kinetic energy loss of the impactor after the three impacts. The energy loss of the sphere is a measure of the energy absorption capability of the structure. In the Table only the 40m/s impact velocity is listed. The energy loss of the ball is tabulated as the percentage of the impact energy.

Table 3. Energy loss of the impactor

G_a(Pa)	E_1/E_0(%)	E_2/E_0(%)	E_3/E_0(%)
∞	98.74	87.39	
1×10^{10}	98.53	87.29	
1×10^9	99.73	89.21	
2×10^8	99.95	90.15	87.53
1.5×10^8	99.96	92.82	76.20
1×10^8	99.96	96.82	73.58
1×10^8	99.94		75.49

The impactor loses almost all of its energy during the first impact. The energy absorption of the beam reaches a maximum at certain value of G_a and then levels off. The contact forces are also reduced if G_a is reduced.

5 CONCULSIONS

The dynamic photoelastic tests, the finite element method as well as the analytical method are introduced and correlated in investigating the response of the laminated beam under impact loading. It is found:

(i) The stiffness of the joint between the different layers has an important effect on the wave propagation and transmission. The transmission of waves from layer to layer is significantly delayed when the interface is loosely bonded or in contact.

(ii) The adhesive layer tends to absorb more
     energy at the expense of possible interlayer
     shear failure. The tendency of the tensile
     break failure of the layer is much smaller in
     transient case than in static case. The
     localised stress concnetration due to the
     contact of the impactor is also reduced.
(iii) The energy absorption capability of the beam
      is determined by the interface condition,
      reaching a maximum at an intermediate bonding
      strength.

REFERENCES

[1] CORRAN,R.S.J., RUIZ,C. and SHADBOLT,P.J.
On the design of containment shields.
Computers and Structures, 1983, 16, 563-572.

[2] CORRAN, R.S.J., SHADBOLT,P.J. and
RUIZ,C. Impact loading of plates - an
experimental investigation. Int.J. Impact
Eng., 1983, 1, 3-22.

[3] SANKAR,B.V. and SUN,C.T. Low velocity
impact response of laminated beams subjected
to initial stresses. AIAA J., 1985, 23, 1962-1969.

[4] GRESZCUK,L.B. in: Impact Dynamics (ed)
Zukas, J.A. et.al.. 1982, John Wiley.

[5] SMITH,P.A., ASHBY, M.F. and PASCOE,K.J.
Modelling clamp-up effects in composite bolted
joints J. Compo. Mater., 1987, 21, 878-897.

[6] XIA.Y. Behaviour of a two-layered beam
under impact loading. OUEL Report, 1716/87.

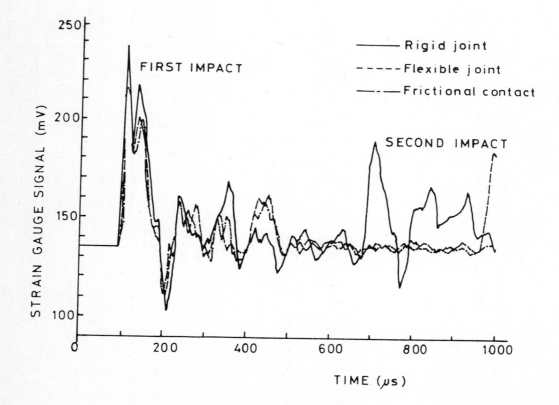

Fig 1   Strain gauge signals

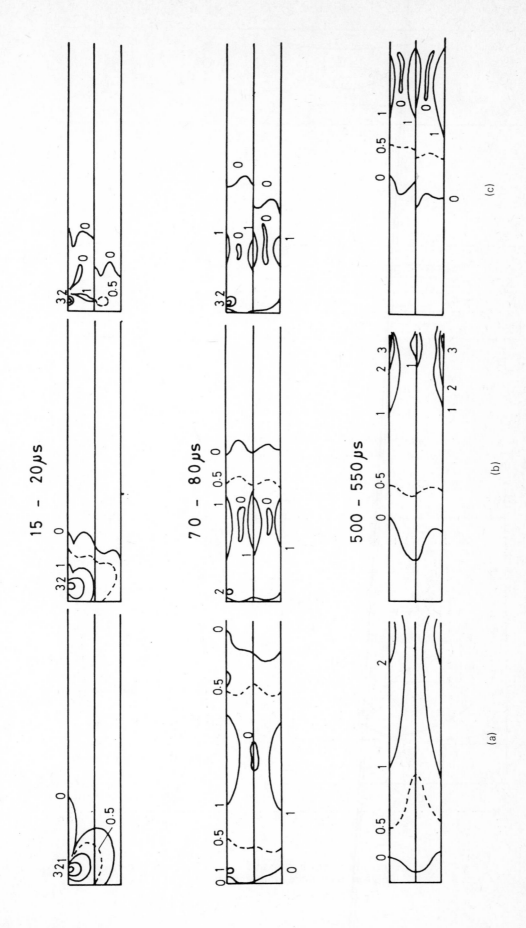

Fig 2 Typical sequence of fringes for a two-layered cantilever beam
(a) Rigid bonding at the interface
(b) Flexible bonding at the interface
(c) Frictional contact at the interface

15 – 20 µs

70 – 80 µs

500 – 550 µs

(a)

(b)

(c)

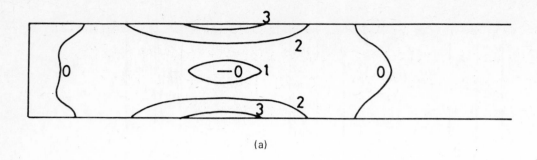

(a)

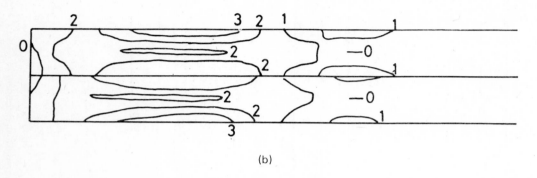

(b)

Fig 3   ABAQUS results for the two-layered cantilever beam
         (a) Adhesively bonding at the interface (at 100µs)
         (b) Frictional contact at the interface (at 100µs)

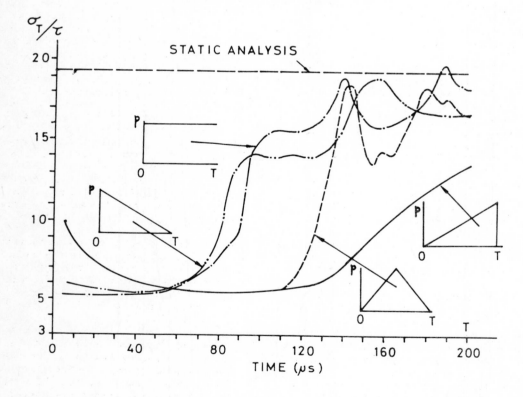

Fig 4   Ratio of maximum tensile stress in the composite layer to the
         maximum shear stress in the adhesive region

C387/012

A design assessment for metallic pressure vessels circumferentially reinforced with a pre-tensioned high-specific strength anisotropic composite overwind

A GROVES, BSc, PhD, CEng, MIMechE and J MARGETSON, BSc, MSc, PhD, CEng, FIMechE
Royal Armament Research and Development Establishment, Westcott, Buckinghamshire

SYNOPSIS A design assessment is presented for thick-walled metallic pressure vessels circumferentially reinforced with a pre-tensioned high-specific-strength anisotropic fibre reinforced composite overwind. However, because of limited publication space, the assessment is restricted to the most important study of evaluating, for five potential composite overwinds, the relationship between the reinforcement thickness and metallic liner thickness to yield a vessel of comparable strength to an all-metal reference vessel. The resulting data is nevertheless used in a series of ancillary analyses, namely weight comparisons, strain to failure studies and detailed stress computations, to establish optimum configurations and, moreover, to identify the most suitable overwinding material. The influence of variations in the considerably lower transverse moduli (radial and axial) of the circumferentially reinforcing material is also considered by repeating the assessment studies for both 10 GPa and 1 GPa transverse moduli composite overwinds.

1 INTRODUCTION

Circumferentially reinforcing thick-walled metallic cylindrical pressure vessels with a pre-tensioned filament overwind for the induction of compressive stresses is not new. Indeed the technique can be traced back many years when wire was used as the reinforcing material (1). However, with the advent of the new high specific strength (strength to weight ratio) fibre reinforced composites, eg GFRP, CFRP, etc, the technique has seen a revival of interest particularly in the construction of lightweight high performance pressure vessels. These composites have resulted in substantial weight savings in many aerospace applications (2,3) and it is likely that they will yield similar benefits in the design of high pressure containment vessels. Unfortunately though, the simplified design techniques and documented behavioural characteristics (1) associated with the early wire wrapped vessels cannot be applied to vessels circumferentially reinforced with these new composite materials because of their underlying isotropic theory. The behaviour and, moreover, the suitability of reinforcing vessels with highly anisotropic composites are therefore unknowns and before they can be adopted as viable reinforcing materials detailed assessment studies must be undertaken. Such assessments must be comprehensive and every attempt should be made to identify the interaction between all of the design variables. These variables include the initial pre-stressing parameters, ie, winding tension and number of layers, material properties, geometry and possibly machining tolerances.

It should be noted that such assessments are further complicated by virtue of the reinforcement material having an almost infinite range of property values through the choice of fibre lay-up and matrix selection. However, in this study, where the composite is used only as a circumferential reinforcement, it is convenient to assume that the reinforcing fibres will lie solely in the circumferential direction. Consequently, circumferential property variations in the reinforcement will be governed essentially by the fibre type selected, though it should be appreciated that different matrix resins will have a significant effect on the very low transverse properties (radial and axial). It is anticipated that these very low properties will have a large influence on the vessels behavioural characteristics and indeed quantifying this influence forms an important feature of the assessment studies.

In this paper such an assessment is presented. To conserve space the underlying stress analyses are omitted but they are nevertheless well documented in reference (4). It should be noted, though, that of the two techniques detailed in ref (4) for analysing the initial winding process, ie an exact discrete approach and an approximate continuous approach, only the latter will be used due, principally, to its greater computational efficiency. Nevertheless, computations have shown that for the vessels under consideration the errors associated with this approximation are very small, typically $\ll 1$ per cent.

Because of the many independent design variables it is not possible, because of restrictions on publication space, to carry out a complete comprehensive assessment. It has therefore been decided to consider the most important study in which metal is removed from the external surfaces of an original all-metal reference vessel (details of which are presented in Table 1) and calculations performed to evaluate the thickness of reinforcement necessary to return the vessel to its original load bearing configuration. Such an assessment also has the benefit of being easily repeated for a wide range of composite types with economical presentation of results. The assessment is repeated therefore for five potential fibre reinforced composites, two glasses (GFRP) and three carbons (CFRP), with two different, but typical, transverse moduli; 10GPa and 1GPa. Material properties pertaining to these composite overwinds with the 10GPa and 1GPa transverse moduli are presented in Tables 2 and 3.

Although this study is confined to a reinforcement thickness assessment it is nevertheless possible to use the resulting information in a series of ancillary analyses, for example, weight comparisons, maximum composite strain to failure strain calculations as well as detailed stress computations. Such analyses are particularly useful for establishing optimum configurations and, moreover, identifying the most suitable reinforcing material.

2   10GPa TRANSVERSE MODULI OVERWIND

Using the Tables 2-3 material property data and the reference vessel data presented in Table 1, the dependence of the reinforcement thickness on material properties and liner thickness has been assessed for an arbitrarily chosen 500MPa winding tension. The resulting computations are presented in Fig 1. Composite circumferential moduli are used to differentiate between the five composite types considered. In addition, for comparative purposes the thickness of original metal required to return the vessel to its original strength condition is also shown. It should be noted that, unless otherwise stated, all curves terminate when the liner yields in compression during winding.

From the figure it is immediately apparent that for reinforcement thickness purposes the CFRPs yield the most favourable design solutions due to their higher moduli. Indeed, the 40GPa GFRP requires approximately twice the reinforcement than that for the 240GPa CFRP. Nevertheless, it is of interest to note that when these reinforcement thicknesses are added to the liner thicknesses all of the vesels exhibit external dimensions less than that of the original monolithic structure. A further and unexpected feature of the assessment was the existence of maxima in the reinforcement thickness vs liner thickness curves for the 180 and 240GPa

CFRPs. Detailed computations revealed that these maxima correspond to the point where the winding induced stresses increase more rapidly than the pressure induced stresses with decreasing liner thickness.

Preliminary calculations have indicated that the CFRPs are likely to yield the most favourable design solutions. However, other information such as weight and maximum composite strain to failure strain also need to be considered. In Fig 2 the weight calculations follow anticipated similar trends to the reinforcement thickness studies since the density of GFRP is greater than that of CFRP, see Tables 2 and 3, with all the CFRPs offering similar weight savings. However, when Fig 3 is considered, where the ratios of maximum composite strain to failure strain are plotted against liner thickness, these trends are modified. In terms of safety it can be seen that the 60GPa GFRP offers the most satisfactory design, with a typical strain ratio of 0.3, while the 240GPa CFRP the least, with a strain ratio in the region of 0.7 (although in excess of unity for 6mm liners or less). In the design of high-specific strength pressure vessels it is recognised though that in order to minimise component weight the constituent materials should be used well into their operating ranges. On this basis Figs 2 and 3 would suggest therefore that the 240GPa CFRP should be used as the reinforcing material. A more rigorous inspection of Figs 2 and 3 reveals, however, that the 180GPa CFRP is likely to yield an even more satisfactory design solution since not only are the weight savings comparable with that of the higher modulus CFRP, but, moreover, the margins of safety to composite failure is some 75% greater. The 60GPa GFRP offers even greater margins of safety, but the weight penalties associated with this reinforcement, see Fig 3, clearly outweighs this potential advantage.

2.2   Stress distribution calculations

A detailed knowledge of the stress distributions through the vessel is important for two reasons. Firstly to identify those regions most highly stressed and secondly to establish whether the stresses are sufficient to cause failure of the composite reinforcement. The former is important from a design point of view in that it may permit the engineer to identify more efficient, and hence, cost effective routes of manufacture. For example, for the very highly stressed regions of the vessel it may be desirable to wind with an expensive, though high modulus composite, whereas for the remainder of the vessel a lower quality and less expensive composite may suffice.

A noteable example is the use of high specific strength sleeves to line conventional medium quality steel pressure vessels. However, such fabrication routes are beyond the scope of these initial assessement studies and will not be discussed further. The second reason, which is of equal importance, arises from the fact that the stresses may themselves cause transverse failure of the composite overwind. Whilst uniaxial composites exhibit very high tensile strengths in the direction of fibre alignment (in excess of 1GPa) (2) their strengths in the transverse directions are very much less, typically 125MPa. Since the Table 1 internal pressure is very much greater than this value, problems may arise at the liner/composite interface where, for particularly thin liners, the interface pressure may exceed 125MPa. Furthermore, it is known that for vessels overwound with highly anisotropic reinforcements the axial stress is non-zero (5). Although these values are likely to be small, they must nevertheless be considered.

In order to undertake a detailed stress analysis it is necessary to identify a suitable geometry. From the previous calculations it is clearly evident that the final geometry is heavily dependent on the selected liner thickness since, when established, the reinforcement thickness readily follows from Fig 1. Previous analyses have shown that for the 180GPa CFRP liner thicknesses as thin as 5mm are attainable; see Fig 1. It must be appreciated, however, that the liner may also be required to support additional loads (possibly due to inertia and thermal effects) which were not considered in that figure. Furthermore, sufficient thickness must exist to take into account any inhomogeneity prevailing in the liner material. Unfortunately for overwound pressure vessels such information is either very scant or unavailable and as a result it is not possible to choose with precision an exact liner thickness. Detailed computations, based on the very limited information available, have, however, shown that liner thicknesses of 20mm or less leave little margin for error and furthermore would be unlikely to support all of the applied loads without yielding. For the vessel under consideration a more acceptable liner thickness would therefore lie in the 20 to 30mm range. For engineering purposes the weight benefits offered by a 20mm liner over a 30mm liner are small, approximately 8 per cent relative to the monolithic vessel, and in view of this fact coupled with the uncertainties associated with the axial loads a 30mm liner was selected as the basis for the stress analysis calculations. Having determined the liner thickness the reinforcement thickness for the 180GPa CFRP readily followed from Fig 1 as 35.5mm.

For overwound pressure vessels the stress state will be essentially the summation of two components. One due to overwinding and one due to pressurisation. A further component resulting from the additional loads described above may also exist, but for the purposes of this study these additional load components will be neglected. Since both of these loads may not be acting on the vessel at any one time it is necessary to look, in detail, at both of the

stress states arising from these two components. For the 30mm liner overwound with 35.5mm of 180GPa CFRP subject to the 300MPa internal pressure detailed in Table 1 the resulting stress components in the circumferential, radial and axial directions are presented in Fig 4-6 respectively. The combined stress state is also given. From Fig 4 it can be seen that the circumferential stress distributions are well behaved in that no steep stress gradients are observed. A further and most encouraging feature is the almost uniform stress distribution in the reinforcement, indicating excellent load transfer under the most severe loading conditions. When the radial stress distribution is considered, see Fig 5, it can be seen that the radial stress at the liner/composite interface is, unfortunately, in excess of the transverse strength of the reinforcement. However, the strength figures quoted are based on tensile loading and the mechanism governing compressive failure may be significantly different. Furthermore, the most highly stressed material is constrained from free movement by external layers of composite operating at lower radial stress levels. This may also have an effect on the radial stress to failure at the liner/composite interface. Such failure mechanisms are subjects for future research. Finally, whilst the axial stress distributions, see Fig 6, are of interest, they are nevertheless very small and for engineering purposes may be neglected.

3   1GPa TRANSVERSE MODULI OVERWIND

The analyses presented in section 2 have been concerned solely with the 10GPa transverse moduli composite overwinds. It was indicated in section 1, however, that the overwinds may, through the resin selection, have an even lower transverse moduli, eg 1GPa. In order to assess quantitatively the influence of such low transverse moduli on the behavioural characteristics of the overwound vessel the reinforcement thickness, weight and maximum composite strain to failure strain calculations described previously were repeated using, in this case, the 1GPa transverse moduli material properties given in Tables 1 and 2. The results to these three studies are presented in Figs 7-9. On comparing the resulting computations with those obtained from the 10GPa transverse moduli overwinds, see Figs 1-3, several markedly different trends were observed. Firstly the relationship between the reinforcement thickness and liner thickness ceases to be generally linear and becomes very non-linear, particularly for thin liner thicknesses. Furthermore, with the exception of the 40GPa GFRP, all of the curves were observed to tend to infinity before yielding the liner in compression. Secondly there exists, for a particular composite, a minimum liner thickness below which a vessel cannot be fabricated to meet its in-service loads and thirdly the vessel weights pass through minima. For engineering purposes the values of these minima can be assumed to be independent of the liner thickness and reinforcement material and are approximately equal to 700 grams per mm length. The relationship between the liner thickness and material properties corresponding to these minima is, however, complex, but computations show that the liner's thickness decreases with decreasing circumferential modulus and vice versa. A further interesting feature is the fact that the most suitable composite overwind for minimum reinforcement thickness purposes varies as a function of the liner thickness. For example, for a 80mm liner the 240GPa CFRP yields the minimum reinforcement thickness while for a 40mm liner the 40GPa GFRP is required.

Whilst the reinforcement thickness calculations and weight studies for the 1GPa transverse moduli overwinds have been found to be markedly different to those for 10GPa transverse moduli overwinds, the maximum observed composite strain to failure strain analyses were found to be similar, see Figs 3 and 9, with the most suitable overwind again being the 60GPa GFRP; the least being the 240GPa CFRP. The only notable feature arising from the figure is that the maximum composite strain is now almost independent of the liner thickness.

For the vessels reinforced with the 10GPa transverse moduli overwinds the 180GPa CFRP was chosen as the reinforcing material by carefully trading off weight benefits against factors of safety. For the 1GPa transverse moduli overwinds the reinforcement selection process is more straight forward since the maximum attainable weight savings are independent of the reinforcing material. Thus in the absence of other over riding requirements the 60GPa GFRP should be selected as the reinforcing material due to its high strain to failure properties.

The features observed from vessels reinforced with 1GPa transverse moduli overwinds are notable and in many respects in direct contrast to those reinforced with the 10GPa transverse moduli overwinds. In order to gain an insight into the mechanics governing these two contrasting behaviours it is necessary to consider, in detail, the manner in which the dominant circumferential stresses are built up during the overwinding process for both the 10GPa and 1GPa transverse moduli composite overwinds. For a 30mm liner overwound with a 180GPa CFRP with 10GPa and 1GPa transverse moduli such studies are presented in Figs 10 and 11 respectively. In both figures the stress distributions presented are those resulting from 10,20,30,40 and 50mm of applied reinforcement. For the 10GPa transverse moduli CFRP overwind the results are as anticipated, that is the compressive stress in the liner is seen to increase with increasing reinforcement, from −160MPa for 10mm of reinforcement to −520MPa for 50mm of reinforcement. Furthermore the loss in tensile stress in the applied layers is seen to decrease almost uniformly as additional layers are introduced. When the 1GPa transverse moduli CFRP is considered

these trends are modified, due principally, to the "squashing" effects associated with the reinforcements very low radial modulus. For the first 10mm of reinforcement both the 10GPa and 1GPa transverse moduli CFRP overwound pressure vessels are seen to exhibit similar trends. When additional layers of reinforcement are introduced two markedly different features are observed. Firstly, the intermediate layers of the 1GPa transverse moduli overwind are seen to loose more of their tensile stresses than those at the interface and secondly the compressive stress in the liner asymptotes to a maximum more rapidly than that of the vessel overwound with the 10GPa transverse moduli CFRP. The low radial modulus of the 1GPa transverse moduli overwind therefore acts as a "load absorber", and prevents the winding induced loads being transferred into the liner material. When the internal pressure situation is considered, the reverse situation occurs, see Figs 12 and 13, where the pressure induced circumferential stresses for the 10GPa and 1GPa transverse moduli CFRP overwound vessels are plotted respectively for the same reinforcement thicknesses considered above. For the 1GPa transverse moduli CFRP, the composite material adjacent to the interface is seen to readily compress thus preventing efficient load transfer from the liner through to the external layers of composite reinforcement. Consequently the benefits of applying more and more layers of reinforcement becomes increasingly small and indeed it can be seen that the pressure induced stress in the liner asymptotes to a minimum after 50mm of reinforcement has been applied. For the 10GPa transverse moduli CFRP a similar situation occurs, though the trends are not so pronounced. For example, although the pressure induced stress in the liner is observed to gradually asymptote to a minimum, this situation has still not occurred after the 50mm of reinforcement illustrated in the figure has been applied.

The radial modulus is therefore an important feature in the design of overwound vessels and due regards must be given to its effects on the behaviour of the vessel. For example, if the combined asymptotic stress state in the liner is greater than that for the resulting strain to meet the Table 1 design requirements the application of further layers will have no beneficial effects. This feature governs the highly non-linear reinforcement thickness vs liner thickness curves observed in Fig 7.

3.1 Stress calculation

Although the preceeding analyses indicate that a 10GPa transverse moduli overwind is preferable to a 1GPa transverse moduli overwind, situations exist, however, where low transverse moduli overwinds may have to be employed. A typical example is in high temperature applications.

© IMechE 1989 C387/012

Since situations exist therefore where very low transverse moduli overwinds may have be employed, this paper would be incomplete if no attempt is made to assess the stress response of such vessels. For a truely rigorous study this would require stress analysing a considerable range of vessel geometries, but for the purposes of this study it is considered reasonable to restrict the stress analysis to that of a typical overwound vessel, namely the minimum weight configuration for the 60GPa GFRP overwound vessel, ie a 46.0mm liner overwound with 63.8mm of GFRP (see Figs 7 and 8).

Contrary to the author's expectations, based on the preceding discussions, the resulting stress distributions were again well behaved and indeed the trends were generally similar to those already observed in Figs 4 to 6. The only notable differences were:

i)   The combined circumferential stress through the composite, though reasonably uniform, is approximately one-half of that for the 10GPa transverse moduli reinforcement.

ii)   The radial stress at the composite/ liner interface is approximately 30% less than that shown in Fig 5.

Both of these features are largely attributable to the increased liner and composite thicknesses. As previously, the axial stress was again very small and can be neglected as a second order quantity.

4   CONCLUSIONS

A design assessment for thick-walled metallic cylindrical pressure vessels circumferentially reinforced with a tensioned high-specific-strength anisotropic composite overwind has been presented. Because of space limitations this assessment has been confined to a study of the relationship between the thickness of composite reinforcement and liner thickness necessary to produce an overwound vessel of comparable strength to an initial monolithic reference vessel. This assessment was repeated for five different reinforcement composites with firstly 10GPa transverse moduli and secondly 1 GPa transverse moduli. Whilst confined to a reinforcement thickness study the resulting information was nevertheless used in a series of ancillary analyses, namely weight calculations, maximum composite strain to failure strain studies and three dimensional stress evaluations, to identify optimums and eliminate unsuitable reinforcement overwinds. These studies clearly indicated that the vessels behavioural characteristics are heavily dependent on the magnitude of the transverse moduli of the composite overwind. This is clearly illustrated in the following observations derived from the pressure vessel design data under consideration:

4.1   10GPa Transverse moduli composite overwind

i)   The reinforcement thickness is inversely related to the composite circumferential modulus, and vice versa.

ii)   A 180GPa CFRP was found to yield the most favourable design solution based on reinforcement thickness, weight and maximum strain to failure strain calculations. This is attributable to the composites comparatively high modulus and good strain to failure properties.

iii) For a 180GPa CFRP, liner thicknesses as thin as 5mm can be achieved. It is unlikely though that such a liner could support any significantly additional axial loads. In practice the liner thickness will lie somewhere between 20-30mm, offering weights savings of approximately 70 per cent of the original monolithic vessel.

iv)   Stress calculations for a 30mm liner overwound with a 180 GPa CFRP indicate that the stress distributions are well behaved with no steep stress gradients being observed. Furthermore, for the combined loading condition, ie overwinding and pressurisation, the circumferential stress was observed to be fairly uniform through the composite, indicating efficient load transfer. Axial stresses were sufficiently small to be neglected.

4.2   1GPa Transverse moduli composite overwind

i)   The relationship between the reinforcement thickness and liner dimensions are very non-linear. Furthermore, but with exception of the 40GPa GFRP, there exists, for a particular composite overwind, a minimum liner thickness below which a vessel cannot be fabricated to meet its in-service loads.

ii)   Vessel weight vs liner dimension curves are observed to pass through minima before increasing rapidly as the liner dimensions are further reduced. The values of these minima are, for engineering purposes, equal indicating that the maximum attainable vessel weight savings are independent of reinforcement properties and liner dimensions. The liner dimensions corresponding to these minima are, however, complex functions of the reinforcement properties and decrease with decreasing composite circumferential modulus, and vice versa.

iii) The most suitable reinforcement material was a 60GPa GFRP due to its high failure strain properties.

iv)   A low radial modulus acts as a serious "load absorber" preventing efficient load transfer from the tensioned composite to the liner during winding and from the liner through the composite during pressurisation.

v)   Weight savings are not as great as those attainable from the 10GPa transverse moduli overwinds.

5 ACKNOWLEDGEMENTS

The authors would like to thank Messrs Parratt, Cook and Hinton and Miss Howard of the Royal Armament Research and Development Establishment for their invaluable discussions and comments and for providing the material property data used throughout this report.

6 REFERENCES

(1) NICHOLAS, R. W. Pressure Vessel Engineering Technology. The Design of Vessels for High Pressure, 1971, Chapter 8, pp 402-473, Applied Science Publishers Ltd, London.

(2) JONES, R. M. Mechanics of Composite Materials, 1975, McGraw-Hill Book Company.

(3) HINTON, M. Unpublished MOD report.

(4) MARGETSON, J., GROVES, A. Analytical Stress Equations for Thick-Walled Pressure Vessels Circumferentially Reinforced with an Anisotropic Composite Overwind. Unpublished MOD report.

(5) STANLEY, P., MARGETSON, J. Failure Probability Analysis of an Elastic Orthotropic Brittle Cylinder. Int. Journ. of Fracture, 1977, 13, pp 787-806.

Table 1 Reference vessel design data and material properties

Dimensions

External radius	300 mm
Bore radius	200 mm

Internal pressure

Internal pressure	300MPa

Fatigue Limiting strain

Maximum permitted bore strain	4.35×10^{-1} %

Material properties

Youngs Modulus	200GPa
Yield stress	1150MPa
Poissons ratio	0.3
Density	7.8×10^{-3} grams/mm^3

Table 2 GFRP material properties

Property	Material	
	40GPa GFRP	60GPa GFRP
MODULI		
Circumferential (GPa)	40	60
1GPa transverse moduli (GPa)	1	1
10GPa transverse moduli (GPa)	10	10
POISSON RATIO's		
Circumferential/ Radial		
1GPa transverse moduli	0.0075	0.005
10GPa transverse moduli	0.075	0.05
Axial/Radial	0.3	0.3
Axial/ Circumferential	0.3	0.3
DENSITY (grams/mm^3)	0.002	0.002
STRAIN TO FAILURE (%)	3	4

Table 3 CFRP material properties

Property	Material		
	120GPa CFRP	180GPa CFRP	240GPa CFRP
MODULI			
Circumferential (GPa)	120	180	240
1GPa transverse moduli (GPa)	1	1	1
10GPa transverse moduli (GPa)	10	10	10
POISSON RATIO's			
Circumferential/ radial			
1GPa transverse moduli	0.0025	0.001666	0.00125
10GPa transverse moduli	0.025	0.01666	0.0125
Axial/Radial	0.3	0.3	0.3
Axial/ Circumferential	0.3	0.3	0.3
DENSITY (grams/mm^3)	0.00156	0.00156	0.00156
STRAIN TO FAILURE (%)	1.5	1.5	0.75

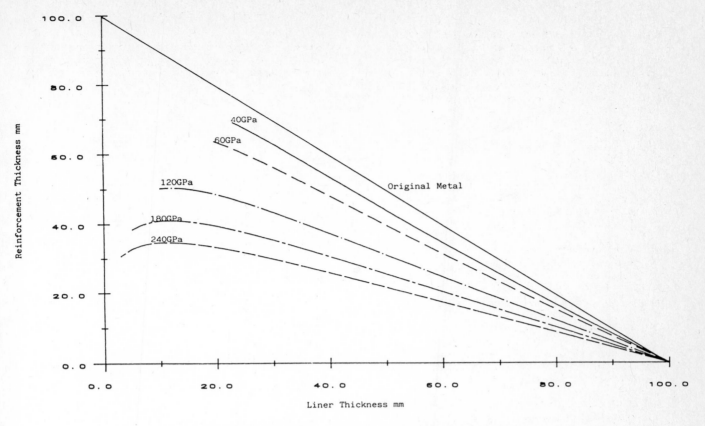

Fig 1   Reinforcement thickness versus liner thickness; 10GPa transverse
moduli composite overwinds

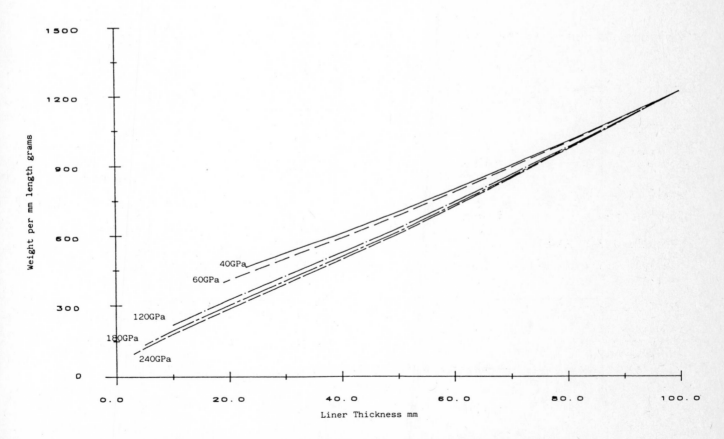

Fig 2   Vessel weight per mm length versus liner thickness; 10GPa transverse
moduli composite overwinds

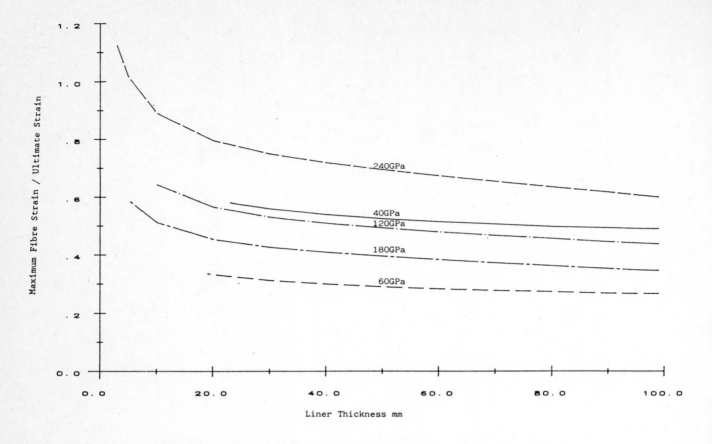

Fig 3   Maximum reinforcement strain/ultimate strain versus liner thickness;
          10 GPa transverse moduli composite overwinds

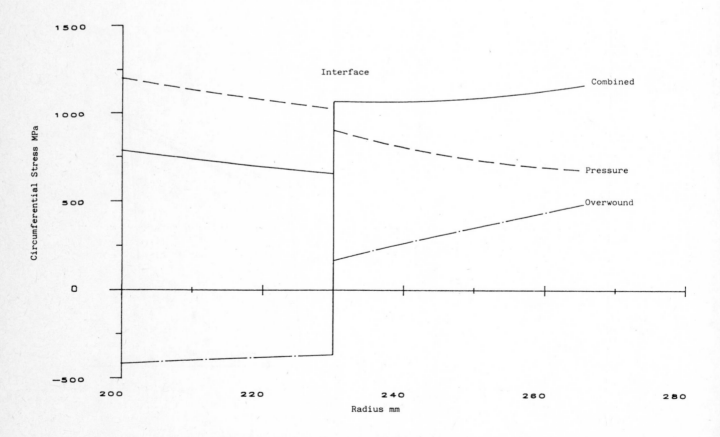

Fig 4   Circumferential stress versus radius for 10 GPa transverse moduli
          180 GPa CF RP overwind

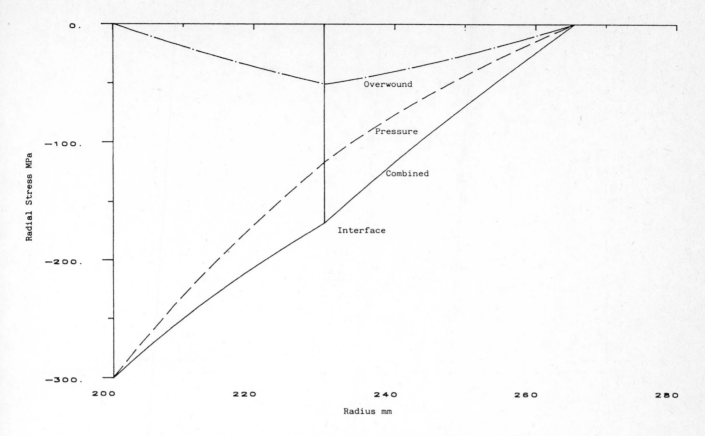

Fig 5   Radial stress versus radius for 10GPa transverse moduli 180GPa
         CFRP overwind

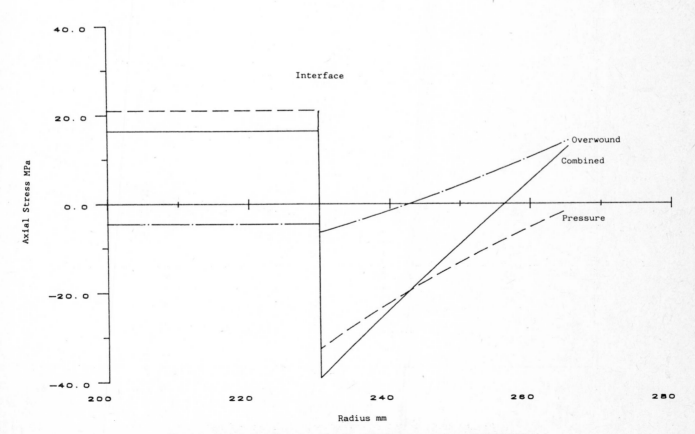

Fig 6   Axial stress versus radius for 10GPa transverse moduli 180GPa
         CFRP overwind

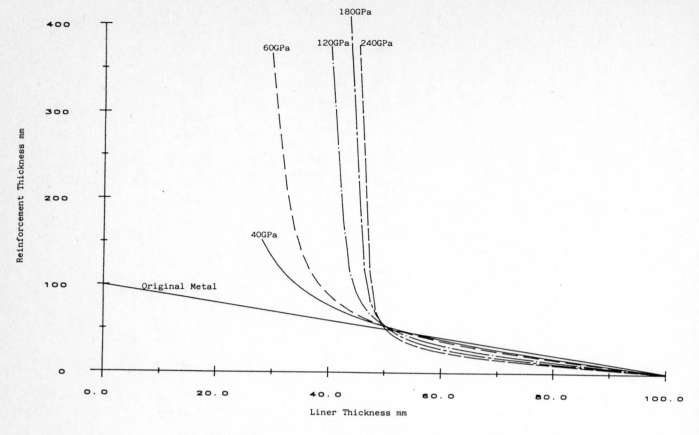

Fig 7 Reinforcement thickness versus liner thickness; 1GPa transverse
moduli composite overwinds

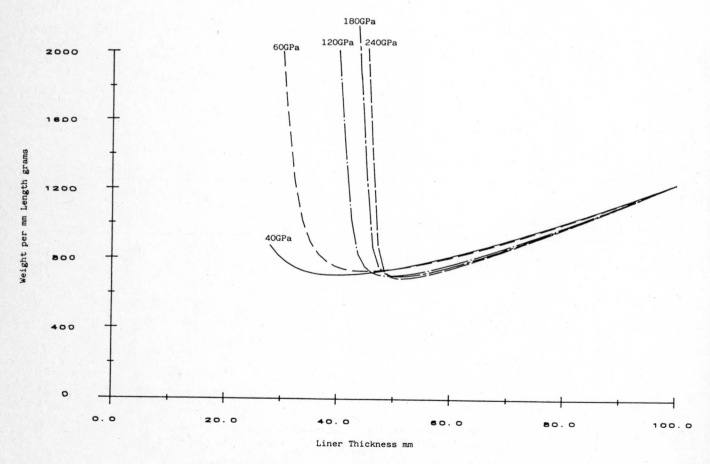

Fig 8 Vessel weight per mm length versus liner thickness; 1GPa transverse
moduli composite overwinds

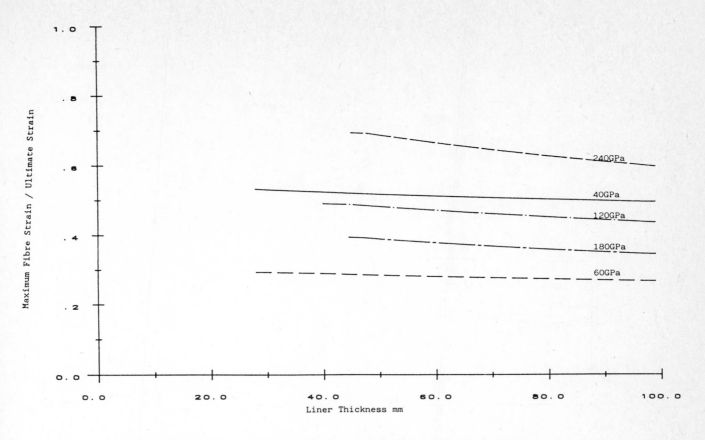

Fig 9 Maximum reinforcement strain/ultimate strain versus liner thickness;
1GPa transverse moduli composite overwinds

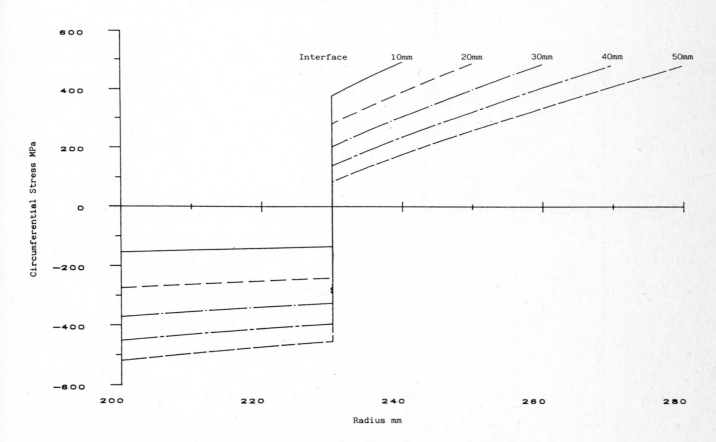

Fig 10 Circumferential pre-stress versus radius for various reinforcement
thicknesses; 10GPa transverse moduli 180GPa CFRP overwind

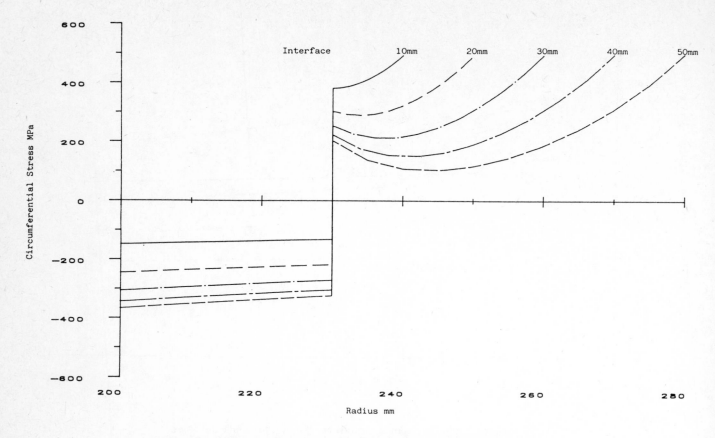

Fig 11 Circumferential pre-stress versus radius for various reinforcement
thicknesses; 1GPa transverse moduli 180GPa CFRP overwind

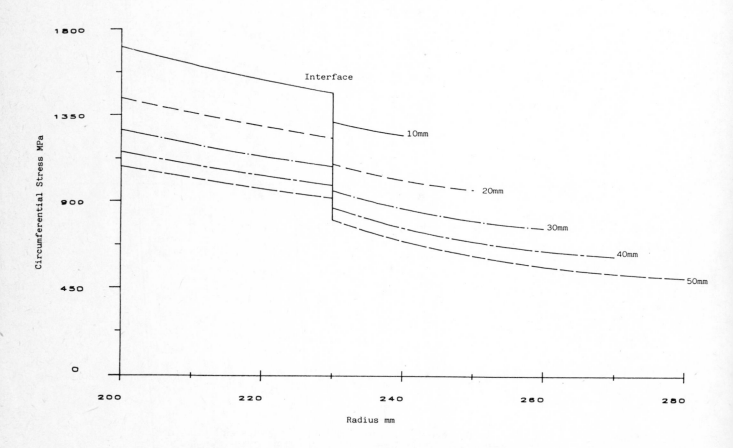

Fig 12 Pressure induced circumferential stress versus radius for various
reinforcement thicknesses; 10GPa transverse moduli 180 CFRP
overwind

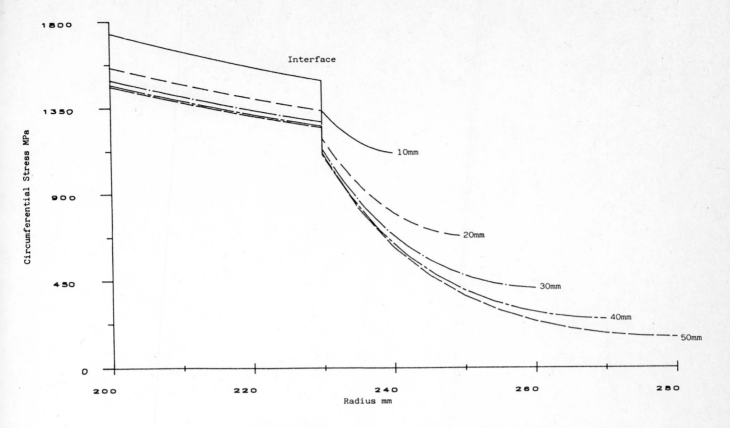

Fig 13   Pressure induced circumferential stress versus radius for various
          reinforcement thicknesses; 1GPa transverse moduli 180GPa CFRP
          overwind

C387/002

The development of resin transfer moulding (RTM) for volume manufacture

M J OWEN, BSc, MS, PhD, CEng, FIMechE, FPRI, V MIDDLETON, BSc, PhD, CEng, MIMechE,
K F HUTCHEON, MA, CEng, FIMechE, FIEE, F N SCOTT, MEng and C D RUDD, BSc, AMIMechE
Department of Mechanical Engineering, University of Nottingham

INTRODUCTION

The automotive industry has been aware for many years of the potential advantages of reinforced plastics and several manufacturers have been able to exploit these materials in low volume, niche market vehicles. Unfortunately, current manufacturing technology dictates that the production of composite parts such as body assemblies has been confined to low volume applications.

The passenger vehicle market is becoming increasingly fragmented into a large number of basic models. These niche markets (10 000 to 50 000 per annum) present problems to the major manufacturers, as the cost of tooling up for steel presswork becomes only marginally economic. One possible solution to this problem is the use of composite materials. Composites offer the manufacturer the opportunity of attacking the high cost of tooling in two distinct ways:

(a) Part and tool integration. A recent study in the U.S.A. (1,2) has shown the possibility of replacing a fabricated part containing 44 individual pressings with a single composite moulding. In addition to the reduced number of sub-assemblies the number of tools required to produce each component is greatly reduced, as composite mouldings require only single impression tooling, while steel pressings often require several hits to produce the final shape.

(b) Low cost tooling. If a suitable low pressure moulding process were to be available, this would enable the use of relatively low cost, lightweight tooling.

The most likely processing route to satisfy the requirements of the automotive industry in the market identified is Resin Transfer Moulding (RTM), also known in the UK as Resin Injection. RTM processes have been used in various forms by several manufacturers for the low volume production of panels and body assemblies, examples being the Lotus Excel and the Renault Espace. The traditional RTM process (Figure 1) requires development in several specific areas before it will be suitable for volume vehicle manufacture.

THE RTM PROCESS

There is no single process which defines Resin Transfer Moulding. RTM more properly describes a family of processes which share the common feature of the injection of a liquid, thermosetting resin system into a closed mould containing a dry fibre preform, but differ in the way the resin is retained in the mould while the air is removed. The traditional concept of RTM is shown schematically in Figure 1. The majority of commercial RTM work is based upon low pressure processes, low investment tooling and cold setting resin systems. This technology, whilst suitable for low volume work, does not enable the cycle times necessary for medium to high volume production to be achieved. One important feature of a viable RTM process is the use of hot-setting resin systems. These enable shorter filling times, gel-times and demould times.

One immediate problem which the traditional process presents to the volume manufacturer is that of generation of waste. The production of waste free mouldings requires preforms which have been trimmed to the cavity dimensions and a moulding process which does not generate flash. A moulded edge can only be achieved by use of a perimeter seal and this presents problems with the removal of air from the mould. This could be achieved by evacuation, in a similar manner to vacuum impregnation. The use of a high vacuum however creates problems of its own, one of which may be boiling of styrene or other volatiles in the low pressure areas, i.e. the flow front.

One possible solution to this problem, where hot setting resins are used, is the displacement of the air by a vapour or 'vapour purging'. In practice, this consists of wetting the fibre preform with a small quantity of a volatile liquid and placing the preform in a heated, sealed mould. The preform is raised to the saturation temperature of the liquid, which then boils. The mould is then vented and the majority of the air is removed with the escaping vapour. The vent can now be closed, leaving only the preform, together with a very small amount of vapour plus residual air in the cavity. The injection process then proceeds with the incoming resin driving the remaining air and vapour mixture to the perimeter, where it is compressed until the saturation pressure of the vapour is reached. The vapour condenses and is absorbed into the liquid resin, while the air is compressed around the perimeter, where it constitutes a negligible volume.

The traditional method of expelling air from the mould is to provide some means for controlled leakage at the perimeter - The Vented Seal process. This may be achieved by allowing the reinforcement to hang outside the mould and clamp it around the perimeter to form a pinch-off. This method results in substantial overspill and trimming. Alternatives include the use of a porous gasket or a rubber seal with discrete vents at strategic points. The Vented Seal process inevitably involves the generation of some flash, but with careful siting of vents and accurate preforms this can be kept to a minimum.

PREFORMS

One of the key advantages of an RTM type process over alternative manufacturing routes such as hot press SMC moulding is the ability to use preplaced, continuous fibre reinforcement in either random or directional orientation in the preform and to maintain the required density and orientation in the final part. Currently, preform technology is based upon the use of tailored continuous filament random mat. This is an inherently wasteful process and even with regularly shaped components, fibre utilisation is unlikely to exceed 50%. Although acceptable currently (in the absence of a suitable alternative), as volumes increase the levels of waste fibre are likely to prove to be an embarrassment. The present forming technology, which consists of a pre-heating cycle followed by stamping causes significant stretching and orientation of the nominally random mat, giving rise to non-uniformity in the preform. The problem of supply of accurate, high quality preforms, preferably produced by a waste free production process is critical to development of a viable RTM process for volume manufacture.

MATERIALS

The requirements of high volume manufacture with the associated short cycle times demand that the materials are well characterised with regard to their processing properties. In order to gain a full understanding of the process variables, a large number of instrumented plaque mouldings have been carried out using state of the art RTM technology. This has provided a comprehensive history of the pressures and temperatures which occur throughout the mould cavity during the moulding cycle.

The aluminium mould used in the production of plaque mouldings (Figure 2) was 548mm x 598mm with an injection gate offset from the centre of the plaque by 25mm. This has been used with a steel moulding frame in order to control thickness and retain a perimeter O-ring seal. The sealing arrangement is shown in Figure 3. The frame reduces the overall plaque area to 508mm x 558mm. The lower mould half was fitted with pressure tappings which enable the cavity pressure to be measured at seven points from the injection gate to one corner at 59mm intervals. Pressure in the injection nozzle was measured using a further transducer. Fibre preforms were prepared from continuous filament random mat (CFRM) and trimmed closely to the cavity dimensions. Thermocouples were laid in the mid-plane of the preforms at positions corresponding to the pressure tapping points. Data logging was provided by a personal computer. This enabled the nature of the moulding cycle to be determined. In later experiments, studies were made of the effects of different materials and process parameters upon the pressures and temperatures encountered during the cycle.

It became clear from early work that the best hope of achieving very short cycle times lay in the use of hot setting resin systems. For this and other reasons, the majority of mouldings have been carried out using premixed hot setting polyester resins at mould temperatures in the range 100 to 130°C. Initial results from temperature monitoring during the moulding cycle showed that mid-plane temperatures of 230°C could occur during exotherm. This explained the occurrence of styrene boil in many mouldings produced in this temperature range, and demonstrated the need, in many cases, to maintain cavity pressure during gelation in order to prevent the occurrence of high void contents in the final mouldings.

Comparison of typical pressure and temperature data from one point in the mould cavity (Figure 4) with saturation pressure and temperature data for styrene (Figure 5) provides a useful indication of the likelihood of styrene boil.

Further study of pressure and temperature results for the full cavity enables the significant events of the moulding cycle to be identified. A typical case is shown in Figure 6.

INJECTION CYCLE

The beginning and end of the injection period are marked by the step changes in pressure at the transducer opposite the gate and the cooling effect of the incoming resin at the same position. As the injection proceeds and the mould becomes filled, the pressure begins to rise across the mould.

Injection must continue at least until the mould cavity is filled. At the instant the cavity becomes filled by the incoming resin (mould fill), the majority of the mould sees only low pressures relative to the injection nozzle. It may be required to continue injecting resin past this point in order to compress or expel residual air, or to pressurise the cavity and assist wet-out of the mat. If the mould is sealed then a hydrostatic condition is pressure is maintained past the 'just filled' condition, as shown in Figure 6. The timing of the end of injection will be determined by the nature of the moulding process but in practice, some form of transducer is required to indicate cavity fill. This may take the form of a proximity gauge, pressure transducer or a strain gauge on the mould itself.

CURE CYCLE

The relative positions of the peak exotherm temperatures indicate the progression of the cure, from the outermost position back to the injection gate. Any disturbance in the order of the peaks is indicative of premature gelation. It is important that the resin system is sufficiently well characterised to enable the mould to be filled before any increase in viscosity due to gelation occurs (wet-through). It is also important that the system is designed to provide the necessary dwell time for the resin to dissolve the binder on the reinforcement and to completely wet the individual fibres (wet-out).

The magnitude of the peak exotherm recorded in the laminate is a function of the heat of the reaction available, the reaction kinetics, the laminate thickness and the thermal conductivity and mass of the system. In general, attempts to speed up the cure cycle result in an increase in the peak exotherms recorded. This effect is shown in Figure 7, where by increasing the reactivity of the resin system, the peak exotherm is increased by 60 degrees. High

exotherm temperatures can cause defects such as voiding, resin cracking and precipitation effects. Furthermore, in the case of shell tooling, a reduction in tool life may result.

QUALITY

Operation of a viable production system demands that the materials are well defined and quality is guaranteed by the supplier. Close co-operation between materials suppliers will be necessary in order to ensure compatibility between all components of the materials system. This goes beyond the normal question of resin/size compatibility, but needs to addres in detail the net effect of each component: fibre, size, binder, resin, additives and fillers upon the process, moulding quality and final material properties.

THE WAY FORWARD

RTM offers a possible route for the manufacture of medium volume automotive components. Currently moulding technology provides a starting point, but, the key areas for development are:

*   Direct production of preforms via a minimum waste route.

*   Development of reinforcement surface treatments and binders to enable complete wet-out within the time available.

*   Resin systems with improved processing characteristics and high temperature performance.

*   A process control system which provides accurate timing of the injection and cure cycles.

*   Component design methods which include processing parameters, material requirements and mould design.

REFERENCES

(1) JOHNSON, C.F., N.G. CHAVKA and R.A. JERYAN, 'Resin Transfer Moulding of Complex Automotive Structures', 41st Annual Conference RP/C Ins., SPI, Atlanta, Georgia, Jan. 27-31 1986, Session 12-A, pp 1-7.

(2) JOHNSON, C.F., N.G. CHAVKA, R.A. JERYAN, C.J. MORRIS & D.A. BABBINGTON, 'Design and Fabrication of a HSRTM Crossmember Module', Advanced Composites III: Expanding the Technology, Proceedings of the 3rd Annual Conference on Advanced Composites, Detroit, Michigan, 15-17 September 1987.

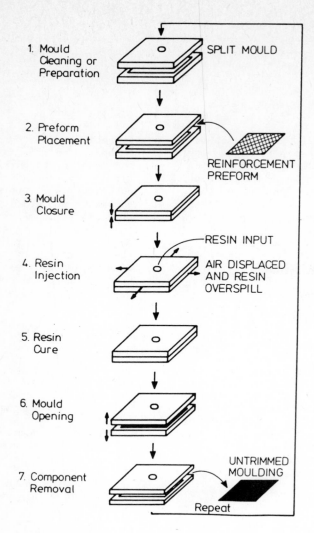

Fig 1   Schematic of the traditional RTM process for a single skinned component

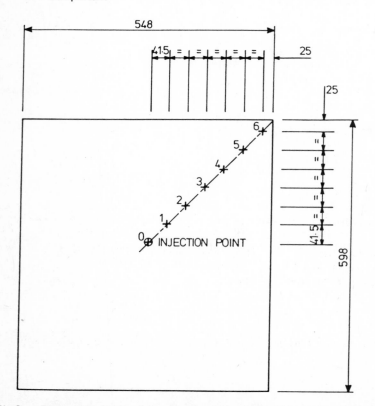

Fig 2   Plaque mould showing positions of thermocouples and pressure tapping points

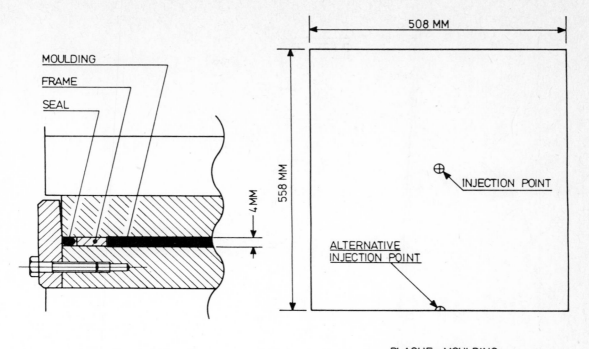

MOULDING

FRAME

SEAL

508 MM

558 MM

4 MM

⊕ INJECTION POINT

ALTERNATIVE
INJECTION POINT

PLAQUE MOULDING

Fig 3

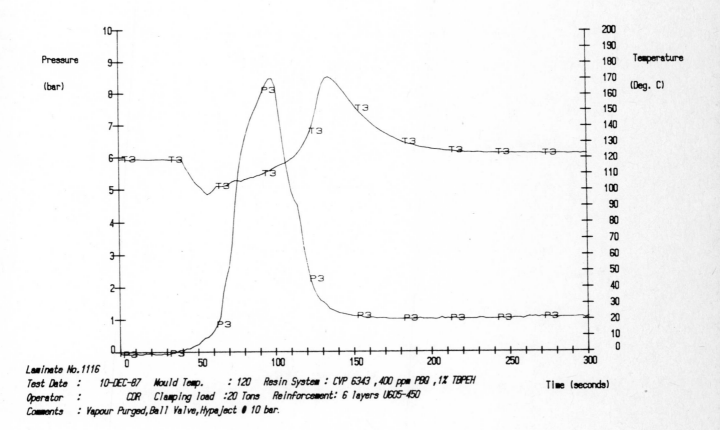

Pressure

(bar)

Temperature

(Deg. C)

Laminate No.1116
Test Date : 10-DEC-87 Mould Temp. : 120 Resin System : CVP 6343 ,400 ppm PBQ ,1% TBPEH
Operator : COR Clamping load :20 Tons Reinforcement: 6 layers U605-450
Comments : Vapour Purged,Ball Valve,Hypaject @ 10 bar.

Time (seconds)

Fig 4   Pressure and temperature during moulding cycle at position 3

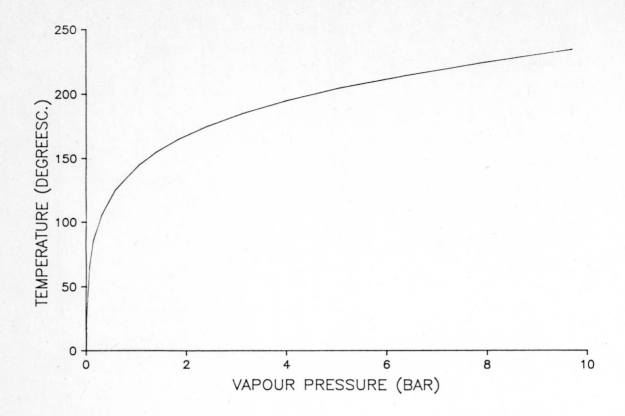

Fig 5   Saturation temperature versus vapour pressure for styrene

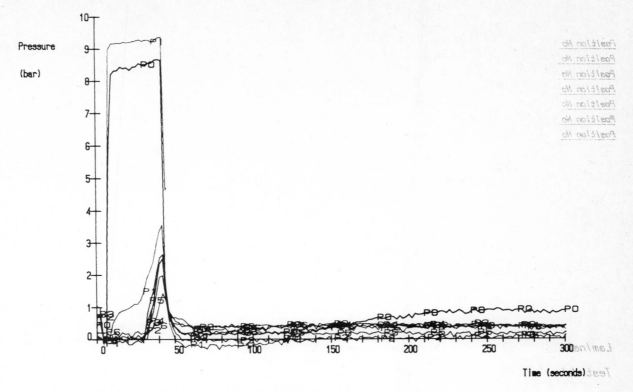

(a) Pressures during moulding cycle; laminate 1141

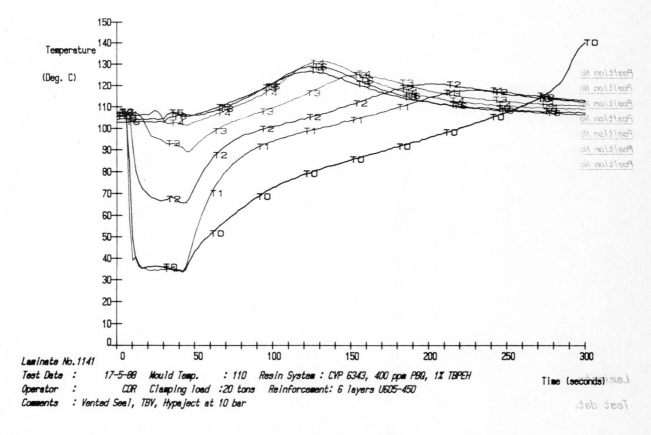

Laminate No.1141
Test Date :   17-5-88   Mould Temp.   : 110   Resin System : CVP 6343, 400 ppm PBQ, 1% TBPEH
Operator :   COR   Clamping load :20 tons   Reinforcement: 6 layers U605-450
Comments : Vented Seal, TBV, Hypaject at 10 bar

(b) Temperatures during moulding cycle; laminate 1141

Fig 6

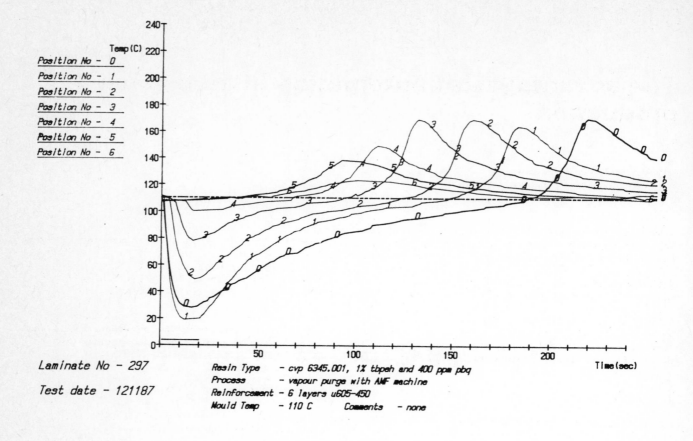

Laminate No – 297

Test date – 121187

Resin Type   – cvp 6345.001, 1% tbpeh and 400 ppm pbq
Process   – vapour purge with AMF machine
Reinforcement – 6 layers u605-450
Mould Temp   – 110 C   Comments – none

(a)   Temperature during moulding cycle; low reactivity resin

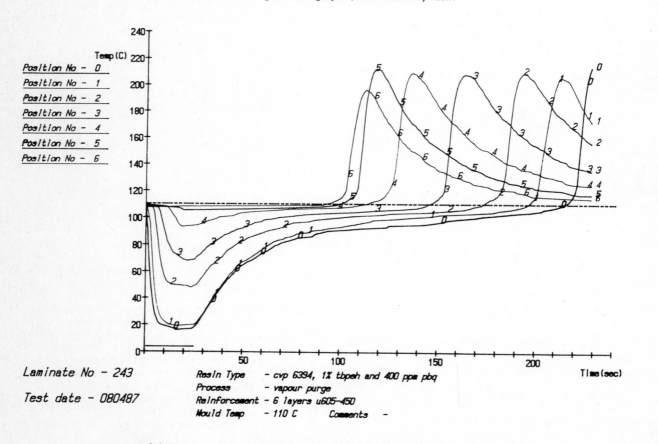

Laminate No – 243

Test date – 080487

Resin Type   – cvp 6394, 1% tbpeh and 400 ppm pbq
Process   – vapour purge
Reinforcement – 6 layers u605-450
Mould Temp   – 110 C   Comments –

(b)   Temperatures during moulding cycle; high reactivity resin

Fig 7

C387/020

The advantages of automation in aerospace production

G W HUGHES, BSc, PhD, MBA
British Aerospace plc, Blackburn, Lancashire

SYNOPSIS   Composite components have been manufactured for aircraft for several years. The main application today is for carbon fibre/epoxy resin composites. In the early days of manufacturing the challenge was to manufacture parts of suitable quality to almost any cost.

With increasing production volumes and the increasing pressure on costs of both civil and military aircraft programmes the emphasis has shifted significantly to one of minimising costs.

An attractive candidate approach is the introduction of automation. This paper investigates various alternative automation options for manufacturing and concludes that the introduction of some plant can be extremely cost effective. However, care must be taken as some means of automation on offer are not worthy of investment on purely cost grounds.

1 INTRODUCTION

Advanced composite materials have been in use in the aerospace industry for some twenty years. In the early days all the emphasis in manufacturing was on the ability to produce components to the right design and quality standards. The components manufactured at this time were generally one off demonstrator components and the manufacturing cost was of secondary importance. However, as composites manufacture moved into the production phase, then an increasing emphasis was put on the reduction in manufacturing costs.

This drive to reduce manufacturing costs is not peculiar to the aerospace industry; in the field of general engineering, a reduction in manufacturing costs is a pre-requisite for the more widespread acceptance of the use of composite materials. In these areas however, the emphasis is on materials of a different form. Primarily woven, knitted or braided fibres are used together with some applications for composites with short fibres. These are also used in the aerospace industry, but for applications to Military aircraft the prime material is un-directional pre-impregnate which offers the best strength and stiffness to weight ratios. This paper will concentrate on automation for uni-directional composites.

The application of automation in aerospace has been a result of an increasing drive to reduce manufacturing costs.

Automated systems have been investigated at British Aerospace to obtain an appreciation of whether these savings are realisable in practice. A number of these will be examined here including flat and contour tape laying, various methods of broadgoods cutting, automated ply location methods and tape winding.

2 PLY CUTTING AND LAYING

Uni-directional pre-impregnated tape is available from suppliers in several widths ranging from 25mm to 1.5m. For hand lay-up narrow widths are used on complex shapes with 'broadgoods' being used for near flat or shapes that can be formed from a flat laminate.

The use of broad or narrow tape also distinguishes the two main routes which have developed towards the automation of cutting and laying operations. The use of narrow tape is the field of automated tapelaying systems where the tape is cut - either by the tapelaying head or in a separate operation - and the material is laid up 'black on black'. Manufacture using broadgoods on the other hand, requires several plies to be cut from a sheet of material which are then kitted and stored for a subsequent lay-up operation. These two routes will now be examined in further detail.

2.1 Automated Tapelaying

The first application of automated tapelaying was to the lay-up of flat laminates. Early machines cut in the laying head, were manually operated, and very slow. Development led to DNC control and automated operation, but cutting was still performed in the laying head and productivity is still very low. The very latest machines currently under development separate the cutting and laying operations so they can be performed in parallel. In this way the laying head can be made of significantly lower inertia with a remarkable improvement in productivity as a result.

The use of automated tape laying machines for laying up in the flat is not as restrictive as it may first seem, even for aerospace components which are almost inevitably curved. The development of forming techniques for composites at British Aerospace has meant that significant numbers of different kinds of components can be laid in the flat and then formed to shape prior to curing. However, there are certain applications where curvatures are too severe for the shapes to be formed from the flat, and in this case the requirement is for a tape layer which will lay directly on a shaped tool - a so called contour tape layer.

Contour tape laying is a recent development and few machines are in existence. The physical problems of machine control over contoured surfaces are much greater than they are on the flat. The associated software problems for controlling the paths to be followed in the laying down of each ply piece are considerable, and many problems remain unresolved. An additional fundamental problem is generated by the geometry in such cases, where there is an inherent mismatch of orientations and gaps/overlaps etc, simply because of the compound curvature. This requires rethinking from the designers point of view because he can no longer specify a single fibre orientation for a whole ply and he must accept that certain gaps and overlaps are inevitable because of the shapes, notwithstanding any tolerances in tape widths or tape placement.

2.2 Broadgoods Automation

If the lay-up operation has to be performed manually then there is clearly a productivity advantage in laying broadgoods rather than narrow tape when this is feasible. Broadgoods have, therefore, been used extensively in the aerospace industry and this has led to developments in automation of the cutting process.

All automated ply cutting techniques, usually driven by NC or DNC, basically involve the same principles. The main difference between competing systems is the actual method of cutting. The most popular system employed in the aerospace industry worldwide is the Gerber type. This is a technique which has been developed from the textile industry where a knife reciprocates at high speed as it passes through the raw material. This has proved quite successful, but is not as fast as some of the systems and does have the limitation that it cannot cut very tight radii.

The use of lasers for cutting CFC tape and cloth has been tried. In fact a system was operating in the US several years ago. This method is relatively slow and does have the disadvantage of degrading the material adjacent to the cut. A further system developed for this application was the use of a very high pressure water jet. This employs a very fine jet of de-ionised water at 60,000 psi with a diameter of 0.008". This system is extremely fast and several layers of pre-preg can be cut at once. Very tight radii can be achieved, the one draw back of this system

being the absorpotion of moisture adjacent to the cut edge. When multiple plies are cut, this means a drying cycle has to be performed before any further lay-up operations take place. The latest development in ply cutting which has none of the disadvantages of earlier systems is the use of a knife blade which is vibrated ultrasonically. This system has no contamination problems, can cut very tight radii and has the additional advantage that it is possible to cut pre-preg without damaging the backing paper on which it is carried. However, this system is limited to the cutting of a single ply whereas the water jet or Gerber systems can cut many plies simultaneously. Further development and enhancements of these systems are inevitable.

In all current aerospace applications the subsequent lay-up of laminates is a manual operation where the pre-preg plies are stacked one on the other by hand. Several systems have been conceived in the automation of these processes, but none as yet is actually in production. One such system is a robotic ply handling system which makes use of standard robots with the aid of various handling devices in order to build up the stack.

A different concept is being developed by Composite Automation Engineering Incorporated employing a roller system for picking up plies and laying them down in the correct position on the stack. The system uses vacuum rollers to effect this and if the system is effective in practice it could lead to increased efficiency in the laminating lay-up phase.

Some development is also evident in improvements to the productivity of manual lay-up operations. For example, the introduction of handling and transportation systems between lay-up stations for kits and tools can be beneficial. In addition, improvements to the lay-up cell itself using vision systems and lasers, giving operators and inspectors information on ply-ups actually on the component, show real promise.

Whichever system, manual or automated, is adopted for lay-up a buffer stock will be required between cutting and laying if material wastage is to be kept within reasonable bounds. This is not a problem with refrigerated storage and the usual mode of operation is to kit a set of plies after cutting, bag and then store until required for lay-up. However, the kitting and bagging operations are also labour intensive and methods are being developed for automating these processes. A system of bar coding with visual ply identification has been developed by CAE where plies are randomly fed into the machine which sorts them and kits them on to trays. A method of bagging the kits afterwards has been developed elsewhere for placing kits, carried on cardboard trays, into the correct size polythene bags for refrigerated storage.

2.3 Comparison of the two Routes

There are several features which are common to all broadgoods systems or all tapelaying systems which will now be compared. Firstly, the material utilisation of broadgoods systems is much lower than for automated tapelayers. This is because, using narrow tape, only small pieces of tape at the end of each run are wasted whereas with broadgoods, material utilisation depends on nesting efficiency but will typically not average better than 70%. This is a major drawback of broadgoods - however the systems can be used to supply kits to hand lay-up where the shapes are too severe for automated tapelaying. Broadgoods too offer more flexibility to the designer in the profiles of internal plies. Virtually any shape can be specified in broadgoods whereas these can only be achieved on an automated tape layer at considerable cost in terms of machine laying rates. in order to achieve high machine efficiencies it is necessary that each ply piece has either a single straight cut or two straight cuts at each end. This is not a major mass penalty as the tape width is only narrow, but it does lead to a staircasing effect which must be allowed for in the design.

Furthermore, as the tape is narrow, the designer must accept new tolerances for gaps and overlaps and for the stagger index from ply to ply. This restriction is even more severe in tapewinding which offers the only means of automation for very highly curved structures and will be discussed separately below.

2.4 Tape Winding

For very severe curvatures, the only practical means of automation is through the use of multi axis winding. There are major problems with the winding of severe double curvatures as there are with contour tape laying. These include problems of laying tape in the mandrel axis direction and normal to it, as well as the positioning of reinforcing or drop-off plies. Coupled with this are the inevitable software problems of coping with compound shapes and several axes.

To evaluate these problems, initial development work at British Aerospace was centred on manufacture of the laser fairing for Tornado. This is a compound double curvature and was originally manufactured in a joint programme with Harwell using a semi-automated technique where some hand control was necessary. Later a joint programme with Nottingham University investigated the full automation of this technique. The technique has also been used on a similar basis on a much larger scale on the Beech Starship, where the complete fuselage which consists of inner skin, non-metallic honeycomb and outer skin, has been manufactured on a winding machine in virtually one operation.

Current development at BAe is centred on the tapewinding of a demonstrator fuselage on a full scale machine. The potential deposition rates of winding are so great - they can be about 4 times faster than tape laying or 40 times faster than hand laying up - that applications of the technique on components of relatively simple shape are very attractive even though they can be manufactured using alternative methods.

The basic winding techniques involve the revolution of the mandrel either continuously or stepwise, with a progressive feeding of the laying head in the mandrel axis direction. The relative speeds govern the ply orientation. Other techniques involve the use of an oscillating mandrel or, for semi closed cylindrical shapes, the use of polar winding. Several different types of components are suitable for winding. For example, flat panels for use as access panels or for subsequent forming operations could be manufactured using, say, 6 per mandrel; and curved panels could be manufactured, say 3 at once. A deep curved panel like a laser fairing would sensibly be manufactured in production as two per mandrel. Even square mandrels can be used: for example, for 'L' shaped panels or for channel section spars, these could readily be made at two per mandrel.

All these applications are primarily focused on <u>tape</u> winding, as these are the primary applications on aircraft structures. However, wet winding on simple shapes is a well established technique and the winding of pre-preg tows also has some application.

3 COST COMPARISONS

The material utilisation of broadgoods manufacture and tapelaying have already been compared - tapewinding is somewhere between the two depending how much of the mandrel covering is required for the final component. The following theoretical comparison is on a direct labour hours basis only.

Consider the hand cutting and hand laying of plies as a datum then the use of broadgoods and DNC ply cutting followed by hand lay-up can theoretically improve this by a factor of 3. Automated ply collation systems for the lay-up phase as well can improve this factor to about 10.

Alternatively, the use of a DNC contour tapelayer or current production flat tapelayer would improve on the datum by a factor of 7 whereas the current development 'fast and flat' tapelayer can give a factor of 14. These potential savings are extremely attractive, but the most efficient means of laying down composite tape is through the use of tapewinding which can conceivably be 40 times faster than hand cutting and hand laying.

Theoretically then the savings in direct labour cost are extremely attractive and automated systems have been or are being developed to exploit them. However, practical experience of these techniques shows that the theoretical factors are not, in practice, achievable.

Some of the realistic times are typically twice those originally predicted. For example, a realisable factor for automated broadgoods cutting is 1.4 compared with 3 predicted. For contour tapelaying the factor is 4.5 compared with 7 and for 'fast and flat' tapelaying 8 compared with 14, when practical considerations are taken into account.

Although in practice the savings realisable are considerably less than predicted they are nevertheless still very significant. Taking the capital costs into account some such systems make attractive investments. As a result BAe is committed to further introductions of automation for the manufacture of composite components although each individual system is considered strictly on its own merits.

NOTATIONS

BAe - British Aerospace
DNC - Direct Numercial Control
NC   - Numercial Control
CFC - Carbon Fibre Composite
CAE - Composite Automation Engineering

C398/009

Composite plastic gears to reduce problems on process plant conveyors

J H PURSLOW
Pilkington plc, Ormskirk, Lancashire

SYNOPSIS   Conveyors in glass producing factories can run on a continuous or cyclic basis, often for 24 hours/day, over a period of many years, depending on their function in the process line.   A torque of 60 Nm is required to drive roller and product, using a bevel gear.   Problems exist with traditional hardened steel spiral bevel gears e.g's replacement downtime, fretting corrosion of roller ends, wear etc.   The development of thick section moulded composite nylon gears to replace the steel units, has alleviated these problems, and resulted in gears which have a significantly lower initial cost.

1.   INTRODUCTION

Three fundamental factors which Pilkington's line management in continuous glass making factories must be aware of are:-
1. Current and future market requirements.
2. Knowing the life of the glass melting furnaces.
3. Reliability of glass processing plant to meet life of furnaces.
Market demand can only be met efficiently on the Pilkington high volume plants by having processing flexibility built into them and when significant market changes and new products are regonised, technology is developed and introduced at the earliest possible time.

Major upgrading and/or repair of plant can only be carried out when the glass melting furnace is shut down for a scheduled "cold" repair or rebuild, which lasts 10-12 weeks. Before the repair period, maintenance and upgrading arrangements are made after examination of the whole plant for areas of deterioration, e.g. main line process conveyor rollers, gears, bearings, drive ystems, etc. Approximately 20 years ago, a furnace's continuous, 24 hour per day production life would be 3 years. Since then, improvements in furnace technology has extended the operational life to between 8 and 10 years, and in addition, the output has nearly doubled, hence an increase in throughput speed.

One element of the automatic production line which handles glass through the various processing stages of cutting, snapping and stacking the glass is the main line roller conveyor.   The conveyor sections can run on a continuous or cyclic basis depending on their function, 24 hours per day, for the life of the glass melting furnace (i.e. 8-10 years).

The conveyor rollers, under acceleration conditions require a maximum torque of 60 Nm to drive a master roller plus 2-idler rollers and glass, using a bevel gear, see Fig. 1 for drive torque/cycle time diagram. Problems exist with traditional hardened steel spiral bevel gears fig. 2, e.g's long replacement downtime, fretting corrosion of roller ends, noise, wear, lubrication, etc. I now come to the subject matter of this paper, the development of moulded composite reinforced platic bevel gears to replace the steel units, which has alleviated the above mentioned problems and has resulted in gears which have a significantly lower initial cost.

2.   DEVELOPMENT OF MOULDED COMPOSITE GEARS

2.1   Background

Initially, proprietary sources were investigated to find a replacement for the steel bevel gear at lower cost, better reliability and with reduced maintenance attention.   It was decided that a gear in a non-metallic material may meet the requirements.   After an extensive search the only moulded gears available were small tooth size used for instrument and domestic machinery or alternatively machine cut to our design. Nobody would guarantee a life of machine cut gears in any material as suppliers had no experience with glass making and associated glass production environments e.g's glass dust and granules, which penetrate drive enclosures. Since there was nothing available "off the shelf", we decided to develop our own non-metallic bevel gear.

2.2   Gear Design and Development

Before starting the design it was essential that several alternative materials were selected to satisfy the main requirements viz:

2.2.1 Tough to withstand bending stresses.

2.2.2 Low friction to keep driving energy to a minimum.

2.2.3 To have low noise/vibration characteristics.

2.2.4 Little or no wear with glass dust/granule environment.

2.2.5 Low cost.

2.2.6 Should be compatible with existing fast-enging methods for quick replacement "on line".

2.2.7 Reasonable dimensional stability.

Looking at plastic materials, Nylon 6 and 6.6 also Acetal were obvious contenders.   To maintain dimensional stability, these materials were also investigated with glass reinforcement in the form of fibres or ballotini (small glass spheres), carbon fibre was also considered. After discussions, it was our opinion that any hard reinforcement media would degenerate the main plastic support matrix of the mating gear teeth and so a non-reinforced material was initially pursued.

A desirable design feature of the gear was to incorporate straight teeth which would enable a split gear feature to be included thereby allowing a quick change operation on a long driver line shaft. The tooth profile was formed to the Gleason system. The drawbacks associated with straight teeth, i.e. meshing noise and single tooth loading/shearing are alleviated by the resilient nature of the polymer material providing a dampened impact tooth engagement and due to tooth deflection load sharing by adjacent teeth, respectively. The finalised design policy was to fit roller ends with non-split gears and driver lineshafts with split gears.

Taking into account the materials physical properties the design resulted in a gear much larger than the available space envelope on existing conveyors. However, it was felt that it was worth pursuing the plastic gear in the event of adopting them on new factory conveyors designed to accept them.

Trials were carried out with experimental gears machined from blocks of Nylon 6 and tested on a "back-to-back" test rig shown in figure 3. The constant torque loading of 60 Nm is the maximum acceleration and deceleration torque applied to the gear during normal production use. Because this start/stop cycle occurs with each plate, the test rig gives an accelerated test period e.g. for an average of 8 plates/min. over a 10 week period the gears would undergo an equivalent on-line operational use of 4 years. Two pairs of experimental straight tooth machined nylon 6 gears were fastened to one end of the rig whilst the other two corners were fitted with hardened steel spiral bevel gears.

One initial coating of general purpose grease was applied to all gears and the rig was started. After 4 weeks the gears were cleaned and examined. No appreciable wear had taken place on any gear. After regreasing the test was repeated with the addition of a metered amount of glass granules/dust. It was found that the steel gears were showing degrees of wear through the 0.3 mm thick hardened surface, whereas, the nylon gears had accepted the glass particles which were embedded in the tooth surface and provided a wear/sacrifical surface.

Acetal gears, although more dimensionally stable than nylon, were less resistant to wear on the tooth profile. The confidence generated with the Nylon 6 gears made us think about trying machined gears designed with the overall dimensions the same as the hardened steel gears. 22 tooth gears were cut from blocks of Nylon 6 and mounted on the back-to-back rig. These gears withstood the endurance testing, including the sprinkling of cullet dust and granules. However, when tried on a production line, teeth were broken off and the experimental gears had to be replaced with the traditional steel bevel gears. it was later found out that the prototype nylon gears were inadvertently fitted with a steel gear backlash of only 0.1-0.15 as against the recommended 0.4-0.5 mm. Due to material expansion the tight backlash was reduced quickly to an interferance fit, hence the failure.

With the failure of the small gear teeth and not knowing about the backlash error, we decided because of the success with the earlier large gear design, that we would reduce the number of teeth from 22 to 20 thereby giving the smaller gear the same large section of tooth. At 200 rpm max. the 20 tooth smaller gear endured the test programme successfully. Subsequently both U.K. and overseas plants fitted small batches of the machined Nylon 6 gears which withstood the operational duties and generated confidence. The machined Nylon 6 gears have since been replacing worn steel gears.

The cost of a pair of 1-solid gear plus, 1-split gear was approximately 60% of a pair of hardened steel gears machined from nylon 6. The next obvious move was to develop a moulded gear to further reduce the initial cost.

2.3 Initial moulded composite gear development

It was decided to initially try a single material moulding. A low cost aluminium mould with water cooling was made from a machined brass gear pattern with shrinkage allowance for moulding the gears in Nylon 66. After the development stage which included changing the flow gate configuration, introduction of vacuum ports at roots of teeth to negate gas pockets, etc. prototype moulded gears were produced. However, with gear body sections in excess of 10 mm shrinkage and distortion took place. A carbon fibre reinforcement (10% by vol) was introduced. The C.F. reinforcement helped to curb the distortion but concern was strong with regards to the fibre ends that would probably degenerate the Nylon 66 base material of the mating gear teeth, hence lead to short life. c.f. reinforcement was placed in abeyance.

Because the gear required the thick sections to withstand the drive pin bearing stress in their performance duty, a solution was required to make the gears 20 mm thick boss section with a maximum moulding thickness of 10 mm.
Moulded cavities were considered, but the mould complexity and weakness of section steered the design toward maintaining a solid section. It was realised that a composite design was the solution, i.e. 2 x 10 mm.

Steel inserts were thought best to try initially, as they could be made with several alternative shape configurations, including deep knurling on the outer surface for shrinkage grip of outer moulded gear shell. From the customer, Engineering Department's point of view, the steel insert would give them confidence in a dimensionally stable bore, keyway and shaft relationship. In addition the steel thick wall insert would provide a good bearing area for transmitting the torque loading from shaft to gear, via a spring steel "roll pin" and a drive key.

Nonsplit gears with steel inserts were moulded. After an acceptable metrology check they were fitted to the "back-to-back" endurance test rig and subjected to 4 weeks torque loading of 60 Nm at 200 rpm. They successfully withstood this trial.

The next step was to try split gears with steel inserts. It was decided to use non-split moulded gears and machine away half of each gear since packers would be an unwanted necessity if the gears were split with a slitting cutter. Because the stressed nylon shell was severed at the split line, the material retracted approx. 1/2 mm from the machined flat steel split face which created a 1 mm gap between the nylon moulded gear shell when two halves were brought together.

It was realised that the insert should be made from the same material as the gear shell if possible, for compatible linear expansion/contraction. Initially, inserts were machined from block and then moulded into the Nylon 66 gear shell. When gears were sectioned through to make split gears, large gas pockets were found see fig. 4, assumed to have been generated by low packing pressure, the cruciform flow gating and the resultant rheology. Endurance rig trials were carried out with these sub-spec. specimens which performed well until the teeth adjacent to the split line, with gas pockets, started to crack at the root. In addition, when the machined inserts were made, no bonding took place between insert and gear shell, other than by mechanical interlocking by way of shallow grooves on periphery of insert.

2.4 Final development of moulded composite plastic gear

At this stage it was decided to invest in a prototype moulding tool to produce moulded inserts which:
a) used same polymer as gear shell, i.e. Nylon 66 with or without reinforcement.
b) could be designed for thin wall sections to prevent cooling distortion.
c) to meet the thin wall section requirements a series of core holes were moulded in which also provided a keying feature hence preventing movement of insert in the gear shell.
d) would enable a keyway to be moulded into the bore of the insert/gear.
e) to prevent retraction of gear shell from the insert at the split line, a dovetail groove to be formed such that when machined at the split line, the remaining half dove tail would prevent this movement. The result would minimise the gap (approx. to 0.15 mm maximum) between the gear shell halves at the split line.
See fig. 5 for moulded insert. After moulding, the inserts were dept dry and were warmed up to 80 degrees C prior to threading them onto the gear cavity mandrel and datumed on a key.

Gears were produced with consistent tooth form for all 20 teeth. Unfortunately, some "weld lines" were found at rear of gear teeth, and in addition, gas pockets were again discovered when gears were machined to make split gears, the bore accuracy was not consistent. The decision was made to modify the mould to leave material in the bore to enable minimal machining to take place with reference to the gear teeth, the flow gating was altered from cruciform to full diaphragm, and a higher packing pressure was used. In addition the nylon 66 was changed to a less viscous grade and KEVLAR reinforcement was introduced. The gas pocket and "weld line" problems were overcome. See fig. 6 for moulded insert, complete gear moulding and dismantled split gear.

The static strength of individual gear teeth was ascertained by mounting a specimen gear on a shaft, meshing a steel peg against one gear tooth and applying force, via load cell, on a torque arm located on the shaft end. the average maximum torque was found to be 5x greater than the maximum duty torque.

Sets of prototype moulded composite gears have since successfully undergone endurance tests and have been recommended to Works Engineering Departments as low cost replacements for the original steel and/or machined nylon gears.

3. CONCLUSIONS

The experience gained over the development period has helped to set down a pattern for investigating/introducing machine components in metallic and/or non-metallic materials. It was difficult in the time prior to this gear development period, to persuade Engineering Departments to introduce non-metallic components as replacements for existing traditional metallic units. However, this attitude has dramatically changed to, if it can be proved on endurance test rigs that it can do the job at less overall life cycle cost, then install it for on line trials. A fundamental fact about on-line trials is that 1/2 ton of saleable glass could be lost during a production line breakdown period, hence trials with new technology must have a high success probability.

As tabulated in appendix 1, the problems experienced, with the originally installed hardened steel gears have been alleviated with the introduction of nylon gears, e.g's reduced plant down time when replacing gears by a factor between 2:1 and 12:1, cost reduction 2:1, etc.

The introduction of the machined nylon gears to the Pilkington Group worldwide, backed up with installation and maintenance information, was a significant break through for engineering plastics. This in turn has paved the way for introducing the moulded 'kevlar' reinforced composite gears with the cost saving incentive.

The major factor in the moulded gear development was that, without the "composit" design approach, the basic requirements for accurate gears could not have been met, i.e. the moulding of thick sections without major distortion effects.

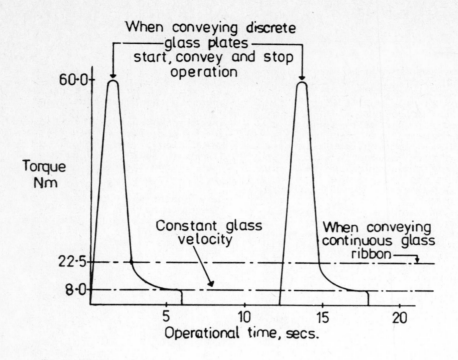

Fig 1   Drive gear duty cycles

Fig 2   Hardened steel spiral bevel gear
         22T 100mm pcd and drivepin

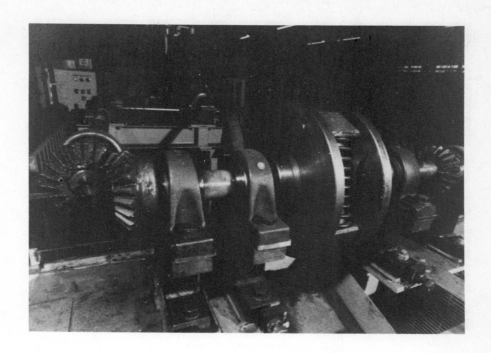

Fig 3   Back-to-back gear test rig

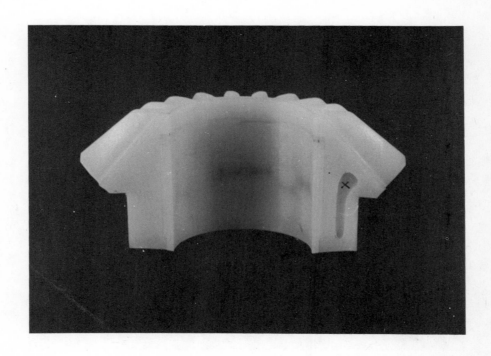

Fig 4   Gas pocket in moulded gears X

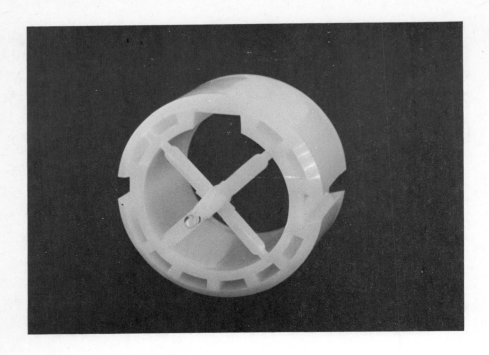

Fig 5   Moulded insert

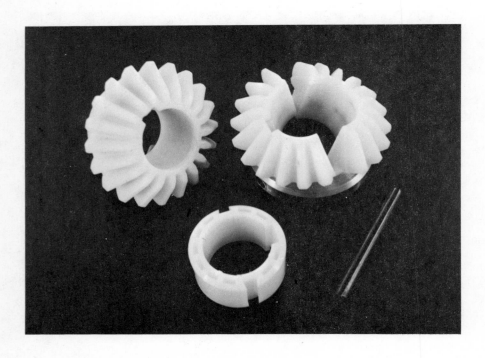

Fig 6   Moulded gear components

124

Factor	Hardened steel spiral bevel gear	Moulded composite polymer bevel gear
Cost	Based on 1,000 pair 1 pair = £57.00 Includes drilling jigs and tooling	Based on 1,000 pair:- No split gear = £20.00 alternatively 1-split + 1-no split = £26.00 Includes tooling and drill jigs
Lubrication	Regular lubrication necessary with general purpose grease. On average 2 x weekly, manual task.	Only one initial application of a general purpose grease. However, life of gear can be extended if regular greasing is given, say 6 p.a.
Performance/Wear Duty	Glass at ribbon speed:- gears at - 14 - 140 rpm High speed plate handling:- gears at 150 - 200 rpm Maximum operational torque - 60 Nm Life expectancy is 10 years depending on operational zone of production line.	Moulded nylon gears are predicted to withstand specified operational duty, as shown opposite for steel gears. However, their actual operational life can only be assertained over 10 years on a production line.
Space Envelope	Conveyors originally designed for rollers driven with steel gears.	Moulded nylon gears developed and tested to carry out specified duty in same space envelope as steel gears.
Setting up	Precise backlash setting required. i.e. 0.1-0.15 mm.	To allow for expansion, due to changes in both temperatures and moisture, a crude backlash of 0.4-0.5 is permissible. In addition the resilient material allows load sharing with adjacent teeth.
Dynamics		With steel backing collar, the plastic gear has a 30% lower inertia than that of a steel gear.
Replacement time from lineshaft location	Because the steel gear has spiral teeth to keep noise and vibration down, it would be an extremely costly machining operation to produce split gear. Therefore to remove a conventional steel gear from a lineshaft, up to 2 hrs. line downtime can be expected i.e. 70 tons of glass diverted to scrap.	The resilient nature of the nylon teeth keeps noise and vibration down to a minimum, therefore straight teeth are acceptable on the gear. With straight teeth of equal number, i.e. 20, the gear can be split at 180º. A solid gear is fitted to roller end which is easily removed by unbolting roller support bearing and sliding gear off journal end. the split gear is fitted on linehsaft with captivating steel backing collar. When a split gear needs changing, the fixing pin through backing collar and base of gear halves is released and the two halves can be removed leaving the collar on the lineshaft ready to receive the new split gear. Approximately 15 minutes are required to change a pair of gears.
Gear pairing/ storage	Pairing is necessary to keep within precision envelope, therefore gears must be paired for life.	Use of resilient material and large backlash allowance alleviates necessity for pairing.
Vibration/ fretting corrosion on shafts	Many cases of fretting followed by wear on roller ends and lineshafts.	Again, resilient nylon material absorbes damaging vibrations, hence reduces fretting and also keeps noise level down.
Consistency of manufacture	Quality control is necessary at stages of machining hardening and tooth grinding.	Q.C. required at moulding of insert and gear composite, also machining of bore and boss.

C387/014

Computer aided filament winding

G C ECKOLD, BSc, PhD, MPRI, **D G LLOYD-THOMAS**, BA and **G M WELLS**, BSc, PhD
United Kingdom Atomic Energy Authority, Harwell, Oxfordshire

SYNOPSIS   This paper describes a design package for composite structures manufactured by filament winding. The main elements of the procedure are 3D graphics for the construction and display of components of complex geometry, applications programs which predict the behaviour of material as it is wound onto a surface, and software for structural design. An important feature of the analysis is the ability to simulate the effect of friction between fibre and the mandrel, which allows the reinforcement to be steered along a path to give optimum winding angles. The mathematical routines employed in the process are quite general and are able to cater for surfaces without symmetry, together with material in a variety of forms, including wet fibre tows, prepregs and reinforced thermoplastics. In the paper the package is demonstrated by application to the design of a pressure vessel and an aircraft fuselage.

1. INTRODUCTION

Filament winding, where continuous fibres are placed onto a rotating mandrel, is an established technique for the fabrication of high quality composite components(1)(2). Accuracy of fibre placement, automated manufacture and the potential for cost effective production are factors which make the process particularly attractive for a range of engineering applications.   Modern filament winding equipment are sophisticated, numerically controlled machine tools offering several independent axes of motion. However, the programming of such machines, apart from the most simple of geometries, is a difficult task and currently limits the realisation of their full potential.

The control of the filament winding process requires careful consideration of three interrelated aspects of composite fabrication;   the constraints imposed by the component geometry, the material behaviour during manufacture and the requirements of engineering design. Current work at Harwell has been directed towards the greater integration of these requirements and the results to date take the form of a computer software package, CADMAC (Computer Aided Design and Manufacture of Advanced Composites). This is a system which incorporates 3D surface modelling to construct and display surfaces of high complexity, filament winding applications programs to calculate non-slip fibre trajectories, and finite element analysis for the assessment of structural integrity.

The design method allows consideration of a whole range of structures, including those of asym tric geometry. By employing the friction that exists between the fibre and mandrel the reinforcement can effectively be steered towards an optimum trajectory and this greatly enhances the flexibility of the system. The use of these procedures allows the engineer to fully examine the range of design options available for a particular component, prior to the generation of machine control instructions and prototype manufacture.

2.   DESIGN PROCESS

The major elements in the CADMAC design process are shown schematically in Fig. 1. As with all design exercises of this nature the procedure begins with a review of the requirement specification for the component of concern. This will usually consist of a consideration of the applied mechanical loadings, geometry, available space envelope and possible materials of construction. In addition, there may be other design criteria dictated by the specific applications, eg. maximum component weight, chemical resistivity or aeroelastic performance. Together these will allow the objectives for the design to be established and define the constraints within which the engineer must remain.

2.1   Surface modelling

The first step in the modelling process is to construct a mathematical representation of the surface of the structure. Within CADMAC this is carried out using a surface modelling technique which employs a polynominal definition of geometrical entities (4). Surfaces of complex geometry are built up from a combination of patches which are in turn created by the user through a series of 'user friendly' prompts and commands. Constraints between adjacent patch boundaries can be controlled to ensure continuity over the surface.

A feature of the analysis is the accuracy of representation which may be obtained. This is an important consideration as it can be shown (3) that the behaviour of winding trajectories can be very sensitive to small changes in geometry. Other modelling techniques, such as those based on facets or the addition of solid primitives, can be comparatively inaccurate and are therefore less suitable if precise material deposition is required.

Once the surface has been constructed the mathematical parameters which describe its geometry can be extracted and used in winding trajectory calculations.

2.2 Winding trajectories

Given the necessary geometric information, the behaviour of fibre as it is wound over the surface under tension can be predicted. At this stage the main criteria for an acceptable winding trajectory are as follows:-

- The fibre must not slip after initial placement onto the mandrel.

- There should be no fibre lift-off as a result of winding over locally concave areas.
- The path should be free of clash.

Stability of the material as it is deposited can be achieved by two means; winding along a geodesic path, or making use of the friction which exists between the fibre and mandrel surface. A geodesic path is a trajectory along which the distance between adjacent points over a surface is a minimum. As a result, such a path is stable as any shift of a segment of tow would require a change in length which would be resisted by the fibre tension. In many circumstances the use of geodesic trajectories can be quite restrictive with respect to obtaining optimum designs, as once the engineer has selected starting conditions, ie initial position and angle, the path is thereafter defined.

The incorporation of friction, however, allows much more flexibility, as the material can then be steered over the surface whilst at the same time maintaining the condition of the trajectory being non-slip. The rate of deviation from the geodesic which is possible not only depends on the value of friction coefficient, but also on the local geometry of the surface. The greater the curvature at a position along the winding path, the greater the normal reaction force which, in turn, increases the available frictional component. Magnitudes of effective

friction coefficients are affected by the materials being used for winding and process conditions. It has been shown (5) that for wet winding, values of between 0.15 to 0.2 can be successfully employed for certain resin systems. For other materials such as prepregs, where there would be a certain amount of stiction between material and mandrel, and thermoplastics, where the rapid solidification of the matrix would prevent subsequent movement, it is anticipated that allowable friction values would be considerably higher.

Within CADMAC, fibre paths are calculated, given initial conditions of position, angle and friction coefficient, by accessing the mathematical description of the surface and using a stepwise solution of a series of partial differential equations. A geodesic path is obtained by using a value of zero for the friction coefficient. Deviations to the left or right of the geodesic are achieved by using positive or negative values for friction. Fig. 2 shows schematically the relationship between different trajectories on a surface. In practice the calculation of a path can be stopped at any point on the surface and the value for friction changed, thereby allowing the angle of reinforcement to be carefully controlled.

Prevention of fibre bridging, which can cause lift off, is ensured in that the program highlights the positions where a trajectory passes over a locally concave area. The interactive nature of the procedure then allows the designer to take the necessary corrective action. In certain circumstances clash can be a potential problem, either between the winding eye and the workpiece or the fibre and the workpiece. This can be detected by using routines within the surface modelling software, which enable intersection calculations between graphical entities to be carried out. Given the predicted fibre trajectory the software then simulates the winding process by displaying tangents of a chosen length at each point along the path. These lines represent the successive positions of the tow during manufacture and by using the intersection routines a winding pattern free of collision can be assured.

2.3 Design assessment

Once the manufacturing feasibility of particular winding patterns has been established it is then possible to carry out a design assessment. At this stage all of the information necessary to undertake design calculations, eg. geometry, fibre angle, laminate thickness, is available. For a component with complex geometry it is probable that the thickness and angle of reinforcement will vary over the surface. To accommodate this in design, numerical techniques will normally be necessary and within CADMAC there are routines which compute the necessary geometrical and stiffness data for such an analysis. These procedures allow the stiffness matrix of the laminate to be derived from point to point along the surface and present the data in the form of a file which may be used as input into a finite element program. For axisymmetric components a mesh generator is also available which calculates nodal positions of both internal and external component surfaces. The results can then be compared with the original design specification and if necessary the winding pattern can be modified to obtain an improved solution.

2.4 Machine control

On conclusion of the design process the coordinates describing the positions of the ends of the tangents representing the fibre tow are written to a file. These coordinates define the position of the feed eye with respect to the mandrel during manufacture. This data is then converted from the mandrel frame of reference to a coordinate system which corresponds to the kinematics of the winding equipment. A series of files is written, one for each degree of freedom, formatted to meet the requirements of the winding machine controller.

The numbers of degrees of freedom which are necessary are dependent on the nature of the component. For most winding campaigns only three are required, ie. mandrel rotation, carriage translation and cross feed arm motion. This is because three axes allow the feed eye to be positioned at any point in space with respect to the

mandrel surface. If tape is being applied an additional axis may be necessary to control the orientation of the feedstock, particularly if the width of the tape is comparable to the dimensions of the mandrel. Further degrees of freedom may be required if there are special problems associated with collision.

3. MATERIALS OF CONSTRUCTION

The filament winding process is a flexible one which in principle can deal with various materials such as, wet fibres, prepreg, tape or reinforced thermoplastics. In the case of fibre and prepreg these can be applied as single tows or in the form of a multiple tow bandage. The choice of material of construction is primarily determined by factors not linked to processability, such as mechanical performance, chemical resistivity or problems associated with qualification requirements. However, with composites the behaviour of the materials of construction during manufacture can be of prime importance. As suggested previously the scope for achieving an optimum design is much increased if large friction coefficients are achievable during winding.

This is one area where the use of thermoplastic composites is of particular interest, as if wound onto a cooled mandrel not only may large deviations from the geodesic be possible, but there is also scope for the application of material into re-entrant geometries.

Mandrel design, particularly for complicated shapes where normal extraction methods cannot be used, is also an important consideration. Depending on geometry there are a number of techniques that may be employed. Simple systems based on disposable materials eg. friable or soluble, or dismantleable fabrications may be employed for low volume production, but for larger quantities a more sophisticated approach may be more cost effective. Examples of these are expandable/collapsible structures and mandrels cast from low melting point materials which can be recycled.

4. EFFECT OF GEOMETRY

As discussed above, the effect of geometry on the range of possible winding patterns is considerable. The degree of symmetry is also important as it can influence the way the design of a particular component is approached.

4.1 Axisymmetric geometry

Examples of components which have an axis of symmetry and may be manufactured by the filament winding process include rocket nozzles, pressure vessels, motor casings, drive shafts and satellite structures.

For geodesic paths the analysis reduces considerably. The winding angle over the surface is given by the well known Clairaut equation:-

$$k = d \sin \alpha \qquad (1)$$

where α is the local winding angle at a position on the surface at diameter d, and k is a constant which can be evaluated from the starting conditions for the path.

If non geodesic paths are required the Clairaut relationship is not applicable and the surface must be analysed in a step wise fashion using the necessary boundary conditions.

Once a path is obtained, acceptable in terms of manufacturing feasibility and design, coverage of the mandrel can be accomplished by repeating the circuit with increments of mandrel rotation. Turn around can be accomplished by incorporating domed sections at the ends of the mandrel or by using friction effects which would allow reversal of fibre direction without slippage. Both of these methods, together with all bandwidth related calculations, can be catered for in the software.

The use of the CADMAC procedure for the design of axisymmetric components using geodesic winding has been demonstrated (3) by the modelling, design, manufacture and testing of a number of components. An example showing the benefits of non geodesics is given in a subsequent section.

4.2 Asymmetric winding

The winding of asymmetric components poses a number of difficulties which do not occur when an axis of rotation is present. Of course, the Clairaut expression has little meaning, but more importantly there are the problems associated with mandrel coverage. Unlike shapes which are rotationally symmetric the concept of a repeatable circuit does not apply. In the most general case ever trajectory required to cover the surface would be unique, as even if two paths had identical starting conditions, except for a slight displacement to allow for the width of a tow, they would eventually be divergent as inevitably they will traverse sections of the surface which are not identical.

To overcome this difficulty the software allows offset paths to be calculated. Given a single trajectory which has previously been steered over the surface to give the desired angles, a second path can be derived which is offset from the first by a predetermined amount. The degree of offset could, for example, be related to the width of the tow. The output of this analysis includes the variation in friction coefficient which is required to wind the trajectory without slippage. This process can then be repeated, either by the operator or automatically within the system. Individual paths can then be linked together to form a complete winding campaign. In certain circumstances, where a shape is particularly difficult, pins inserted into the mandrel may be used. By winding fibre around pins individual trajectories can be decoupled and then added together in the most appropriate manner.

5. THICKNESS CONTROL

The build up of local wall thickness on a filament wound component is dependent on a number of factors, eg. geometry, tow cross-section, number of circuits and the local fibre angle. For axisymmetric shapes the thickness can be calculated simply from the winding angle and component diameter. For example, thicknesses will increase as the winding angle approaches the hoop direction and decrease as the diameter becomes larger. This variation, which occurs as a natural consequence of the winding procedure, can be advantageous in certain circumstances, eg. bending or torsional loading where the reduction in section stiffness due to a smaller diameter may be compensated for by an increase in thickness, but in other cases, eg. membrane loads due to internal pressure, the effect is the reverse of that required for optimum design.

Given a particular geometry, control of wall thickness can be achieved by a number of mechanisms including:-

- Variation in fibre angle
- Preferential reinforcement over local areas
- Reduction in the number of plies deposited over sections of the surface

Section wall thickness can be very sensitive to the direction of reinforcement, particularly at high winding angles. Employing this method would require a compromise between thickness, ie. minimum weight, and section properties.

In certain components where areas of high stress can be readily identified some form of preferential reinforcement may be used. For example, in a pipe tee joint where the design of the intersection requires the consideration of stress concentrations which arise due to internal pressure and applied bending moments, a two stage winding campaign can be envisaged. The first would result in coverage of the main pipe sections whilst the second would allow a build up of material in the junction region.

For other shapes where the geometry is more uniform, eg. conical sections, fuselage and wing components, and constant thickness is a design requirement ply drop off may be a more appropriate technique. Here the number of tows or tapes applied to a surface varies with position and a means must be found of cutting the material, retaining the position fibre on the surface after cutting, holding the fibre within the winding head and then reapplying it at a pre-programmed position on the surface. Thermoplastic composites where the ability of the material to remain fixed in position after placement are particularly attractive in this respect.

6. EXAMPLES OF SOFTWARE APPLICATION

To demonstrate the effectiveness of the CADMAC software two examples are given. The first is a pressure vessel of axisymmetric geometry which requires non geodesic trajectories to allow coverage and minimise stress concentrations, and the second is an aircraft fuselage where asymmetry requires that special consideration be given to mandrel coverage and design.

6.1 Pressure vessel

Consider the design of the pressure vessel shown in Figure 3. When subjected to internal pressure a combination of meridional and circumferential stresses will be generated the magnitude of which will depend on geometry. Elementary analysis (6) shows that the ratio of these two stresses away from junctions are as per Table 1.

Section	Ratio*	Angle
Cone	2	±55°
Cylinder	2	±55°
Ellipsoid		
φ = 0	1.76	±54°
φ = 15	1.67	±52°
φ = 30	1.55	±51°
φ = 45	1.34	±49°
φ = 60	1.18	±47°

*Ratio of circumferential and
  meridional stresses

Table 1 Stress ratios and winding
        angles for pressure vessel

Also shown in Table 1 are the optimum
angles for each stress ratio and the
objective of any design would be to
achieve these at the appropriate
positions on the surface. Winding using
geodesics, equation 1, would not be
possible as when the diameter decreases the
winding angle would increase, the opposite
of what is required. To compound this
difficulty the surface could not be
covered as, assuming an angle of ±55° on
the cylinder, a value of 90° would be
reached at 0.82D compared with the nozzle
openings at 0.5D and 0.75D.

Fig. 4 shows how the use of non geodesic
winding not only allows the shape to be
covered, but also produces a winding
pattern close to that described in Table 1.
A feature of Fig. 4 is the large change in
angle achieved over the small torispherical
region connecting the cylindrical and
conical sections. This demonstrates the
influence surface curvature can have when
determining non-slip trajectories.

In addition to the membrane stresses
described above there are local bending
moments and shear forces where the shape
changes geometry. These arise due to the
requirement to maintain continuity of
displacement and rotation at each junction.
Although these stress concentrations decay
over a short distance,(7) typically at $2\sqrt{Dt}$
from the junction they can be considered
negligible, they can be significant in
terms of the overall design.

Two methods can be employed to accommodate
these effects. Additional reinforcement
could be added in these positions to reduce
stress levels to within acceptable limits
or, alternatively, the circumferential
stiffness of the cylinder could be
increased so that its displacement on
pressurisation would equal that of the
vessel ends. This latter solution has the
added advantage in that if the edge moments
are reduced there will be a corresponding
reduction in the through-thickness and
interlaminar stresses which accompany them.
These secondary effects can be important in
composites as transverse normal and shear
strengths can be low. It can be shown that
an increase in cylindrical shell stiffness

of approximately 16% would allow cylinder
and ellipsoidal displacements to be
matched. This could be accomplished by
either using a high winding angle as the
junction is approached, ie. using friction
to steer the path as necessary, or by
incorporating a thin layer of hoop
reinforcement within the laminate. Both of
these methods could be catered for in the
design procedure. At the conical end it is
likely that additional reinforcement will
always be necessary due to the radial
component of the meridional load at the
junction.

Additional control of laminate thickness is
not required for this component as,
although it will increase as the diameter
changes, the build up of material will be
necessary to reinforce the end
openings.

Fig. 5 shows details of the winding path
described in Table 1 together with tangents
which represent the fibre tow.

6.2 Fuselage

Fuselages are examples of large aerospace
structures which may be filament wound (8).
Most aircraft components of this type are
subjected to a complex series of loading
combinations, but these are normally
dominated by bending and torsion. In
practice it is common to cater for these by
employing a balanced construction such as
(0°, ±45°, 90°) (9). The relative
proportions of each laminate being
dependent on the particular fuselage under
consideration.

The problems of winding such a
structure are as follows:-

- Maintenance of winding angle over
  surface.
- Coverage to give constant
  thickness.
- Inclusion of local design
  features, eg. stiffeners, into
  the construction.

Due to the asymmetry of the shape, non
geodesic trajectories will be required in
order to wind at a constant angle along the
profile. Fig. 6 shows the variation in
friction coefficient along the fuselage
length necessary for this to be achieved
and as can be seen all values are below
0.15, which is considered allowable for wet
winding. If a structure of high stiffness
is required a honeycomb material can be
incorporated in the design.

Due to the changing cross-section
variations in wall thickness are possible.
It can be shown that potential change in
thickness along the profile which will
occur as a natural consequence of the
winding process will be approximately 30
per cent. To prevent this, ply drop off
where certain circuits only traverse part
of the length of the mandrel, would have to
be employed. For the circumferential
reinforcement this would be relatively
straightforward, but for the other

laminates the material would need to be cut and retained in position whilst the carriage carrying the fibre deployment mechanism returns to its initial position and starts another circuit. For thermoplastics or prepreg tape this could be accomplished as a result of the ability of the material to remain in place due to matrix solidification or stiction, but for wet winding a mechanical system would have to be devised to prevent recoil of the tow once the tension is released on cutting.

As stated above, honeycomb could be included in between laminates to increase flexural and torsional rigidity. Circumferential stiffening rings could also be included either internally, on a suitably designed mandrel, or between the skins of a sandwich construction. If necessary additional material could also be applied in other areas to cater for local loads and attachments, together with any reinforcement required for openings. Fig. 7 shows the fuselage with a winding pattern superimposed on its surface.

7 SUMMARY

This paper has described a computer software package, CADMAC, which forms an integrated design and manufacture system for filament wound composite structures. Each stage of the procedure has been described including initial consideration of the design specification, surface modelling, computation of feasible winding patterns and structural analysis. The process is capable of dealing with components of either axisymmetric or asymmetric geometry, together with the special requirements of diffent materials including wet fibre tows, prepreg tows and tapes, and thermoplastic composites. A feature of the software is the ability to compute non-gedesic trajectories which, due to the friction which exists betweeen the material as it is depositied and the mandrel, are non slip. This allows fibre trajectories to be steered over the surface so that fibre directions can be carefully controlled. To demonstrate the capability of the procedure two example components have been described; a pressure vessel and an aircraft fuselage section. In each case it has not only been shown that filament winding is a feasible means of manufacture, but also that optimum designs can be achieved.

8. ACKNOWLEDGEMENTS

The authors wish to acknowledge the enthusiastic support of Mr T Thorpe and Mr E Brown of the Composite Fabrication Laboratory, Harwell, for their assistance during the course of this project. Financial support from the Department of Trade and Industry is acknowledged.

9. REFERENCES

(1) Bowen, D.H., Filament winding in the 1980's, Fibre Reinforced Composites '84, University of Liverpool, 3-5 April 1984.

(2) Owen, M.J., et al, Developments in filament winding, Advanced Composites: The Latest Developments, Michigan, 18-20 Nov. 1986.

(3) Bezier, P., Essai de definition numeriques des coubes et des surfaces experimentales, Theses d'etat, Paris IV, Feurier 1977.

(4) Wells, G.M., and Eckold, G.C., Computer aided design and manufacture of filament wound composite structures, 1st International Conference - Automated Composites, University of Nottingham, 10-12 September 1986.

(5) Wells, G.M., and McAnulty, K.F., Computer aided filament winding using non-geodesic trajectories, ICCM VI, Imperial College, 20-24 July 1987.

(6) Eckold, G.C., Design method for filament wound GRP vessels and pipework, Composites, 1985, Vol. 16, p41-47.

(7) Gill, S.S., Stress analysis of pressure vessels and pressure vessel omponents, 1970, Pergamon, London.

(8) Wood, A.S., The majors are taking over in advanced composites, Modern Plastics International, April 1986.

(9) Ling. Y., and Zukany, M., Optimum design based on reliability for composite laminates, Composite Structures 4, Paisley College of Technology, 27-29 July 1987.

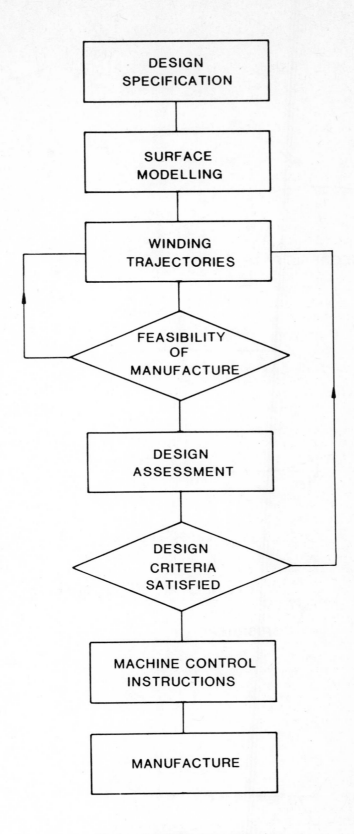

Fig 1   CADMAC design procedure

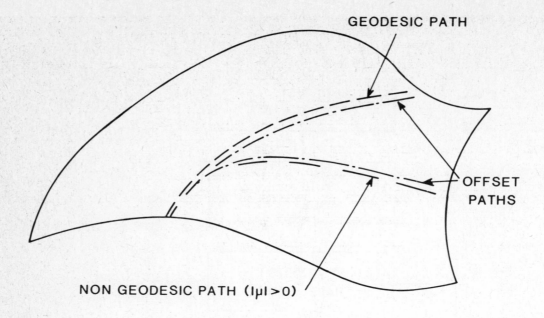

GEODESIC PATH

OFFSET
PATHS

NON GEODESIC PATH ($|\mu| > 0$)

Fig 2   Fibre trajectories

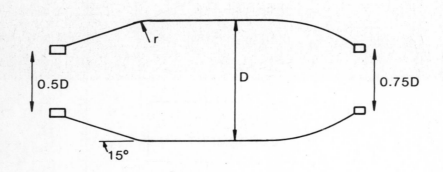

r

0.5D

D

0.75D

15°

Fig 3   Pressure vessel section

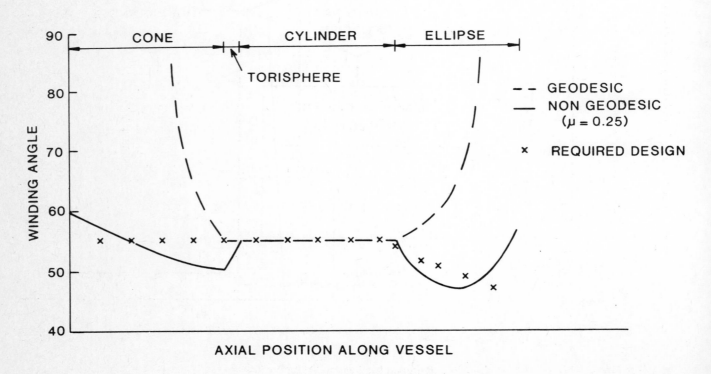

Fig 4   Pressure vessel winding trajectory

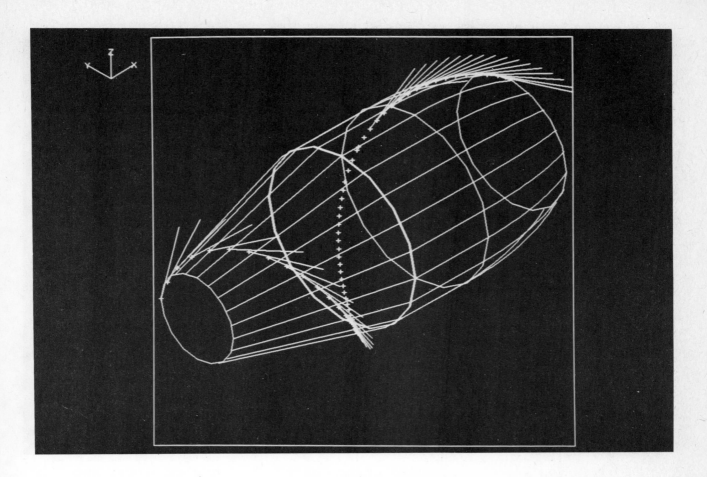

Fig 5   Pressure vessel with winding pattern

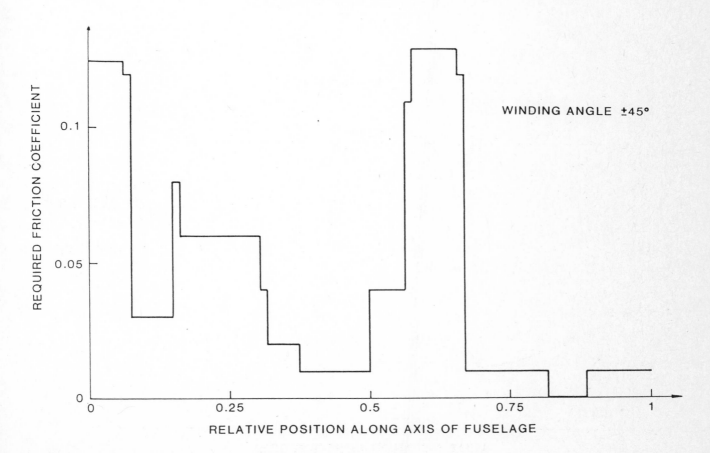

Fig 6   Required friction coefficient for fuselage

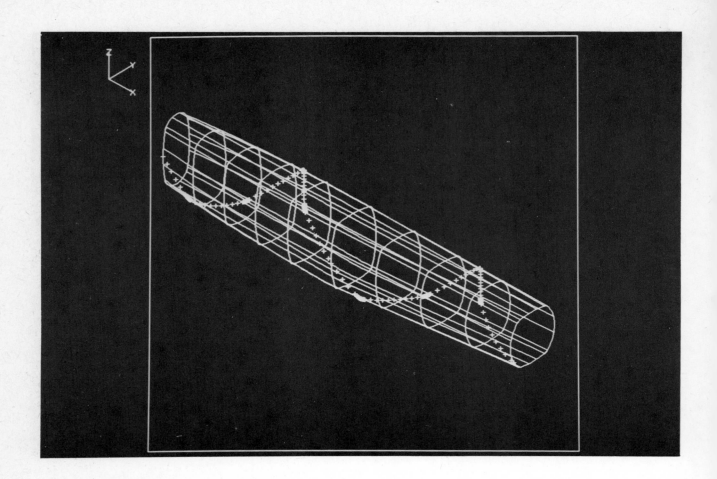

Fig 7   Fuselage with winding pattern

C387/001

Filament winding of non-axisymmetric components

V MIDDLETON, BSc, PhD, CEng, MIMechE, M J OWEN, BSc, MS, PhD, CEng, FIMechE, FPRI,
D G ELLIMAN, BSc, PhD, CEng, MIEE, MBCS and M R SHEARING, BEng
Department of Mechanical Engineering, University of Nottingham

SYNOPSIS

Filament winding permits the near optimum use of material when fabricating artifacts from glass or carbon fibre based composite materials. It is relatively straightforward to establish part-programs for numerically controlled machines for simple tubular shapes.

This paper describes a CAD system capable of producing NC part-programs for non-axisymmetric bodies, including branched shapes. Geodesic or controlled-angle fibre paths may be generated and locations where fibre slippage may occur are highlighted. The system which produces finished part-programs ready for direct loading and running on an NC machine will also be capable of producing data ready for entry into a finite element stress analysis package.

INTRODUCTION

Filament winding, the mechanised process for the production of fibre reinforced plastics (F.R.P.s) has a history that dates from the turn of the century. In its most basic form a filament winding machine is similar to a lathe, except a payout eye is substituted in place of a cutting tool and some type of mandrel for the work piece. As the mandrel is rotated resin impregnated filaments are pulled onto the surface via the payout eye which is mechanically manipulated. The relationship between mandrel rotation and payout eye movement govern the winding pattern produced on the mandrel surface. On completion of the winding the resin is cured and the mandrel removed to leave an F.R.P. shell. As mandrel shapes become more complex, so the requirements of the capability of filament winders increases, demanding more sophisticated movements of the payout eye relative to the mandrel. With the recent advance in multi axis computerised numerical control (C.N.C.) this requirement has been satisfied.

The filament winding programme at the University of Nottingham makes use of a five axis C.N.C. machine, manufactured by Pultrex Ltd. (figure 1). The overall program has been split into six Science and Engineering Research Council (S.E.R.C.) funded programmes, two industrially funded programs and one University funded program. The primary overall objective is to develop the technology for designing and manufacturing complex shaped filament wound components. Given that the hardware exists for this technology the major developments that are needed lie in the software techniques for programming machines, and in the development of suitable economical Computer Aided Design and Computer Aided Manufacture (CAD/CAM) systems. Labour intensive methods such as teach-in, which may have the immediate advantages of being able to generate part-programs for complex shapes today, require the machine for large amounts of unproductive time, and consequently should be avoided.

CAD/CAM systems while they are expensive to develop and have a long lead in time will eventually be cost effective as they provide a user with the facility to design and simulate manufacture 'off line', freeing the winding machine for production runs only. However, when developing a CAD/CAM system, the requirement to invest in large computers must be avoided so that such technology is affordable by small production units. The method reported here is based on a CAD/CAM system that can generate part-programs for axisymmetric or non-axisymmetric mandrels. The coverage patterns may be based on geodesic or non-geodesic (controlled angle) fibre paths generated on a remote computer, utilising a graphics workstation costing less than £10 000.

THE WINDING MACHINE

The winding machine is a Pultrex MODWIND 1S-5NC (figure 1) with a single spindle and five independently numerically controlled axes of movement (mandrel rotation, 3 mutually perpendicular carriage movements and a rotary movement of the payout arm). The machine can accept mandrels up to three metres long and one metre in diameter. The maximum speed of a linear axis is 60m/min and the max speed of a rotary axis is 200r/min. The machine is controlled by a G.E. Fanuc 11M machine tool controller. The controller uses standard CNC commands to position the axes, the majority of which are redundant because the payout eye is not coincident with the surface of the mandrel as in conventional cutting machines.

DEVELOPMENT OF SOFTWARE FOR WINDING

Extensive software development was undertaken based on winding techniques, theoretical analysis and part programs for a variety of simple and complex shapes. Four separate routes were identified for developing part programs for the Pultrex winding machine.

1. Theoretical: using customer parametric cycles with CNC commands.

2. Graphical: off line programming using drawings.

3. Teach-in: on line program development.

4. CAD/CAM: off line generation of part-programs using modelling techniques.

Where the geometry of a mandrel becomes more complicated than a cylinder, or a winding of varying helix angle is required, it is difficult and extremely time consuming to define the winding pattern manually either by graphical or teach-in methods. An iterative sequence of trial windings is usually necessary to achieve acceptable results, and the part programs comprise of a long and unwieldy series of co-ordinate positions. Modification of one part of the program usually requires re-developing all subsequent code. Constant material thickness is not obtainable on complex mandrels so that judgements have to be made about the degree and position of overlap between passes. These decisions cannot be left to the machine operator in high performance applications. In these circumstances the use of CAD/CAM techniques are not merely a productivity aid, but an essential pre-requisite in producing the finished part. A suite of software has been devloped which covers all aspects of the design and manufacturing cycle. The component development cycle has been cut from days to a few hours depending upon the complexity of the winding required. Further important advantages of the CAD approach are that the machine is not tied up for long periods of time carrying out unproductive trial runs, and material wastage is much reduced.

CAD/CAM FOR THE FILAMENT WINDING PROCESS

The current software for filament winding exists as two distinct packages. CADFIL^{TM} is a complete CAD/CAM package for filament winding axisymmetric mandrels using coverage patterns based on geodesic paths over the surface. It is capable of modifying mandrel geometries for subsequent winding patterns and interfacing other packages for the calculation of strength properties. A second system currently nearing completion removes the axisymmetric limitation by using a more general mandrel surface modeller and also expands the way in which coverage patterns may be generated by incorporating a non-geodesic/controlled angle path design feature.

A flow chart for the system is shown in figure 2. The first stage of development is to define the shape of the mandrel. The format for the input of mandrel data is as a series of XYZ co-ordinates describing a series of cross-sections. The X and the Y co-ordinates describing the profile of the cross-sections and the Z co-ordinate the position of the section along a spine. Cross-sections are assumed to hang perpendicular to the direction of the spine. Figure 3 illustrates the concept of points defining cross-sections and cross-sections hung on spines. This data is usually generated by a surface modeller and passed as a data file to the CAD system. Having edited in all the mandrel data, it may be viewed as a wire framed model to check for errors. Figure 4 shows a wire framed model of a branched mandrel with no hidden line removal. The only restriction for the model is that each section must have the same number of points defining it.

This information is used to build a surface model of the mandrel surface comprising of flat triangular patches, as shown in figure 5 with some hidden line removal. Triangular patches were chosen as it is straight forward to predict a geodesic or a non-geodesic path across a plane patch with only three sides. A geodesic path is calculated on the mandrel by extending the fibre path in a straight line to the boundary of the current patch.

CADFIL ^{TM} is a registered trademark of Crescent Consultants Limited, Nottingham, England.

This patch is then rotated by its common boundary with an adjacent patch, the one that the path is about to proceed into, until the two patches are co-planar. As a geodesic is a straight line on any developed surface the path can be extended into the second patch, and the process repeated under the control of the operator, with the fibre path being displayed as it is calculated. The situation is only slightly different for a non-geodesic/constant angle path. The definition of a constant angle path is the direction taken by a fibre across a patch that is at a fixed angle to a reference plane. This reference plane is defined by the starting position, the patch surface normal and the mandrel axis. Again the fibre path is incremented around the mandrel axis a patch at a time, its progress being shown on a graphics display. A 45° controlled angle path is also illustrated in figure 5.

The fibre path is stored as a stream of co-ordinates corresponding to the position of the intersections with the patch boundaries. The direction cosines of the tangent at each of these positions is also stored to facilitate the calculation of the payout eye path.

Once a fibre track has been designed it must be duplicated many times in order to obtain coverage of the entirety of the mandrel surface. Unlike generating coverage patterns for axisymmetric shapes, it is not merely a case of repeatedly indexing the design path. The nature of a non-axisymmetric shape implies that each pass along a mandrel's surface follows a unique route and consequently each fibre track must be individually designed. The path designed by either the geodesic or the constant angle methods can be used as a template for the coverage pattern. Paths adjacent to the template are then repeatedly designed until total coverage is achieved. Each adjacent path becomes the template for the next path, its offset from the template being the circumferential distance, at that axial position divided by the number of passes required for total coverage.

The constant angle path based coverage pattern, since it is unlikely to be a geodesic, is then examined to discover whether it is likely to slip out of position during the winding process. Local predictions are made for geodesic paths from the constant angle path points and the direction cosines of the path previous to this point. If the constant angle path and the geodesic path are found to differ significantly then the operator is warned and a note of the position made for inclusion in fibre assisted placement assessment by the post-processor.

The payout eye path is calculated taking the equation of the tangential line from each path point, the path direction cosines, and calculating the intersection with a control surface that surrounds the mandrel. The locus of these points is the desired payout eye path.

GENERATING A PART-PROGRAM

The payout eye path is the raw data from which the part-program is derived but in order to keep this of a reasonable length some of the points are discarded.

A table driven post-processor is used to generate the specific command lines in the part-program as these will be specific to the winding environment. This utility transforms the payout eye path to machine co-ordinates and adds the codes necessary to set up the machine feed rates and other initialisation parameters. The size of the part-program depends upon how many passes are required to produce the coverage pattern and upon the mandrel complexity. As each pass is unique, none of the program may be repeated and it generally means that part-programs far outstrips the machine memory size. A tape stream loader enables the part-program to be fed piecemeal to the machine controller as and when more data is required, and relieves any program size restrictions.

COMPLETE COVERAGE OF A BRANCHED MANDREL

From the winding tests performed so far it is clear that generating complete coverage of a branched mandrel will have to be performed in several stages. Developing a single pass over such a mandrel is not difficult (see figure 5) but its at the subsequent stage of coverage pattern development that problems occur. The techniques earlier described, which can produce complete coverage patterns for non branched shapes, begin to break down when adjacent passes begin to be laid on the branched section. The use of inserts to fill areas of difficult access, perhaps positioned by robots and then overwrapped by the winder presents one possible solution. Alternatively a totally designed coverage pattern using a mixture of geodesic and controlled angle winding paths, making no use of repetition techniques, could be developed. However, it might prove to be difficult to obtain total coverage with a good quality laminate using this method. These techniques are currently under review and development under the filament winding project at Nottingham.

INTERFACING WITH STRESS ANALYSIS AND STRENGTH PREDICTION ROUTINES

The direction of fibres is known for all points on the mandrel surface and in principle it should be possible to derive a matrix describing the anisotropic material properties for any patch and to use finite element stress analysis package to calculate stress and stiffness. In practice however the variation of properties with winding pattern is not sufficiently well defined. At Nottingham a data base of properties is being established in parallel with winding work covering static and fatigue characteristics. A simplified thin shell analysis is carried out to estimate the direction and magnitude of principal stresses and the number and thickness of layers is adjusted until the shell is sufficiently thick to meet the design specification, with an adequate margin of safety. It is likely that an initial design will have areas that are of a much greater thickness than is necessary as a result of satisfying design criteria in another region. This effect can often be reduced or eliminated by redesigning the coverage pattern at this stage.

ENHANCING THE WINDING ENVIRONMENT

Enchancing the filament winding environment has highlighted some practical problems. A major difficulty is the problem of slippage and its prevention. Using the CAD system it is possible to predict where slippage is likely to occur and in order to prevent a fibre moving from its intended position a Fanuc-S1 robot has been introduced to the winding environment. A flexible manufacturing cell for filament winding is now being developed. The cell comprises of a three axis winding machine with a dedicated controller specifically designed for the filament winding process, the Fanuc robot and its controller. The robot interfaces with the machine and provides a 'tacking' service to locate a fibre and prevent it from moving from its desired position. The robot movements are introduced to the part program by a second stage post-processor. This post-processor takes the form of a simulator, modelling the winder and robot environment and illustrating graphically how they move together, warning of any potential collision. The simulator enables the whole manufacturing cycle to be inspected before any production takes place, reducing the part program development time and the number of prototypes required. An example of the simulator is given in figure 6 where it is seen modelling the winding of a single pass over a branched mandrel.

NECESSARY COMPUTING POWER

The CAD/CAM and simulator packages require the use of high resolution colour graphics in order to produce intelligible displays on a terminal screen. Memory mapped graphics with at least two displayable pages is also desirable for realism in simulation of machine and mandrel movements.

Other parts of the system involve extensive floating point arithmetic that is best carried out on powerful machines with hardware arithmetic unit if a reasonable interactive response is to be achieved.

A digitiser tablet or mouse is needed to drive "pop-up menus" and window managing facilities. These two factors provide an interactive working interface that is simple and appealing to use.

It has been found that the Whitechapel MG1 workstation provides a cost effective system for this application, using a colour terminal in conjunction with the main console. However the software is now being developed to run on Sun 3/60 workstations where it is expected to achieve faster response times because of the computer's greater power.

After initially using Fortran 77, the C language was adopted for the project. The programs have been found to be highly portable between Vax, Whitechapel, Tourch, Sun and even IBM PC's, and should be easily transferred to the next generation of Reduced Instruction Set Computer (R.I.S.C.) workstations.

CONCLUSIONS

Filament winding is a powerful manufacturing technique which allows composite structures of very high strength to weight ratios to be produced. Modern CNC machines have extended the application of this process to complex geometries. The use of CAD/CAM systems expedites the development of part-programs eliminating many laborious and expensive processes, however the development cost is quite high.

CAD systems for solids of revolution have been enhanced to include non-axisymmetric shapes with coverage patterns based on constant angle designs.

A flexible manufacturing cell, devoted to filament winding, is being developed along with appropriate software that should allow the complete design and simulation of the manufacture of a component to be performed 'off line' reducing the number of prototypes required and overall component cost.

REFERENCES

(1) OWEN M.J., MIDDLETON V., ELLIMAN D.G., REES H.D., EDWARDS K.L., YOUNG K.W. and WEATHERBY N. Filament Winding for Complex Shapes on F.R.P., S.E.R.C. Polymer Engineering Directorate Review Conf., Loughborough, 1985

(2) EDWARDS K.L., Advanced C.N.C. Filament Winding of Complex Shapes, Ph.D. Thesis, Mechanical Engineering Department, Nottingham University, 1985

(3) YOUNG, K.W., Computer Aided Design and Manufacture for Filament Wound Reinforced Plastics, Ph.D. Thesis, Mechanical Engineering Department, Nottingham University, 1986

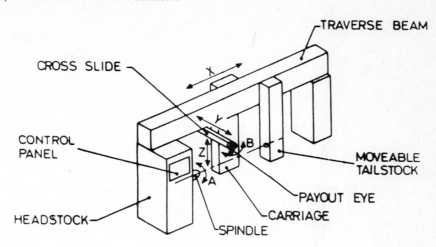

Fig 1   Schematic of filament winding machine

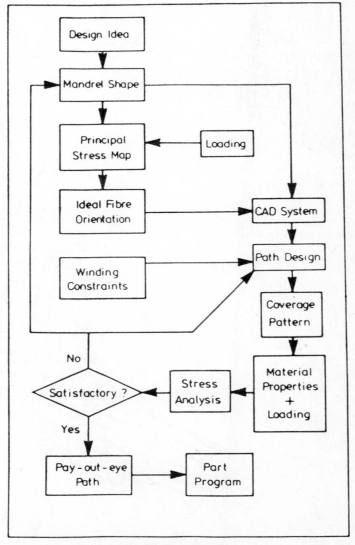

Fig 2   Design loop

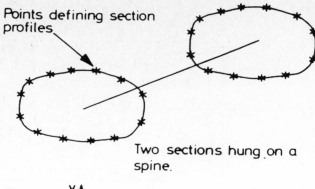

Points defining section profiles

Two sections hung on a spine.

Fig 3   Paints, sections and spines

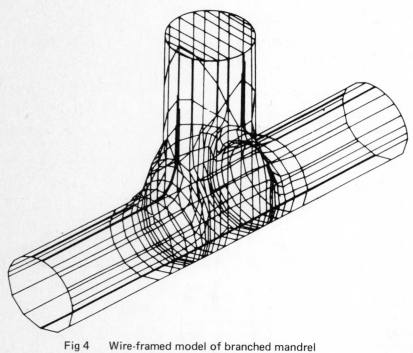

Fig 4   Wire-framed model of branched mandrel

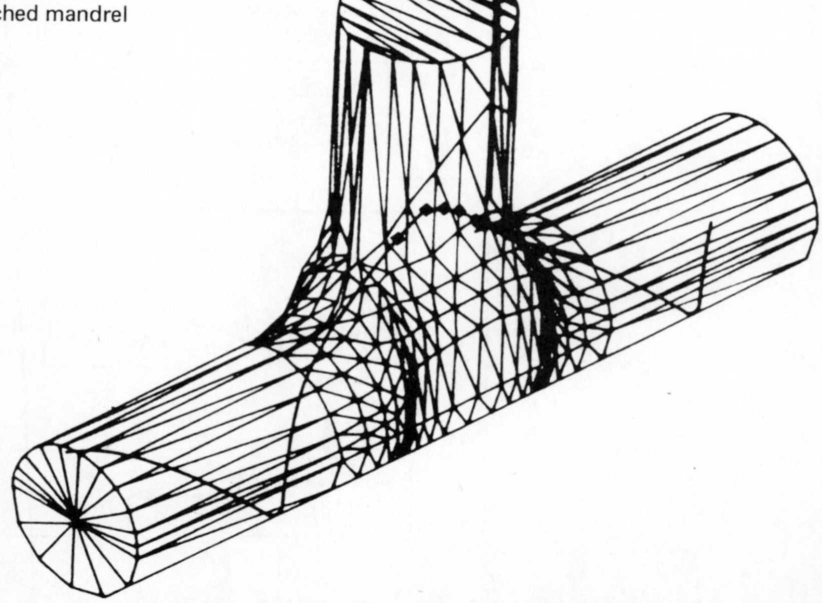

Fig 5   Patched branched mandrel showing 45° pass and robot interaction points

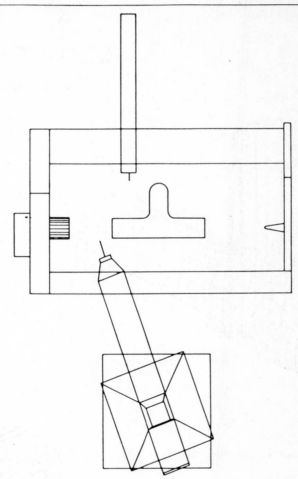

Robot and Winder Position Data		
Robot Joint Angles	Robot Position	Winder Position
THETA = − 25·00		
W = 10·00	X = 765·50	X = 200·0
U = − 20·00	Y = 180·59	Y = 0·0
BETA = 0·00	Z = 128·97	A = 40·0
ALPHA = − 30·00		

Fig 6   Simulator scene with branched mandrel winding machine and robot